LEADERSHIP

MANAGING IN
REAL ORGANIZATIONS

McGraw-Hill Series in Management

Fred Luthans and Keith Davis, Consulting Editors

Levin, McLaughlin, Lamone, and Kottas: Production/Operations Management: Contemporary Policy for Managing Operating Systems

Luthans: Organizational Behavior

Luthans and Thompson: Contemporary Readings in Organizational Behavior

McNichols: Executive Policy and Strategic Planning

McNichols: Policymaking and Executive Actions

Maier: Problem-Solving Discussions and Conferences: Leadership Methods and Skills

Margulies and Raia: Conceptual Foundations of Organizational Development

Mayer: Production and Operations Management

Miles: Theories of Management: Implications for Organizational Behavior and Development

Miles and Snow: Organizational Strategy, Structure, and Process

Mills: Labor-Management Relations

Mitchell and Larson: People in Organizations: An Introduction to Organizational Behavior

Molander: Responsive Capitalism: Case Studies in Corporate Social Conduct

Monks: Operations Management: Theory and Problems

Newstrom and Davis: Organizational Behavior: Readings and Exercises

Newstrom, Reif, and Monczka: A Contingency Approach to Management: Readings

Parker: The Dynamics of Supervision

Pearce and Robinson: Corporate Strategies: Readings from *Business Week*

Porter and McKibbin: Management Education and Development: Drift or Thrust into the 21st Century?

Prasow and Peters: Arbitration and Collective Bargaining: Conflict Resolution in Labor Relations

Quick and Quick: Organizational Stress and Preventive Management

Reddin: Managerial Effectiveness

Rue and Holland: Strategic Management: Concepts and Experiences

Rugman, Lecraw, and Booth: International Business: Firm and Environment

Sartain and Baker: The Supervisor and the Job

Sayles: Leadership: Managing in Real Organizations

Schlesinger, Eccles, and Gabarro: Managing Behavior in Organizations: Text, Cases and Readings

Schroeder: Operations Management: Decision Making in the Operations Function

Sharplin: Strategic Management

Shore: Operations Management

Steers and Porter: Motivation and Work Behavior

Steinhoff and Burgess: Small Business Management Fundamentals

Sutermeister: People and Productivity

Vance: Corporate Leadership: Boards, Directors, and Strategy

Walker: Human Resource Planning

Weihrich: Management Excellence: Productivity through MBO

Werther and Davis: Human Resources and Personnel Management

Wofford, Gerloff, and Cummins: Organizational Communications: The Keystone to Managerial Effectiveness

LEADERSHIP

MANAGING IN REAL ORGANIZATIONS

SECOND EDITION

Leonard R. Sayles

Graduate School of Business
Columbia University
and
Center for Creative Leadership

McGRAW-HILL BOOK COMPANY

New York   St. Louis   San Francisco   Auckland   Bogotá   Caracas
Colorado Springs   Hamburg   Lisbon   London   Madrid   Mexico
Milan   Montreal   New Delhi   Oklahoma City   Panama   Paris
San Juan   São Paulo   Singapore   Sydney   Tokyo   Toronto

This book was set in Palatino by the College Composition Unit
in cooperation with General Graphic Services, Inc.
The editor was Kathleen L. Loy;
the production supervisor was Janelle S. Travers.
The cover was designed by Warren Infield.
R. R. Donnelley & Sons Company was printer and binder.

LEADERSHIP
Managing in Real Organizations

1 2 3 4 5 6 7 8 9 0 DOC DOC 8 9 4 3 2 1 0 9

ISBN 0-07-055018-2 (hard cover)

ISBN 0-07-055017-4 (soft cover)

Library of Congress Cataloging-in-Publication Data

Sayles, Leonard R.
    Leadership: managing in real organizations.

    (McGraw-Hill series in management)
    Includes index.
    1. Leadership. 2. Management. I. Title. II. Series.
HD57.7.S29 1989   658.4   88-23145
ISBN 0-07-055018-2 (hard cover)
ISBN 0-07-055017-4 (soft cover)

TO KATHY:
Excellent Manager
Astute Observer
Aide and Gentle Critic

CONTENTS

PREFACE

The first edition of this text was written because I felt that American society undervalued the extraordinary challenge of managerial work. Organizations which coordinate the work of large numbers of technical and professional personnel and which develop and absorb new technologies, products, and systems are taken for granted in this country. Managerial work is viewed as remunerative, even prestigious, but it is not usually perceived as creative, nor demanding of substantial talent.

Traditionally, management has been depicted as an analytical profession whose practitioners systematically move from larger objectives to detailed execution by means of thoughtful decisions and well-reasoned plans. When these rational and logical procedures fail, it is because of personnel "frictions"—problems of motivation, communication, and politics.

But over the years, in a variety of research studies, I came to appreciate the extraordinary complexity of the managerial tasks. In seeking to describe what managers actually do in real-life organizations, I recognized the discrepancy between the principles of "good management" portrayed in most texts and the pressure-filled, fragmented, uncertain world which confronts contemporary executives.

It was to address this discrepancy that I wrote the first edition of *Leadership*, and now to readdress the old issues and to consider some new ones I present this new edition.

This book, like its predecessor, is designed for a dual audience: real managers struggling to cope with one of the most difficult professions (often with tools and expectations unequal to the task) and students seeking to develop themselves for managerial careers.

First-rate managers are, above all else, men and women of action. They seek to orchestrate through their own behavior the contributions of aggregations of personnel, some motivated but many obtuse and recalcitrant. The nimble and complex behavior patterns of these superb managers is a delight to behold as they move to motivate, integrate, and modify the structure and work habits of the people that surround them. Yet few texts capture the spirit of excitement and challenge inherent in these tasks. More often the reader is confronted with the forbidding and abstract concepts of the behavioral scientist or the uninspiring principles of formal organization. Few readers of texts on management will ever glimpse the extraordinary human adventure and accomplishment of the managerial role.

It is hardly surprising that students planning a career in administration have little conception of what they will be doing. And many managers themselves are bewildered by the job that confronts them because it differs so from the placid "clean-desk" world they had been led to expect. Even the novel, the theater, and TV have forsaken modern managers. Scientists and politicians are portrayed with a modicum of realism; never managers.

For a number of years, I have sought to accumulate, through fieldwork, firsthand accounts of managerial work. My research has ranged from extended studies of such major organizations as NASA and IBM to more modest excursions into smaller public and private enterprises. My purpose here is to try to summarize those formal and informal studies as they relate to managerial behavior and to integrate this with other published work on leadership.

The book's focus is middle management and the skills and conceptual understanding required to orchestrate five critical tasks, often simultaneously: monitoring work flows, motivating subordinates, negotiating lateral relationships, working the hierarchy, and introducing change in structure and technology.

It has been gratifying to hear readers of the first edition comment that *Leadership* "rings true" and "tells it like it is," that it accurately describes the organizations they know and the unique problems they confront—the conflicting, often ambiguous demands of their time-constrained world.

I owe a substantial, largely unpaid, debt to two distinguished anthropologists with whom I had the good fortune to collaborate in research quite early in my career. The conceptual underpinnings of this work draw heavily on the seminal ideas and writing of Dr. Eliot Chapple and Dr. William Foote Whyte. Much more recently, several members of the staff of the Center for Creative Leadership in Greensboro, North Carolina, have been enormously helpful. It is a pleasure to express appreciation to Drs. Robert Kaplan and Morgan McCall (now with the University of Southern California) and Wilford Drath. Over many years I have been stimulated and enriched by a continuing dialogue with Robert Wright, who heads his own consulting firm. I have also received valuable comments from the following reviewers: Richard Grover, Indiana University; Avis L. Johnson, University of Akron; Virgil G. O'Connor, Lindenwood College; Michael T. Quinn, California State University at Long Beach; and David Schoorman, Purdue University.

With friends like this, research and writing almost become easy, particularly if one has a patient editor like Kathleen Loy.

Leonard R. Sayles

LEADERSHIP
MANAGING IN
REAL ORGANIZATIONS

1

THE MANAGERIAL WORLD: EXPECTATION VERSUS REALITY

We live in a world of organizations. Aside from art, some crafts, and individual practices in medicine and law, almost all the work of our society gets done through human organizations. Even highly individualistic professional work is increasingly practiced through partnerships, clinics, and laboratories requiring managerial abilities that complement the technical skills of the surgeon or attorney.

Both public and private organizations appear to have an insatiable appetite for new executives. Even in periods of recession, most organizations keep looking for "better" managers; universities, corporations, hospitals, and government agencies constantly complain about their lack of effective "leadership" and the difficulty of obtaining truly effective managers.

In business, with its ability to measure results, there may be even more pressure to upgrade managerial capabilities. After all, most companies compete openly and without secret formulas, protected markets, or impenetrable patents. Both the sophisticated stock market investor and the casual observer recognize that there are extraordinary differences in performance among firms in the same industry. Given the relatively equal access to technical and managerial knowledge, what makes for such extraordinary differences in performance? Managerial skill!

One is continually surprised by the number of obvious and costly errors in leadership. For example, an acquisition-minded company pulls together a number of units in the same industry still run by their entrepreneur founders. A new group vice president destroys their motivation both by being unavailable and by failing to consult them on a whole series of new policies. In a short time the organization is in disarray and many of the previously profitable components are sold. In another case, the finest and costliest new hotel in America hires as chief operating officer a man who has been running another long-established, elite hostelry. Unfortunately, he has neither experience nor skill in coping with the start-up traumas associated with opening a new facility that is loaded with construction and personnel problems. Before it is discovered that the new manager can't deal with change, the result is near financial disaster.

Yet, in truth, the missing managerial skills do not represent profound or abstruse techniques. There are tens of thousands of tracts, as well as more erudite publications, setting forth the principles of good management. Reduced to their essential components, most research findings about good leadership seem obvious—even commonsensical, if truth be told—and not that difficult. While there are some subtle differences among them and a few "sophistications," most of the counsel, the research findings, and the pronouncements have a rather obvious central tendency. Good managers plan ahead, select qualified subordinates, and reward the best performers; they maintain open communications and encourage feedback, and so on. It seems easy.

What, then, explains the shortage, the scarcity of good managers? Are the requisite abilities so arcane that only a small number of human beings have the talent embedded in their genes? Are the compensations too modest to attract men and women away from more desirable pursuits? Do organizations somehow constrain or perversely destroy the practice of good management?

WHY IS MANAGEMENT SO DIFFICULT?

Why, then, should management be so problematic and good managers so scarce? Why should a rather obvious, straightforward task be mishandled so frequently? Why is it that what appears simple may actually be very complex? We think there are answers to this paradox.

1 The organizational setting within which managers must manage is more recalcitrant than one first imagines. While we live in a world of organizations and could not survive without them, as Peter Drucker has so ably documented, these institutions impose extraordinary constraints on managerial effectiveness. We shall explore this in the chapters to follow, but it's difficult to resist one example:

> Even the President of the United States, with the august power of that imposing office, can be overwhelmed by the incredible obdurateness of the organization. The *New York Times* relates how, after assuming office, Carter detected mice in the Oval Office, the very focal point of the Presidency. He called the General Services Administration who then came and handled the matter. Shortly after Carter continued to hear mice but worse, one died in the wall and the stench was quite noticeable during formal meetings. However, when he again called the G.S.A. he was told that they had carefully exterminated *all* the mice; therefore any new mice must be "exterior" mice, and exterior work is apparently the province of the Interior Department. They at first demurred but eventually a "joint task force" was mounted to deal with the problem.[1]

2 Many managers are induced or seduced into trying out rather simplistic models of the manager's role, and each of these assures failure.

3 Where managers seek to go beyond these obvious models, they will have difficulty in getting help. Until quite recently organization researchers were more entranced with assembly line workers and insurance clericals than with executives. But, more damning, the studies that have been done have tended to stress what managers should think and what they should achieve. Ignored is the real pay dirt—*how do you do it?*

4 When they first begin their careers, managers are often shocked and dismayed by what they find. The reality of being a manager is far different from the expectations. Most of the differences between the rhetoric and the reality and the preconception and the firing line relate to the pressured, time-constrained, fragmented, and energy-consuming daily routine of administration.

[1] *New York Times Magazine*, Jan. 8, 1978, p. 29.

5 Unfortunately, behavioral scientists and students of management, like managers themselves, have no language to describe or concepts to analyze this hectic interactional world. The concepts and models that they use are more likely to relate to the world of professions, to the statics of occupational knowledge, than to the dynamics of human interaction. Management bears little resemblance to any other profession, if indeed it is a profession. It represents an extraordinarily challenging skill that must be played on a confounding "field"—the complex organization. Efforts to professionalize it, to reduce it to a set of things to know, as distinct from actions to do, further increase the gap between what managers are told and what they must really learn to do.

6 Rather than responding to the reality and the complexity, many managers retreat to one or another simplistic but appealing model of the managerial role:

The all-powerful boss. Taking Machiavelli and the Mafia seriously and recognizing that power-hungry and politically savvy individuals have always been able to make it, many managers reduce management to simple power politics. They insist on complete loyalty and punish the deviants; they divide and conquer, demonstrate raw courage, and know how to wheel and deal. It works in a one-boss operation and in a few remaining political fiefdoms, but not in a complex institutional world.

The complete bureaucrat. These managers have learned their textbook lessons well. To them management is applied rationality, clearheaded good sense, and a taste for legalism. Just as Frederick Taylor and Max Weber suggested, they try to define tasks clearly, avoid overlapping responsibilities, and make sure everyone has only one boss; the staff is purely advisory, and the line has the authority. They write off all the difficult human problems of getting cooperation and coordination by defining them away in their crystal-clear job descriptions. Everything is normatively correct, but human beings don't operate in normatively correct patterns.

The sophisticated technician. Here are the managers looking for complete and well-packaged cures to the human problems that the bureaucrats ignore in their machinelike precision. They assume that consultants and business schools turn out ready-to-install cures for organizational ills. Whether it is a management-by-objectives (MBO) plan, job enrichment, organizational development (OD), or whatever, they want the newest and the fanciest. Unfortunately, they ignore the fact that there are no easy ways to compartmentalize "fixes." MBO deals with almost the entire organization: structure, leadership styles, controls, and much more. Depending upon who uses it and how, it can be almost anything. The same is true of the other methods; they have no meaning analogous to a finance department's decision to develop a new capital budgeting technique. Almost every management technique really affects the entire organization and can be shaped or misshaped to do pretty much what the managers want. None have independent reality, and most have no independent validation. Not only are they a conglomerate of half-digested procedures, they are not operationalized. OD in one organization means something totally different from what happens next door (even though the same consultant is being paid).

The rejectionist. And then there are those managers who are embittered and confused with how difficult organizational life appears. They argue that there are no rules of the game for their crazy, mixed-up organization. While the person next door may be dealing with rational people in a sensible organization, they must confront a ship of fools.

THEY NEVER TELL YOU HOW

Managers seeking guidance form the academic world and the experts will discover that what first appears useful and relevant has a fatal shortcoming. The books and speeches emphasize what the good manager should be thinking and/or the results he or she should be achieving. They tend to omit the critical "how" to do this—how to think and how to achieve.

Why Managers Do What They Do

A significant share of the writing on management seeks to differentiate effective from ineffective managers on the basis of differences in perception: how they view the world around them and themselves.

Thus good managers are supposedly those who:

- Trust and have confidence in both the capabilities and the motivation of subordinates and believe that they want to accept responsibility and work hard[2]
- Believe that shared authority (participation) is both desirable and useful
- Seek achievement and legitimate power
- Are reasonably self-confident, assured, optimistic, sensitive, and alert

What a Good Manager Should Achieve

Alternatively there is the traditional emphasis on what good managers accomplish: they are effective in planning ahead, delegating, coordinating, staffing, organizing, even making profits. In other words, "good" managers make "good" decisions that work out to be sensible plans, embodying reasonable delegations and yielding desirable results.

The traditional management textbook was largely devoted to what you were supposed to accomplish. In contrast, the organizational behavior approach stressed what you were supposed to think (of yourself and others). Almost no recognition was given to the rather obvious point that probably everybody wants to accomplish the same thing. Few managers *don't* want to plan well, staff well, or coordinate well. The problem is *how*. Since Weber and Taylor, it's been an open secret that organizations ought to utilize techniques like planning and delegation. Similarly, most (but surely not all) managers want to be confident, achievement-oriented, and respectful of the motivations of subordinates. But such desires are often thwarted by the frustrations of organizational life: the apparent recalcitrance of individuals and groups, the willful refusals and distortions, and the apparent reluctance to place private interests behind group goals. Again the question

---

[2] Douglas McGregor is most frequently cited for distinguishing between a Theory X and a Theory Y manager. See his *Leadership and Motivation*, MIT Press, Cambridge, Mass., 1966.

that gets begged is *how* to manage so that the results encourage trust, delegation, and participation.[3]

How: The Significance of Process

Thus it's the middle that is typically neglected, the "how do
you transform intentions into results?" Not even in psychoanal-
ysis does it do much good to be told what you *should* think
about yourself or others. In large part, motivations and beliefs
are either deeply ingrained or the result of immediate experiences. In either case, it's not usually fruitful to try to change
yourself unless the situation changes. In that case, attitudes *follow* behavior; they don't lead it! Subordinates or colleagues are
trusted more *because* the situation is less frustrating and there is
more cooperation, not the reverse.

In the same vein, almost every manager who is a product of
Western, industrialized culture believes in the maxims of good
management: planning ahead, objective personnel decision
making, rational weighing of factors before deciding, utilizing
feedback to evaluate earlier decisions, etc. But most managers
are distressed because they can't seem to make the results turn
out that way.

This is the reason most management principles appear (and
in fact are) so simplistic. Without elaboration, they can be written on one page. But knowing the end result doesn't help much
in getting there. The principles of management neglect everything that's problematic in converting good intentions into
good results. The middle ground, between motive and results,
is the critical *and* the neglected area of training.

An interesting aside is the increased recognition in the social
sciences of the fact that process is a crucial level of analysis. It
would appear that both to learn about social systems and to
cope with them the appropriate working level is the process
level. This means that managers and researchers alike need to
concentrate on the behavioral interaction that underpins organizational life.

---

[3] There is some evidence that managers who adopt the more participative
styles are, in fact, able to do so because their groups were better-performing to
begin with. See George Faris, "Chickens, Eggs and Productivity in Organizations," *Organizational Dynamics*, vol. 6, no. 4, Spring 1977, pp. 2–15.

Why (motive)	How	What (results)
Desire for achievement, institutional power	?	Intelligent plans; trained, responsible work force
Belief in individual capability and willingness to accept responsibility		Profitability; sound organizational structure

RHETORIC VERSUS REALITY

Neophyte managers are mystified (or angered) when the organizational world is so different from what they had been led to expect. New executives anticipate not a vague, ambitious, "systems" world, but a simple, rationalistic, clearly bounded world comprising:

Clear goals, preferably one or two

Results quick in appearance and unambiguously associated with effort (on the theory that hard work consistently produces measurable performance and a sense of closure or completion)

A good deal of time for reflective analysis and decision making

Subordinates who are deferential and responsive

A premium on planning time

Resources comparable to responsibility assigned

A unified management team with shared goals

Rules, procedures, and objectives that are mutually consistent, relatively fixed, and clear-cut

Greater status and greater deference through promotion, with fewer people to challenge or constrain decisions

Authority commensurate with, and therefore capable of fulfilling, responsibility

The "Professional" Manager

The term "professional" manager has come into increasing use, and it's no wonder. While few managers have illusions (or delusions) of being intellectuals or technical impressarios, they do view their managerial role as the equivalent of a professional's task. Success stems from knowledge and critical, thoughtful decisions. Their cognitive skills entitle them to command the resources and the responsiveness which will enable them to complete their assigned tasks.

The professional image is a worthy substitute for the more militaristic concept of manager as commander. Such absolute authority is inconsistent with our society, which demands rights for workers, the community, and other parties at interest. To many managers, professionals get the same deference as their more authoritarian forebears, but they are more deserving of the followers' loyalty. Respect should come from the manager's professional competence to utilize balanced judgment and compassion (as do good doctors or lawyers). New and ever-growing knowledge in the management sciences and the more specialized fields of finance, marketing, and personnel reinforces the professional manager's self-image: the astute, impersonal, respected decision maker who works for the larger interests of others—the organization and subordinates—and for broad goals like "sustained, balanced growth."

Society rewards honorable professionals who abide by the code of impersonally devoted duty to client needs in a context of sophisticated technical competence. The professionals are given status, deference, autonomy, and the opportunity to work in an environment that encourages sustained attention and careful, even meticulous, completion of tasks.

But in the real organizational world these rewards sometimes more readily fall to the staff experts. While in theory more dependent and constrained, the staff experts are in fact, much less enmeshed in a web of interdependent and conflicting requirements. They have the opportunity to do reflective analysis, removed from the hurly-burly, day-to-day crises. They are free to make convenient assumptions about all those sticky imponderables that drive managers wild and, given these presumptions, arrive at unambiguous "solutions" which they recommend, Q.E.D. Completed staff work is the professional's ideal, but only a naive manager seeks to emulate this.

The Appeal of Expert Decision Making

Expecting to be thoughtful, respected decision makers, accepting responsibility for tough choices but getting clear deference in return, many managers are not able to accept the real world of managerial action that confronts them. There is little that appears "professional." But, as we shall see, that makes the challenge all the greater.

One of the hidden embarrassments of most schools of administration is the students' attraction to staff work and consulting, in contrast to line management, roles.[4] Students want to be technical experts in capital budgeting, portfolio theory, OD, or policy analysis. They eschew the managerial role (which was originally the raison d'être for schools of public and business administration) and the present curricula show this with the large number of highly technical courses. The reasons for the new emphasis may be these:

1 The rhetoric of management itself is not designed to appeal to very many of today's college youth. It sounds either trivial or lacking in intellectual guts and substance (just read the older "management principles" text if you doubt this)—in effect, child's play suited to the dull not to the gifted and ambitious.

2 The manager's role appears antisocial. David McClelland correctly senses that too many people misunderstand or misconstrue the role and function of power.[5] Business executives (or power-hungry bureaucrats) particularly are both satirized and condemned for preferring power to accomplishment. The presumption in materials produced by the media and permeating our entire culture is that managers are self-seeking, petty (or not-so-petty) tyrants who prefer to use organizational position for personal gain rather than for selfless accomplishment.

Whatever the source—and one can only speculate—too many of the better students want to be professionals: university teachers, researchers, lawyers, or staff experts. They can't comprehend the challenge and the social contribution of a management career. To be sure, schools of administration are bursting at the seams because this is where the jobs are and many students fervently hope for a career in management (to take the place of that desired but unrealistic academic, legal, or engineering career). But they see the truly managerial component of these careers as a small part of the job; the lion's share is technical knowledge—knowing as distinct from doing.

As we've said, of course, the doing part is as often trivialized as the knowing component. It means either a "doing in"

---

[4] The exception is the small cadre of students who wish to go into business for themselves—to become entrepreneurs.

[5] David McClelland, "Power Is the Great Motivation," *Harvard Business Review*, vol. 54, no. 2, March–April 1976, pp. 100–110.

through wheeler-dealer maneuvers, or a rather elementary "doing for," through good human relations and common sense—e.g., treat people well and don't give them responsibilities they're not ready to assume. In a world stressing knowledge, the fruits of academic exposure, it's no wonder that so many prefer to work in a professional field like market research rather than become just another manager.

A SYSTEMS WORLD

The reality of organizational life at executive levels is a work *process* that seems at odds with the "whys" and the "whats" the professional managers bring to the job. Managers want to have a neat, static, compartmentalized world of clear goals, clearly identified resources, and obvious performance measures, and instead they find almost the diametric opposite. Some never learn; some spend most of their time seeking to make reality resemble rhetoric; most cannot comprehend the managerial skills relevant to operating in the real world.

Contradictions

In addition to being hectic, fragmented, and sharply different from society's portrait, the manager's job is also contradictory, or, at least, appears so.

• Subordinates need to be given a clear understanding of their jobs and their boundaries, yet jobs inevitably overlap and boundaries are blurred.

• Managers need to establish routine and regularization to obtain efficiency, yet routines and stability must be purposefully sacrificed to introduce change.

• Controls destroy the validity of information, but no manager can function without controls and valid information.

• Organizations are hierarchical, but in larger institutions managers spend most of their time coping with lateral relations.

• Managers need to be decisive, but it's often difficult to know exactly when a decision has been made, and many decisions must be reconsidered and remade.

• Managers must be able to comprehend the underlying continuity of their job and of their organization in a setting characterized by extreme fragmentation.

• Time is of the essence, yet most tasks must be repeated just as most problems are not solved but only "contained."

• Managers must have a strong need for achievement yet receive little sense of closure, or completion (not unlike the homemaker's problem of starting over each day).

• Rules and standards are important constraints that can't be ignored, but, inevitably, they are also inconsistent, and the manager must be able to violate or ignore some to meet others.

Rhetoric	Reality
Thoughtful decision making is the priority in a manager's workday.	Most of the workday is devoted to interaction with other people—getting and exchanging information, persuading and negotiating.
Clearly scheduled and logically planned workdays are the rule.	Impromptu, sporadic, and unplanned contacts are the rule; one jumps from issue to issue and from person to person.
Efforts are devoted to "leading" subordinates, who defer to higher status.	Most of the time is spent with outsiders, and even subordinates frequently challenge the manager's authority.
Decisions are made through rational judgment by an individual in position to evaluate all the factors.	Decisions are the product of a complex brokerage and negotiation process, extending over time and involving large numbers of interested parties.
Objectives and goals are clear and consistent.	One is faced with a multiplicity of goals identified with different groups and interests that are conflicting and even contradictory; priorities often change.
Results are proportionate to individual effort and capability; one sees steady progress and decisive accomplishment.	Results are the product of many uncontrollable forces which are slow to emerge and difficult to predict; progress comes in incremental steps—two back, three forward.
Authority is equal to responsibilities.	There are significant deficiencies in the power to command resources and in permissions necessary to fulfill assigned objectives.
Clear goals are established and are subdivided into milestones and benchmarks.	While managers need to break down larger activities into explicit goals and subgoals, in fact, most of the managers' tasks have no beginning or end; problems flow through, and there is often little possibility of neatly completing activities or solving organizational problems "once and for all."

Is Administration Nonwork or Chaos?

Given the great disparity between the brave, powerful rhetoric of management and the reality, it's hardly surprising that many talented individuals eschew managerial careers. Expecting to command and constantly make big decisions, they are appalled by the need for behavioral skills involving extraordinary patience, endurance, continuous interaction, spontaneous compromises, and negotiation. Spending so much time on the unanticipatable and repetitive "working" of relationships, rather than directly solving problems, can produce low self-esteem, a sense of time wasted, and nothing to show in accomplishment. Each day does not bring clear-cut victories and problem solving but more hours of painful persuasion, listening, and accommodation.

This peripatetic flurry, the quality of movement and activity, is not, as many naive managers assume, the result of poorly planned days, disorganization, or difficult personalities. There is no "over-the-rainbow," placid, sedate, harmonious world for the winning executive. Management is and has to be an active, interactive role, both more difficult and more demanding—not to mention more frustrating—than the role that dispassionate management scientists seek and describe.

What Managers Say about Their Work

Thus most of management is fragmented and unfinished—administrative work that appears tomorrow little changed from today. It is the "keeping-house" style where faucets almost always drip and dust reappears as soon as it's wiped away that discourages the would-be "professional" manager. As Robert Calkins put it:

> If administrators are asked to nominate the aspects of the task that are most time-consuming and frustrating to the exercise of their responsibilities, they will agree that they are preoccupied with distractions; with inconsequential little things that push themselves ahead of important issues; with the tyranny of the telephone; with the relentless flitting from one issue to another; with the ceaseless procession of interviews and ceremonials; with the pressure of circumstance and deadlines; and the absence of time to collect one's wits, much less to think or reflect.[6]

[6] Robert D. Calkins, "The Decision Process in Administration," *Business Horizons*, vol. 2, no. 3, Fall 1952, p. 20.

While Calkins was right about the appearance of trivia, he was wrong about its relevance. Indeed, most managers find difficulty in justifying their day. "After all the flurrying around, all those calls and talks and interruptions . . . what did I accomplish; where am I ahead as compared to yesterday?" What Calkins didn't understand and managers need to understand is that often the distractions are the reality.

Managers would do well to listen to a highly mobile member of middle management in a large, demanding, science-based organization describe his job:

> I have a terrible time trying to explain what I do at work when I get home. My wife thinks of a manager in terms of someone who has authority over those people who work for him and who, in turn, gets his job done for him. You know, she thinks of those nice, neat organization charts, too. She also expects that when I get promoted, I'll have more people working for me.
>
> Now, all of this is unrealistic. Actually, I only have eighteen people directly reporting to me. These are the only ones I can give orders to. But I have to rely directly on the services of seventy-five or eighty other people in this company if my project is going to get done. They, in turn, are affected by perhaps several hundred others, and I must sometimes see some of them, too, when my work is being held up.
>
> So I am always seeing these people, trying to get their cooperation, trying to deal with delays, work out compromises on specifications, etc. Again, when I try to explain this to my wife, she thinks that all I do all day is argue and fight with people.
>
> Although I am an engineer, trained to do technical work in the area encompassed by this project, I really don't have to understand anything about the technical work going on here.
>
> What I do have to understand is how the organization works, how to get things through the organization—and this is always changing, of course—and how to stop trouble, how to know when things aren't going well.
>
> As for doing a lot of planning ahead, well, it's foolish. In fact, I usually come to my office in the morning without any plans as to what I am going to do that day. Any minute something can happen that upsets the works. Of course, I keep in mind certain persisting problems on which I haven't been able to make much headway.

The constant anxieties that surround not getting work done and fighting time are misplaced, because management, in large measure, is dealing with the unexpected that interferes with routine, with unanticipated crises and petty, frustrating little problems that appear to require much more time than they are worth.

There is the appearance of a fatal flaw when an executive who is responsible for the wise expenditure of great sums of money also has to worry about parking lot and plumbing problems. The manager may well go from a budget meeting involving millions to a discussion of what to do about a broken decorative water fountain.

And then these petty problems turn out to be interminable, a Byzantine maze of interdependent relationships, personalities, and ambiguity:

> I can't tell you how many hours we wasted coping with a plumbing problem. There was water coming into the ground floor and threatening our equipment. Maintenance said they couldn't cope with it because the water company had to get permission to dig up the street, and when we finally could get the excavation done they still couldn't fix it because they announced that a nearby electric cable was causing the copper lines to disintegrate because of a current leakage through the moist ground. And the electric utility wasn't willing to admit responsibility.

In somewhat similar terms a distinguished psychiatrist-administrator sought to alert his colleagues—many of whom were being thrust into managerial roles—to the problems that arise because management was perceived as "unprofessional":

> If the administrator's image in the professions is eroded, his self-image generally as an administrator is even more diminished. I am referring here to physicians, psychiatrists, who become administrators. Their career patterns, their training and aspirations have generally been toward clinical work, teaching or research. Those are "respectable" fields. It is not unknown for an administrator to come home and when asked by his wife, "What sort of a day did you have?" to say, "It was a complete waste of time. I spent three hours with the Community Mental Health Board and then two hours with the Assistant Commissioner of Hospitals in regard to our affiliation contract, spent the lunch hour with the site visit team in order to lend my weight to a member of the department whose research application's being reviewed. Then an hour negotiating between the service group and the teaching group in regard to a program, and on and on and on. A complete waste of time." Perhaps the truth is that this is the most difficult and most important task of the day—

the managerial task. Few people have the sensitivity, the strength and the perspective to see it through.[7]

Thus, while hoping to be a commander, the manager can easily face lowered self-esteem as a glorified "go-fer." But that need not be.

Relationships: The Core of Managerial Work

Until recently, we knew more about how assembly line workers and insurance clericals spend their time than we knew about the process of management—the work of management. This has partially been rectified by a series of studies concentrating on the actual behavior of working managers.[8] The conclusions are inescapable: managers are peripatetic; their working life is a never-ending series of contacts with other people. They must talk and listen, telephone, call meetings, plead, argue, negotiate.

The pace is fast, pressured, and demanding. A first-line supervisor may have hundreds of contacts per day—many lasting less than a minute—while a "slower-paced" chief executive may have twenty or thirty. Even at that imposing level, Mintzberg reports that half of their observed activities had a duration of fewer than nine minutes.[9] Two European studies found that it was unusual for chief executives to work on any one thing for as long as a half-hour.[10]

Thus managerial work is hectic and fragmented and requires

[7] Alfred Freedman, "The Medical Administrator's Life—Administration Here Today and Here Tomorrow," *Archives of General Psychiatry*, vol. 27, September 1972, pp. 418–422.

[8] The best summary of such studies is Henry Mintzberg, *The Nature of Managerial Work*, Harper & Row, New York, 1973, chap. 3. An earlier empirical work that also summarized the research of the period is Leonard Sayles, *Managerial Behavior*, McGraw-Hill, New York, 1964. Other important research studies in this field are Rosemary Stewart, *Contrasts in Management*, McGraw-Hill, London, 1976; Ross Webber, *Time and Management*, Van Nostrand, New York, 1972; and Eliot Chapple and Leonard Sayles, *The Measure of Management*, Macmillan, New York, 1961. For an excellent view of the role of the general manager, see John Kotter, *The General Managers*, Free Press, New York, 1982. Dr. Jane Hannaway's research demonstrates how each additional executive multiplies required contacts for all others. See her *Managers Managing: The Workings of an Administrative System*, Oxford University Press, New York, 1989.

[9] Mintzberg, op. cit., p. 33.

[10] Sune Carlson, *Executive Behavior*, Strombergs, Stockholm, 1951; and Rosemary Stewart, *Managers and Their Jobs*, Macmillan, London, 1967.

the ability to shift continually from person to person, from one subject or problem to another. It is almost the diametric opposite of the studied, analytical, persisting work pattern of the professional who expects and demands closure: the time to do a careful and complete job that will provide pride of authorship. While the professional moves logically and sequentially to fulfill an explicit or implicit work plan, the executive responds to one unanticipated event after another and even at high levels is at the mercy of the situation—fulfilling an open-ended job.

Managerial work is behaviorally demanding, in its own way as demanding of behavioral skill as professional athletics. It is *doing* much more than reflecting. It requires the ability to shift from one style and set of movements to another in a matter of moments, as the need to listen to a nervous subordinate proposing a new project is superseded by the need to renegotiate terms with a key customer.

Why is management so much action, contact, and relationship? Succeeding chapters will provide many answers, but at this point we shall emphasize three:

1 Most importantly, management is a contingency activity; managers act when routines break down, when unanticipated snags appear. In the modern organization, particularly within management itself, the growing division of labor—the number of specialists (product, function, and administrative) who have a legitimate interest in any question—produces a contact explosion, a sort of domino effect, whenever a modification or new element appears:[11]

> We wanted to change the size of the first shipment. Would you believe I had to inform or get permission from eight different department heads, each of whom probably had to call several other people and they in turn a few more. By the time everyone in marketing, production, and our control staff was aboard, I had shot a good share of the day and still had five calls I hadn't returned on the matter.

It is no wonder that the manager finds it difficult to comprehend what has been accomplished and what is the day's product or to justify the energy expended and (if terribly conscientious) the salary earned: "I spent the whole day running but I'm not sure what I can show for it."

---

[11] This issue will be explored more fully in Chap. 9.

2 Almost as important an explanation can be found in human needs. People in organizations demand contacts. The manager wants to see firsthand, not to rely solely on written analyses; the subordinate wants to hear the boss's reaction, to learn from direct contact that his or her work is still appreciated. Information gets relayed best, attitudes assessed, and problems negotiated in face-to-face confrontations. After all, managers fly thousands of miles instead of relying on letters because meetings produce information and results that are far superior in most cases. While someday video "picture phones" may aid this process, human beings still require human contact to clarify and legitimate feelings and decisions.[12]

3 The third reason for so much interaction is the composition of most management issues. While economists and quantitative specialists seek methods to provide impersonal, objective answers to organization problems, answers that can be obtained by feeding data into equations, most managerial questions do not appear to have acceptable equations. The multiplicity of competing values, subgoals, special interests, and perceptual biases requires most decisions to be worked through human problem solvers. Most managerial choices arise out of interpersonal processes—advice solicitation, negotiation, persuasion, sounding out, and consensus building. Partially it's because people must agree before a decision can be implemented, but, just as importantly, it's because there are no "production functions" for most important questions.

Time: The Scarcest Resource

Perhaps the most demanding aspect of managerial life is the pressure of time. Of course, organizations function largely in terms of time; time is the cement which holds the whole thing together. Activities must be performed to coordinate, and this means an emphasis on what should be done when. But, in addition to that reality, managers in all but the smallest or most routinized situations find themselves deluged with demands for their time.

[12] These needs are analyzed more fully in Chap 4. Also see John Short, Ederyn Williams, and Bruce Christie, *The Social Psychology of Telecommunications,* Wiley, London, 1976.

Revising Expectations: The Beginning of Knowledge

New and old managers alike, as well as professionals contemplating a shift to administration, need more than a shocking dash of realism regarding the managerial role. In fact, management is much more than housework and what appears to be relentless trivia, and the victory of the silly over the important is actually rather profound. The problem has been the inability to find proper pigeon holes, to both describe and explain what managers do. But a shifting to the "*how*-you-do-it" requires a whole new set of conceptual tools. These, in turn, can provide both pride and understanding.

The modern organization, as we shall see, creates the most demanding roles in our society because of the very elements that at first blush seem so inconsistent with challenge and status. The very quantity of contact and interaction, the breadth and diversity of relationships which must be both initiated and maintained, the constancy of action and energy expenditure— all serve to make managerial jobs both the most difficult and the most deserving of acclaim. It is not simply that almost nothing happens without management, but rather that, while many can talk a good game, few are able to play it.

Predictable Behavior beneath the Chaos To naive managers, as we've noted, the real world of the executive suite is confusing chaos—obviously the product of a mixed-up organization that will someday (it is hoped) be rescued by a systems and procedures "fix." There is just too much running back and forth; countless contacts; confusing, contradictory cues; and conflicting interests.

Beneath the surface is a pattern of interaction far removed from the static world of plans and policies, executed orders, feedback loops, and thoughtful decisions. The pattern of give-and-take, demanding exquisite timing and coordination, is prescribed and required by the division of labor within management itself.

What appears to outsiders and naive managers as irrational turmoil and unplanned chaos is in fact the necessary concomitant of the complex division of labor inherent in the very nature of the modern organization. Unfortunately, while a great deal of lip service is given to the concept of *system* in modern management, few have recognized that management jobs are *system* jobs. While the remainder of this book will explore the meaning of that, we need to say here that "systems" means *interrelating, dynamic, active,* and *interfacing.* Typical managerial jobs represent focuses for a large number and broad variety of relationships—with subordinates, other managers sharing work flow responsibilities, centralized service groups, superiors, and staff groups—representing a conflicting variety of definable interests and goals. Relationships have to be worked and reworked if the work of the organization is to go forward. Managerial work gets done by verbal exchange and personal contact and by chains of interdependent bargains and explorations. It is not a discrete, static, one-decision-at-a-time process at all. There is a timed "ebb and flow" of meetings, requests, pressures, and negotiations that is inherent in the structure of the organization and the division of labor. The successful manager both understands—conceptually and cognitively—that systems process and has the behavioral skills to perform its demanding requirements.

It Takes Skills and Energy   While leadership is not the simple heroic act the romantic management writer would have you believe, it is a vital and responsible role. While much acclaim goes to the expert with ideas, answers and intellectual technique, nothing really happens until these programs and solutions get implemented and worked into operating routines that can sustain them. It's easiest to identify and glorify the good idea, but the tough job is getting it accepted and keeping it working. As we noted at the beginning, most organizations learn (to their sorrow) that there is an extraordinary scarcity of men and women who can do this. Business is best known for its constant search for executives, but government and not-for-profit organizations may have an even more difficult time of it. They are suffused with professionals who find it easy to belittle and berate the "pencil pushers." Of course, the pencil pushers don't push pencils and the professionals' skills would be useless without managerial intervention and support. However, our basic theme is not "Isn't it too bad that good managers don't get more recognition or their just deserts?" Rather it is that both the supply and quality of managerial leadership can improve and become teachable if its basic characteristics are understood. Many of the failures in leadership stem from misjudgments in both personnel selection and training, stemming from the belief that the rhetoric of management is the reality. Knowing what managers need to do provides the starting point for helping find managers who can be trained to do it (and who can be evaluated and corrected when behavior is inconsistent with requirements).

With all the brave words of Max Weber and his disciples about the importance of organization and bureaucracy, the status of management, and the deserved perquisites of high office, our society still doesn't accept those views:

> It is one of the modern mysteries that, although so much is owed by our times to the organizing and productive genius of management, the world must constantly be reminded of this fact, which it seems so obstinately reluctant to learn and believe. And curiously, it is precisely in the world's intellectual enclaves—in the universities, and among writers and journalists—that this obstinacy reaches its apex. Somehow, results are presumed to happen as if by immaculate conception.[13]

The old cliché "Workers do; managers tell" is just that—a silly misconception. Managerial work requires more energy, more activity, and more synchronization than any auto assembly line. The white collar is in motion; it is not simply a support for a mouth. It's this work of management to which we shall turn in the chapters to come.

CONCLUSIONS

The widespread failure to understand the job of the manager/leader has broader ramifications for our society as a whole. By failing to comprehend the complexity and the difficulty of these roles, society is very easily able to make management the scapegoat for all the ills of our age. Our problems are presumed to be the result of self-aggrandizing leaders, operating in highly autocratic, secretive organizations (in which hierarchical pressures produce lockstep conformity). The leader's lust for power and

---

[13] Theodore Levitt, "Management and the Post-Industrial Society," *The Public Interest,* no. 44, Summer 1976, pp. 74–75.

money, combined with an unwillingness to change priorities to stress the public good rather than selfish or parochial goals, produces all our problems. And thus the solutions are simply changed goals and unselfish leadership.

Totally misperceiving the complexity of most modern institutions, lacking any understanding of the cross-pressures, conflicting objectives, and ambiguities focused on any leader, ignoring the pluralism inherent in our diffuse profession-filled and specialist-influenced organizations, the public at large sees evil individuals and stupid decision making as the source of our widespread malaise.

Regrettably, there may be something of a self-confirming prophecy here. My experience with students of both business and public administration and my contacts with executives suggest that they are not immune to these nostrums and misperceptions. If they are going into administrative careers, they are cynical about what they will find, and their own motivations are belittled. ("I don't expect to like it, but I'll make good money and get my kicks outside" is not a minority view.) More worrisome yet, many of our best students and young managers want out because they don't believe that administrative careers provide intellectual challenge, personal fulfillment, or opportunities to serve the public good. Instead, they seek to avoid the contamination of the organization by becoming experts, professionals, the self-employed—who can be true to their conscience and always solve the problem "correctly."

How naive and how sad this is. No one doubts we live and shall continue to live in a world of organizations. In fact, increasing interdependence created by technology, by crowding, and by improved communications (and sensitivity to the total-systems implications of our decisions) will steadily increase the significance of organizational solutions to our economic and social problems. Yet many of our most able young people forswear the careers that are most relevant to our world or organizations, and even those who do intend to become managers see themselves as "selling out"—opting for more money and a less demanding life (how naive) in return for bondage to the organization.

I would argue that we badly need better means of communicating the real nature of modern organizations and the challenge of administrative positions. For two decades I have studied managerial jobs in a wide-ranging variety of settings: corporations, labor unions, courts, and public agencies. I have been struck with the enormous intellectual challenge of these roles; the energy, initiative, and range of human qualities necessary for effective performance; and the degree to which these institutions are more dynamic, more open, and more complex than popular myth recognizes.

My own experience is that the printed word is best at communicating the salacious or the oversimplified. Some years ago, *The Organization Man* gripped its readers (sophisticated students of business and laypeople alike).[14] But condemnatory tracts about government and business throttling individuals and shortchanging the public have always found a ready and responsive readership. Shakespeare made leaders come alive for his time, but we have had precious little since that has not demeaned or caricatured this most demanding of all occupations. I think it is possible to dramatize both sensitively and validly the challenge, the frustration, and the human demands of management. Further, I think we can portray the public executive and the private business manager in congruent terms, and perhaps the university administrator as well. A world of organizations, of increasing interdependence and complexity requires a society that understands something about its central institutions and the men and women who must operate them. If there is gross misconception and, on top of that, little respect for the intellectual excitement and demands of managerial roles, we can only expect increasing cynicism and increasing pressures for quick, once-and-for-all answers. And the vicious circle will be complete as our best people forswear those very positions which are central to the real problems of our time.

One final note: I believe there is more congruity and consistency in our culture than popularly assumed. Business hierarchies and public bureaucracies are not unprincipled, undemocratic exceptions to our rules. Executives in all of these spend more time seeking a consensus, negotiating conflicts, and just interacting, talking, persuading, and learning than in pronouncing orders, enumerating policy, and making shrewd

[14] William H. Whyte, Jr., *The Organization Man,* Simon and Schuster, New York, 1956.

deals. The number of parties at interest in any decision, the difficulty of predicting (or controlling) the future, of measuring performance, all of this provides an open system that is basically democratic and healthy for individual development. To be sure, there are many exceptions, illicit activity, and foolish autocrats, but the underlying point is that the basic framework of our institutional life makes these the exception, not the rule. (As sagacious Walter Lippmann observed long ago in *The Good Society*, the division of labor simply makes monolithic control of the individual untenable in our modern organizations.) Our organizations are not simple hierarchies, ruled by the passions of dolts or evil geniuses. They are, in microcosm, the mirror of the complexities of our heterogeneous, unpredictable age, and the managers who must seek to make "the system" work have on their shoulders the most difficult assignment of our age.

CHAPTER 2

AN OVERVIEW OF MANAGERIAL WORK

It is not sufficient for managers to know that life is different from what they imagined and is more demanding than they would have hoped. Nor is it adequate to have a feeling for modern management jobs in contrast to those simpler roles in traditional organizations. Managers need explicit guides to action—and to proper allocation of time, since so much of managerial work is unconstrained, that is, unprogrammed. Therefore, in this chapter we shall provide an overview of what managers do—sketchy and undocumented—and then, in succeeding chapters, we shall spell out both the reasons and the criteria for their work.

THE LOGIC OF MANAGERIAL WORK

We have seen the often harried, diffuse, fragmented—even frenetic—pace of managerial work and contrasted the reality of management with its antecedent, rational but unrealistic theory and principles, as well as with the character of professional work. Regrettably, many managers consider themselves both professionals and students of scientific management. They are prepared to move consecutively from problem, to plan, to execution and feedback, just like the laboratory scientist or the student of management cases. When the extraordinary behavioral requirements begin to conflict with this ideal, they are disconcerted, frustrated, and then condemnatory toward the shortcomings of their organization, personnel, and superiors.

A more constructive approach requires the manager not only to predict and accept the reality but to understand its own logic. There is a theory of management that squares with the reality of managerial action, and it is neither esoteric nor surprising. Of course, it's not shockingly original either. But the obvious need not be trivial, and common, or uncommon, sense can be useful.

THE ROLE OF THE MANAGER

Managers are concerned with making the organization function as an organization, that is with evolving routines (the source of efficiency) and making these routines relative to the purposes of the organization (effectiveness). Put another way, their major job is to facilitate the recombination of elements separated by the division of labor. At the same time, they want to keep changing these routines, either as persisting internal problems make them unworkable or as new external problems or opportunities require accommodation. In other words: keep "it" going and keep adjusting "it." (The "it," of course, is the work system.)

Thus two basic elements of systems management appear: (1) contingency responses and (2) uncertainty reduction.

Contingency Responses

In the perfect organization, confronting neither internal problems nor external change, the managers would act like those classical management paragons: plans would be converted into procedures and assignments, and the forthcoming work processes would be maintained by automatic interworker coordination. The managers would simply be announcing where to go and how, and everyone would charge along. Each step would follow the other.

But, of course, nature (and a lot of other things) often conspires to destroy that clockwork perfection. Subordinates get testy; they fail to complement one another; other departments are unable to fulfill their commitments; breakdowns and shortages (or surpluses) occur. The manager's job is to get the system going and keep it going by his or her own actions.

These contingency responses—the coping with potential or actual threats to the integrity of the work system and its ongoing regularities (i.e., the movement of people, materials, and ideas from step to step in a self-maintained rhythm of interaction)—are the behavioral components of administration. These unanticipatable, "going-into-action-when-needed" responses involve:

Working the hierarchy, the vertical interchanges required by a multilevel organization. (See Chapter 7.)

Working laterally, the other managers who support, feed, control, impact, and interface any manager's area. These lateral negotiations are required because none but the simplest and smallest organizations are able to give managers all the resources needed to fulfill the unit's responsibilities; rather these resources are dispersed. There is rarely, in other words, perfect decentralization and perfect autonomy so that the managers deal only with the hierarchy: subordinates and superiors. (See Chapter 5.)

Improving motivation by utilizing leadership skills to gain increased subordinate responsiveness where its absence is detected. (See Chapter 4.)

Handling special projects where all or nearly all the resources come under the jurisdiction of other managers. This requires mastering the special and distinctive skills of the project manager, exercising leadership "at a distance," so to speak. (See Chapter 10.)

And, of course, managing a control system, which is implicit in all of the above and which involves the ability to measure, assess, and evaluate where these managerial contingency interventions are required. (See Chapter 8.)

Uncertainty Reduction

But managers do more than keep the system going; they also seek to improve the system and adapt to ever-changing external (to the unit or the organization) circumstances. In simplest terms, this is the introduction of change—but change with a purpose: to cope with threatening instabilities. Both economists and psychologists have long observed this characteristic of both the firm and the executive's world. Uncertainties are psychologically oppressive and economically costly; they are the instabilities that require expensive and debilitating managerial interventions—difficult negotiations with unpredictable outcomes. Just as the firm seeks to integrate vertically to assure constant and predictable sources of supply and uses for its output, managers reach out to increase the regularity of operations and to adapt to threats appearing on the horizon that may destroy the basic rhythms of the organization.

Uncertainty reduction requires:

Applying controls to ascertain where administrative interventions are not working or are too costly—often because one of the parameters of the system has changed and some new structure or plan is necessary. (See Chapter 8.)

Working the hierarchy to evolve a consensus, to "sell" or disseminate a new plan or direction to cope with these problems or new opportunities. (See Chapter 9.)

Moving outward to change the underlying structure of lateral relationships with other managers that create excessive (at least to the manager involved) uncertainties—stressful, erratic, and irregular needs to respond to other managers' demands. This is more self-serving than the other managerial actions we have considered: it is the quest for organizational power, which is really, as we shall see, uncertainty reduction. (See Chapter 6.)

Most importantly, introducing these changes, implementing, and making something workable in an organizational context in which routine (short-run efficiency) has been rewarded. The shifting of gears from regularity to system destruction requires extraordinary skill and a heavy investment of managerial time. (See Chapter 9.)

MANAGERIAL ACTION IN REAL TIME

One must always work within the context of reality. In the following case we wish to illustrate the admixture of longer-run, more strategic executive actions (uncertainty reduction) with short-run, crisis-responding, and "fire-fighting" tasks (contingency responses) that make up a typical day's agenda. As we noted in Chapter 1, to the untutored eye, real managerial behavior may appear to be random in pattern—a manager runs this way and that, never seeming to catch up. But lack of the sequential and the discrete—after all, planning is not separate from doing, and the manager isn't allowed to proceed logically ·from problem to solution—should not cause a manager to despair of achieving any real patterning in his or her work.

A description, extracted from our research files, of a portion of the managerial workday reveals a dynamic patterning of activities that is in sharp contrast to the static view inherent in traditional management principles. In this case we observe a woman who heads a product service department handling short-run contingencies at the same time she seeks to improve operations and the work system for which she is responsible. She "works the hierarchy" and fields a variety of lateral relationships with peers while endeavoring to motivate subordinates. Many of these things occur almost simultaneously, and the pace is fast. It is this almost frenetic pace, diffuse pattern of relationships, and simultaneous "juggling of many balls" that gives managerial work its unique character among the professions.

See if you can identify the real pattern underlying the *apparent* confusion in the manager's actions. Note also her priorities: what is dealt with immediately, what is postponed, and what, if anything, is ignored. You may not agree with all her split-second, real-time decisions, but you should be able to see that allocations of time and energy is one of the most difficult—and important—kinds of managerial decisions: what to do when, and how, and with whom.

CASE: A Couple of Hours in the Life of a Manager

Jane Rao heads product service for the Elgard Company. Elgard sells insurance, produces a variety of industrial equipment, and has recently begun selling a small number of consumer items derived from their commercial lines. Rao has several hundred employees, about half of whom work in the head office, fielding phone calls and letters requesting product information or registering complaints. The other half are in geographically dispersed repair centers. Some work there is done on the premises, but a field repair staff works on-site for large corporate customers.

One afternoon Rao decides to sample one or two of the numerous pink slips that her secretary has placed on her desk in a folder marked "Unsolicited Customer." There is no reason for Rao to talk with customers; her service representatives are well trained, and there are half a dozen supervisors to deal with difficult problems. However, Rao's name is on the company stationery and occasionally a persistent or impatient customer will try to reach "the boss." She knows that responding to a few of these will give her some feeling for how the reps are doing, what they're up against, and how well they're handling the pressure-packed problems.

As luck would have it, the first call Rao places turns up a totally unanticipated issue. She expected to reach a corporate office but is instead connected to a residential number. The customer has recently purchased the #36 model electronic typewriter which has some features of a stripped-down word processor. The customer is angry. In response to his first complaint, he was told ("rudely," he says) that there was nothing Elgard could do about his malfunctioning machine because the warranty had expired. The customer claims that at the store where he purchased the machine *and* on the guarantee slip in its packaging, he was assured of a 24-month warranty, and he wants the machine fixed or his money back. He is prepared to mail it wherever appropriate, but he is not prepared to wait any longer.

Rao assures him that she or one of her people will look into the matter and get back to him within a day or two. Immediately she calls one of her supervisors to inquire about the 24-month warranty. When the supervisor agrees with her that the normal company warranty is for twelve months, Rao decides to go out on the floor herself to one of the computer terminals used by telephone-response personnel in order to find the most recent information on the #36 model. Though she finds no mention of a 24-month guarantee there, she is delighted to see that the new hardware and software have greatly expanded the amount of information a clerk can access and that the system is working smoothly. (In fact, one of Rao's reasons for going out on the floor was to work the terminal herself, and to see the new system in operation.)

The efficiency of the new system aside, Rao's problem remains. Perhaps the 24-month guarantee is one of those new promotions that marketing has undertaken without informing service. Rao vaguely remembers hearing something about an extended warranty being offered as a part of a promotion package that marketing was considering "to jazz up" flagging #36 sales. In fact, just weeks before, she was involved in a minor skirmish with marketing over another promotion. They had developed a rebate procedure which required the customer to return the store receipt, part of the packaging, and a questionnaire that dealt with some market research data. Not only were the requirements for getting the rebate complicated (and easy to misconstrue), but the rebate was being handled by a vendor known for slow service. As a result, Rao's people had been flooded with calls from irate customers who wanted to know either why they hadn't received their rebate or how to handle the application. Her staff had had trouble handling the questions properly because marketing had failed to provide them any advance information as to what was being done, how, and when.

At the time of the trouble, Rao had gone to her boss to complain about marketing's failure to coordinate their plans with her department. But Green hadn't given her much support. In fact, he had indicated that marketing might be inclined to avoid working with service simply because Rao was always finding fault with their proposed campaigns, always pointing out how this or that feature would be troublesome from a service point of view. Rao had been stung by that criticism because she thought service was now a high-priority value at Elgard and that their involvement up front was essential to make sure that high service standards were upheld. When she tried to say something about how important service was in retaining the customers that marketing might attract, Green had brushed it aside, saying that he expected his managers to be "team players."

Remembering all of this, Rao is not surprised when she calls Brown, her counterpart in marketing, and learns that they indeed have implemented an extended warranty on the #36. When Rao duly registers her complaint that her department has not been informed of that fact, Brown tries to pacify her with the information that the new guarantee has not created extra sales and that "no more than two or three thousand units" have been sold under it.

Rao's next call is to Gil Trump, liaison between service and marketing systems. She tells him to be sure that the systems people are aware of the fact that some #36 units are now being sold with a 24-month warranty.

It is not long before Rao receives a call from Green asking her to have her staff keep track of the number of complaints received about the #36 units. Apparently, Rao infers, there are problems here, and Elgard, anxious to make it big in this new consumer business, is touchy.

To find out what's really going on, she calls Al Cohen, her friend in engineering. From Al she learns that engineering is already aware that there are problems, and that the problems are centered in a small auxiliary motor. The motor is a new, low-cost component that was added when the #36 was developed from the very successful #821 machine. The #821 had been designed for high-volume commercial use, and because it was assumed that the #36 machine, designed for the typical "at home" consumer, would be used much less intensively, it was produced with less robust components than its predecessor. Al also tells her that they are now making the more powerful motor available to their sales and service centers around the country, and if a customer "really complains," the more durable motor is to be substituted.

Al has a suggestion: "You know, if your service clerks could get some idea of what kind of users the #36 complaints are coming in from, we might find out whether these machines are getting into the hands of commercial firms that are just beating them to death, or if they are really failing in normal 'home' usage."

As she hangs up, Rao wonders whether she should tell Green that she is thinking of undertaking this informal survey for engineering. And she thinks again of a plan she has been considering for some time—that it would be very useful for service to have some kind of direct access to engineering. There would be many advantages to having her service personnel in direct contact with an engineering representative. At times there are technical questions that her people can't answer; at other times the literature displayed on their video monitors is out of date. Direct contact with engineering would clear up a lot of questions—and would also add to the prestige and visibility of the service jobs. Rao knows that over the years the reps have developed increasing technical competence, but she hasn't been able to get their salaries increased correspondingly; management still thinks of them as just a telephone-answering service.

Rao's reveries are interrupted when Trump calls to say that despite his best efforts, systems can't do anything about updating the #36 screens for at least a month. The software, which had recently been redesigned at some significant cost, lacks the flexibility to add different or extra warranty data, a flexibility no one had thought of in design stages. It's the third time in the past two weeks that Rao has heard that the new upgraded software is more rigid than she had been led to believe. Apparently, it can't display multiple prices or show rebates either, although both are important factors in Elgard's marketing efforts and she had asked for that capability. She wonders how much of this is due to Trump's ineptness and lack of prestige in systems and how much is due to the fact that systems likes to think they know it all.

Rao calls systems herself and asks that all screens for their consumer products henceforth display one line in caps across the bottom of the screen: CHECK CATALOG FOR ADDITIONAL PRICE, REBATE, AND WARRANTY DATA. This will alert the clerks that the screens are incomplete and that they should look elsewhere for the information. The systems manager she speaks to is firm: "That request will have to go into the queue and take its turn," she tells Rao. But Rao knows a reasonable amount about programming and systems and she is sure her request could be honored in five or ten minutes by an experienced programmer. There is no way she can get it done without a good contact, however, and that's where Trump stands in her way.

She's also sure that systems is not anxious to start fussing with bits and pieces of their support software when it looks as though marketing is initiating a major effort to get new product features, many of which will call for systems support. Rao knows that systems isn't getting much more notice than she about what's coming down the pike, and their tactic might well be to wait until the dust settles and then deal with as many changes as possible at one time.

Both because she needs to relax and because she struggled to get the appropriation for the hardware through, Rao now goes back over to the telephone area to watch the clerks use the new video monitor that allows them to access six different databanks simultaneously, bringing up materials for display in separate windows at the same time. Her supervisors have said it's working well, but she wants to see for herself and get the feel of how the work flow is being affected. She also knows that being out on the floor and talking with the clerks helps cement relationships; they seem delighted when upper management cares enough to watch and question them.

Being on the floor also gives Rao a chance to watch Jane Atchley in the process of fielding calls. The customer whose complaint has prompted all of this had made some reference to having been cut short of time to explain his story. Rao knows that Jane has been criticized for curtness before, and while she may not have been the clerk involved this time, she still bears watching.

Indeed Jane's supervisor, Alice, has been reluctant to stay on top of personnel problems. Besides, Alice should have picked up on this #36 problem. Rao has told all the supervisors that during this break-in period when customers request information not available on the new equipment and software she should be informed. But not a single item has yet been brought to her attention.

Rao's mind wanders; she could easily spend a dozen hours getting Jane to be a more considerate clerk and Alice to be a more alert, more energetic supervisor, but there are so many other things to do. And what are the solutions anyway? Some might be tempted to let Alice go. She's made a number of mistakes in the past, but she's a long-service employee. Her departure would only hurt morale. Actually, there's always the chance of encouraging Alice to accept a job in accounting. She worked there when she first joined the company and they liked her—and there are openings in that growing area.

But Rao quickly puts aside the temptation to move Alice out of her department. She is concerned with adding staff, not fine-tuning its quality. Elgard's push into consumer products is adding to service's workload beyond the levels anticipated. Her budgeted staffing levels were developed on the basis of a long-standing formula relating number of units sold to service calls. In fighting for personnel at the last budget go-around she failed to anticipate what seems obvious now. Consumers, less sophisticated and less pressured for time than commercial customers, were much more likely to call in miscellaneous requests and complaints. Her performance indicators, which Green watches like a hawk (e.g., how long a customer has to wait for an answer) are already trending down. And there's worse to come. She fears that marketing is about to encourage a number of new "knock-offs" of existing commercial products to be sold to consumers—although, to be honest, she recognizes that since she has not been included in strategy discussions, that presumption is more guesswork than anything else.

Her boss, to this point, has little sense of the crush of new service calls. All he sees and judges by is a single weekly number: average customer waiting time before call answered. That "average" hardly gives an accurate picture. Certain hours on Monday and Friday are very busy, but those long delays are covered up by quick response times during the slow hours and days. Further, the standard her boss likes—a response under twenty-five seconds—is "helped" by the number of consumers who simply give up, either because they get a busy signal or because the phone rings and rings with no answer. (These "abandoned" calls are not counted in the average.) Rao has often wondered whether she should risk sending up some "bad" numbers to make her case for some kind of relief.

Now as she leaves the floor to go back to her office, Rao runs into Jim Kit, one of her best supervisors. Kit has a problem. The mainframe is down, and without it he can't finish the monthly report service has to prepare for headquarters. One of the major items headquarters looks at is monthly service costs, an item that relates regional labor and parts allocations to centralized refunds and parts and unit shipments. Rao tells Kit that he should be able to do the whole thing on his minicomputer, given the software Rao has had developed for her people. "But," Kit explains, "we're supposed to match every expenditure with the data-entered case-disposition material, and with the mainframe down I can't do the matching." In a split second, Rao makes her decision: "Just don't announce that to anyone. The most important thing is getting in a report—any reasonably accurate report is better than none."

Though Kit wonders what will happen (and to whom) if anyone finds out the data haven't been cross-checked, Rao placates him. She will deal with that problem, if and when it arises; in any event, it is a lot better to be found lax in following a procedure than to miss a deadline on a closely watched report.

Rao looks at her watch. Almost two hours have passed since she talked with the dissatisfied customer. It is now 3:45; she has to get some charts ready for a meeting with the divisional VP in the morning, and there is still a lot of correspondence that has to go out before 5. As she mulls this over, she sees her secretary waving; that can only mean that there is an "important" call waiting. If she's lucky, she can dispatch it in five minutes. As she moves to her office to take the call, she asks her secretary to call the customer with the complaint and reassure him that the company will repair his machine.

In thinking about this brief interval in Rao's workday, one has to be impressed with the managerial challenge of her job. How does she place priorities on the many demands for attention? What are the most pressing issues, and which can she afford to "put on the back burner"? Nonmanagers must wonder just how much of this pulling and hauling one can tolerate in a given day, and just what personality strengths are required. Such considerations will be addressed in Chapter 11.

CONCLUSIONS

Note that we have said little about that critical managerial function, planning. But planning is involved in many of the action patterns described in the case above: in ascertaining where there are problems; in gaining the knowledge and input of technical experts in lateral relationships; in gaining acceptance through the hierarchy; and in being aware of the implementation problems to come so that they may be built into the plans and not be an afterthought.

To summarize—we are dealing with managerial behavior: action in time. Even when managers are thinking and planning they need to understand such things as lateral relationships, impediments to change, building commitment, and much more.

So let us now turn to an analysis of the various elements that make up the behavioral repertoire of modern managers. Our emphasis will be on how managers can perform the tasks necessary to successful leadership. In sharp contrast to the usual discussion of what managers should achieve—somehow—we shall stress the actual behavior utilized by effective leaders. Operating on a contingency basis and learning what it takes to reduce uncertainty are the key constructs, but the behavioral pattern of the effective manager has many other aspects.

CHAPTER 3

ASSERTING AUTHORITY

In the modern organization, as students of management constantly remind us, the manager must earn authority and deference; it's not just given by title or fiat. Thus the manager must be concerned with asserting influence and power—the power to command and to expect responsiveness.

Regrettably, this basic leadership requirement, this skill, is often ignored in the management literature on the assumption that subordinate satisfaction is the primary concern of the leader, the further assumption being (quite correctly) that satisfied followers admire and thus defer to their leaders. Sources of subordinate satisfaction are not, in fact, identical with the skills of initiating action—that is, asserting authority.

To exercise authority, leaders/managers must learn how to:

1 Arouse followers to accept orders and initiations
2 Gain credibility as a legitimate source of initiations
3 Cope with confrontations in which orders are ignored or disputed

UNDERSTANDING PRIMITIVE LEADERSHIP: THE ELEMENTAL SKILLS

We shall consider leadership in its simplest and most primitive form to obtain some insight into the basic relationship of leader and "led." Anthropologists have viewed the leadership role cross-culturally and through the ages. If we examine their findings, a clear pattern emerges.[1]

Leaders manifest their distinctive position by periodically— only rarely and briefly—initiating to all subordinates, getting them to be responsive *simultaneously* to the order (in what is called a "set event"). Such simultaneity is essential to both reinforcing the position of the leader and accomplishing the goals of the group. (Quick, adaptive, simultaneous accommodation is necessary in order to cope with an external challenge that cannot be dealt with by a one-on-one, sequential chain of commands or initiations.)

But this group response must be preceded by a series of "pair events," one-on-one initiations from manager to subordinates that occur with much higher frequency and greater intensity than do set events. Pair events are necessary to bring the subordinates to a point where they will respond synchronously to the initiations of their leader.

Handling Pair Events

Leaders actively encourage the bringing of problems and requests (gifts and tribute in more traditional societies). Wherever social scientists have studied groups, high-status individuals *receive* the most initiations, which is both a mark of their position and a support for it. How is this accomplished?

Leaders are responsive to requests for aid, assistance, commiseration. They are more likely to be willing to devote the time and to have the requisite social *and* technical skills to satisfy these demands. They can provide both organizational and technical "fixes" that aid the other person (and provide appreciation and a sense of indebtedness in return).[2]

Leaders also have the energy and perseverance to keep circulating among their followers. (Remember the example of Jane

---

[1] This section is derived, in part, from the seminal work of Conrad Arensberg, as elaborated by F. L. W. Richardson, Jr., and W. F. Whyte. The basic theory was first developed in Eliot Chapple and Carlton Coon, *Principles of Anthropology*, Holt, New York, 1942.

[2] Peter Blau in his classic study of a public agency shows leaders as being the most sought after for assistance in solving difficult work problems. See Blau's *The Dynamics of Bureaucracy*, University of Chicago Press, Chicago, 1955.

Rao in the case study in Chapter 1.) Their very presence and encouragement enable these "followers" to talk freely and easily—a source of pleasurable release and satisfaction to the follower. (Lower-status persons get satisfaction from being able to initiate to higher-status individuals.) By maintaining free access and proximity and by encouraging such contacts, leaders become the focal points for information, natural "databanks" to which anyone can turn in order to obtain the most current and comprehensive information. In turn, this enables the leaders, in both "pair" responses and "set" order giving, to provide more sensible direction. Thus, by skill and location, astute leaders encourage people to come for assistance and problem resolution. In turn, providing satisfying responses to these requests builds up a reservoir of goodwill and a consensus as to who really is of highest status. Prestige—and later deference—is assigned to those to whom most people initiate.

Leaders do more than give information and aid; they also dispense adjudications that resolve conflicts and stalemates and relieve pent-up tension among subordinates. Whether in the courts of a Solomon or the office of a project leader, followers want arbiters who will be both sagacious enough and respected enough to terminate upsetting disagreements. (This resolving of stalemates will be further discussed in Chapter 7.)

Handling Set Events

Whether one observes a primitive group of warriors or fishermen, a street gang or an agricultural cooperative, one can find a centralized source of direction to accommodate to external change and challenge. To be sure, leaders may simply be announcing a previously arranged consensus, but the clear statement of that new decision, followed by the simultaneous responsiveness of all, is essential for group survival.

Given the information, the loyalty, and the status that result from acting as the focus for these initiations, leaders are then in a position to get subordinates to be responsive to orders and decisions. The mark of leaders is the ability to redirect the actions and goals of followers. Such a source of "new" decisions has been found to be essential to the survival of every human group. ("No, Virginia, there are no leaderless groups," contrary to what some would hope or assert.)

The formal order or decision is often preceded, as shown in studies of primitive as well as of sophisticated societies, by an intensity of interaction. Leaders literally "work up" the group to prepare them to be responsive:

> In primitive societies this takes the form of ritualized dancing and chanting, the showing of symbolic relics and other physical manifestations of the power and mystery of the leader. As the chief or priest senses the increased arousal and attentiveness of the group, the basic "beat," the frequency of his initiations increases; in turn, the frequency of response increases—the followers "lose" themselves in the ceremony. As the pitch of excitement and expectation peaks, the leader can request almost anything—the dramatic climax—launching a battle, an enormous sacrifice, great personal risk taking.

In more modern groups, leaders have the persistence and dominance to keep talking to what at first may be somewhat dubious and easily distracted groups. They have the ability to talk down opposition and to speak rapturously and engagingly on the advantages of the new course of action, the problems that will be resolved, the extraordinary gains for all that will be obtained. Like their primitive counterparts, they will use emotional symbols and metaphors to enhance their responsiveness:

> As you know, we face very serious problems—problems which could destroy us—but they're not going to, because we will do things together that will enable us to come out stronger than ever—like a great football team.
>
> We stand for the best, our department is the best, our people are the best and we are going to continue to show the best results because we're the premier marketing division in this corporation.
>
> If you will support me in launching this development project by providing some budget and personnel, I can promise you that you will be getting in on the ground floor of a development that will keep your divisions in clover for a decade or more. This is going to be so successful, so important, so profitable that every one of you will become famous.
>
> Remember how we did with Project 280? Well this is going to be just as rewarding; it will be more rewarding. It's going to be another 280 all over again.

Enhancing Order Giving Then, if the leader has done his or her job well, subordinates go into action, simultaneously and synchronously. The chances that the decision/order will lead to what they all will perceive as a successful outcome is enhanced by the leader's position and behavior:

1 Being central to communications, the leader knows more than the others about the situation and individual capacities.

2 The simultaneous, and thus mutually cooperative and complementary, response of followers increases the likelihood of their accomplishing the goal, fulfilling the mission.

3 The "working up" by the leader increases the subordinates' drive and determination, the very momentum of the new activity.

4 And, of course, should the endeavor prove mutually rewarding, this result will enhance the status of the leader, increasing his or her ability to give both more and more difficult or controversial orders in the future.

5 Success breeds success in increasing the self-confidence of the subordinate group—they have the ability to follow through successfully, to "win," to be the chosen ones.

In addition to these five sources of impetus in carrying through the "set"—the simultaneous response—to what will be perceived as a successful outcome, the leader has another advantage. Many studies of organizations have shown the enthusiasm and motivation that are derived from the sense of jointly responding to a common disturbance or enemy, or toward a common goal. The very physical, behavioral awareness of being part of a mutually complementary, coordinated, harmonious effort is itself exhilarating:

> Those first few weeks, when the agency was new and we had to establish all our rules and procedures and deal with that enormous backlog of cases, was the happiest and hardest I've ever known. Everyone helped everybody else; there was no complaining or back-biting, just cooperation. We all had the sense of being part of a team that was going to conquer the world.[3]

---

[3] Author's interview with a social agency member recounting the period in which the agency got established under a highly respected leader.

Thus winning begets winning, not simply because of the self-confidence engendered, but because human beings are both aroused and satisfied by experiencing a mutually responsive group. Of course, this is no different from the frequently observed euphoria generated within the audience at a great artistic or athletic performance, the heightened emotion of an enraptured crowd which acclaims by shouts, applause, and "rising as one" the glory of the occasion. The sense that one's colleagues share the same response and the same basic rhythms engendered by the same central stimulus enhances the stimulus. Drummers and great orators, demagogues and thespians have all used this phenomenon of group arousal to multiply the effectiveness of their performances. There are few who don't savor this kind of "dancing in public to a common drumbeat."

The rhythmically maintained, simultaneous response also eliminates potentially interruptive or abrasive individual differences. Fully absorbed in the group response, the individual no longer has the compulsion or need to wrangle or dissent. "When everyone is working so harmoniously, so busily and effectively, I just forget myself and throw myself into the job. It's like we were one person."

To summarize, the basics of primitive leadership are these:

1 The coming together in pair events of the leader and the led
2 The leader's "working up" of subordinates and the enunciating of an order or decision—the "set event," as we have termed it
3 The following through by simultaneous response, i.e., the concerted action of all subordinates to fulfill the command or request

Before and After Events This leadership triad (pair response, set initiation, and subordinate group action leading to a successful outcome) requires behavioral bolstering to be workable over time. Successful leaders must learn to:

1 Legitimate their position to receive initiations from deferential subordinates and to give orders
2 Cope with potential or actual nonresponse (the threat that some will be unwilling to accept the orders and status of the leader)

In a sense, (1) is before the fact and (2) is after the fact—developing the potential for coping with threats to one's position after order giving.

LEGITIMATING THE LEADERSHIP ROLE

How do managers gain acceptance for their right to give orders, their right to higher status and deference?

Demonstrating Ability

Leaders must demonstrate superior ability, whether it be technical skill or organizational sophistication. Their skills and knowledge should entitle them to the position. Thus professionals expect that their bosses will know more about the field, professors that their department heads will be acclaimed experts, artisans that their supervisors will be expert in the trade.

Achieving Credibility

In addition, bosses are expected to know the "rules of the game," the norms, expectations, and values of the group to be supervised. Knowing the norms means being able to communicate: "Since I know your world, I'll do right by you." Thus promotions from within, the use of "straw bosses" (working supervisors), will increase the chance that new leaders will not violate expectations or prove themselves a threat to "all we hold dear." (Working bosses both know the norms and are more vulnerable to work-group pressures to live up to them.)

In strange situations, leaders learn to co-opt "lieutenants"; that is, they give status and recognition to those with preexisting positions which assures deference and responsiveness. By funneling some (but not all) of their orders through lieutenants who know how to convert or translate the request into some terms consistent with group norms and whose own acceptance of these assures responsiveness, they obtain the best of two worlds. Not threatening but enhancing the informal leaders' position assures their support for the formal leader's position.

Further, the lieutenants' "endorsement" or translation assures conformity.[4]

> When I was first made a supervisor, as a college-trained social worker, I didn't know what people expected. I didn't know how they had been working and whether new cases should automatically go to certain caseworkers or not. But I was fortunate; Hank had been there for years, knew the ropes backward and forward, and I could, by working closely with him, make requests that would seem reasonable. In six months I felt confident enough to do much more on my own.

Representing and Buffering

Nothing legitimates and substantiates the position of leaders more than their ability to handle external relations. Above all else, leaders control a boundary, an interface. From the point of view of subordinates, the leaders typically are the link with the outside world, whether the world of financial support (the bankers and investment community) or the world of upper management (where salary increases and increased budgets are born).

Respected, admired leaders are those who can deal profitably with outsiders and bring back benefits and protection. Protection consists of preventing the outside world from making pressure-filled demands and pushing around the insiders, violating norms, and interfering with predictable and comfortable routines.

> Our department does the office moving for the entire organization—desks, files, equipment, even partitions. Everyone wants theirs done yesterday. Since it's usually the brass who calls, when we had a pushover as boss we were always scheduling one job and doing another because someone higher than the first would demand priority. Now we have a boss who stands up for our needs and our schedule. He insists on first come, first served unless they can get an OK to interfere with us from the president.

Thus bosses who can buffer their employees and who can go against the organization's grain, against the chain of command,

---

[4] If all orders are channeled through the lieutenants, the leaders become too dependent, too easily manipulated and controlled. They need to develop the capacity for a reasonable number of direct initiations to the group.

to win benefits and get oppressive rules changed or ignored earn loyal followership—even when their other leadership characteristics are inadequate. We have seen many short-tempered, oppressive bosses who would "fight to the death" for their people and who were beloved by appreciative subordinates. Nothing proves more about the right to command than the ability to defend.

Although the phrase is now almost a cliché, managers are people "in the middle" (except for chief executives). The meaning is simple. Executives will be caught between the conflicting demands and expectations of those above and below. But reconciliation is not a passive process of somehow, analytically or rationally, proving that everyone wants the same thing. (This is the way naive executives used to try to handle labor relations: simply show the unions that more profits mean the ability to pay higher wages and provide greater job security—we both want the same thing, after all!)

Rather, being "in the middle" involves an interface or boundary role which must be played out behaviorally more than cognitively:

1 Get demands modified; sometimes take the chance of reinterpreting.

2 Defend subordinates (cover up at times?).

3 Get thing laterally—from groups that control resources and permissions—and from higher management.

Thus representation becomes *advocacy*. The modern organization actually consists of a number of semi-independent fiefdoms that are competing for budget and perquisites with each other. Few benefits get bestowed without powerful, articulate, patient advocates who are skillful at formal presentations and informal infighting. The last thing subordinates respect is managers who simply sit as judges, seeing themselves as outsiders who support those requests from their group that will most easily be accepted by outsiders (peers) and upper management.

The fervor and animal energy that produce loyalty are well portrayed in the following quotation from a division vice president of a high-technology company, who had just been informed that top management was considering moving the responsibility for certain activities from his division to another. He was asked what he was going to do:

> You've got to be more aggressive than they [i.e., the competing department] are. You've got to be farther down the road than they [the corporate planners whose analyses help shape these decisions] are. You've got to convince [top management] that you're the best God-damned engineers to do the job. You've got to fight every step of the way.

Later he commented on an earlier experience:

> Nobody wanted the [product] when we first came up with the idea. But we went back again and again. We went through a blood bath to get it accepted. . . . [5]

"Anointing"

In some measure, status is transferable. New leaders can be authenticated by someone who already has status in the eyes of their potential followers. Thus the political candidate seeks to be seen shoulder to shoulder—even embraced—by the party's top figure: a governor or senator, or better yet, the President. Heads of organizations can and ought to install—with ceremonious flourishes—all new supervisors to call attention to their formal endorsement of the appointment.

Manipulating Social Distance

New leaders must successfully manipulate the social distance, the gap that separates them from their followers. Here, too, expectations matter. In United States culture (and increasingly throughout the more industrialized world), managers are expected to minimize the social distance separating them from their subordinates. They do this by such techniques as:

1 Being willing to jump into a problem and "get their hands dirty" by doing some of the work themselves, not waiting for a subordinate

---

[5] R. R. Ritti and Fred Goldner, "Professional Pluralism in an Industrial Organization," *Management Science,* vol. 16, no. 4, December 1969, pp. B233–246. Ritti and Goldner even describe the dress rehearsals of astute managers practicing their formal presentation skills. We have observed the same theatrical frills in most organizations we have studied.

2 Having subordinates use the same form of address they themselves use, typically first names

3 Keeping their office doors open, not insisting on appointments

4 Sharing eating or parking spaces, and participating together in social events

Higher levels of leadership are allowed more exclusivity—opulent offices, restricted entry, more formal forms of address. In fact, their status may well be enhanced by their admired, but not to be emulated, "high" living and grand isolation—by figuratively or literally "living like a king." But significantly, in many new "high-tech" firms, top management has few status symbols.

Setting Consequential Goals

Influential bosses are also those perceived as being able to accomplish things internally, within their own work areas. To their subordinates they are not like the proverbial cork bobbing aimlessly in a rough sea. The "seas" are indeed rough, but in the midst of apparent chaos, as we have seen, leaders can establish goals and move their organizations toward them.

Goals perform a number of critical functions in cementing the leadership position of the manager:

1 They help reduce the amount of time taken up by interruptions, distractions, and problem solving. Some simple technical or structural change can often eliminate the source of a problem bothersome to both manager and subordinate. When the manager is less buffeted by work imperfections, he or she can spend more time doing leadership tasks.

> Every day I was spending 10 percent of my time tracking down people who could solve our printer problems. I was finally able to get a capital budget request approved that brought us new and reliable equipment. My people are less frustrated, and we have freed up almost an extra hour a day to give to other projects.

2 They can focus the efforts of subordinates so that they become more mutually cooperative. Most jobs have somewhat ambiguous requirements or, at least, a variety of ways in which they can be performed. A clear focus, reflecting goals firmly stated and consistently rewarded, increases the likelihood that subordinates will do their jobs in ways that complement the work of others:[6]

> I've never worked so hard as when we had to change locations. Our boss had set the date of the third Monday in March for beginning work in a new location, and we had agreed with that, knowing it would be tough but also realizing why it was necessary. Well everyone pitched in; no one said, "This isn't in my job description," and the enthusiasm was contagious. Because Jane would do anything to help me, I would knock myself out for anything she asked.

3   The subordinates' perception that the group is being mutually responsive to the direction (goal) set by the leader and that there is momentum toward the goal redounds to the credit of the leader. He or she has thus proved an ability to lead, to get the group to respond, to make progress, and to accomplish a new objective.[7]

Giving Technical Aid

Managers, to be accepted as leaders, are expected to provide aid and assistance to employees with difficult on-the-job problems. Being able to demonstrate this kind of facilitation requires not only knowledge about the technologies being supervised but also the willingness to use scarce time resources to be responsive to such requests. Obviously it isn't realistic to expect the manager to solve all such problems, nor is it desirable that subordinates become excessively dependent. However, managers who can be helpful derive substantial loyalty from appreciative subordinates.[8]

Showing Persistence

It used to be said that Communists seeking to gain power in the Western democracies often won political victories by sheer en-

---

[6] One of the best examples of this mutual reinforcement to meet a clear and shared goal is the design of a new computer at Data General, as described by Tracy Kidder in *The Soul of a New Machine*, Little, Brown, Boston, 1981.

[7] For a review of the research on goal setting and its effect on motivation, see M. E. Tubbs, "Goal-Setting" a Meta-analytic Examination of the Empirical Evidence," *Journal of Applied Psychology*, vol. 71, 1986, pp. 474–483.

[8] For an extensive discussion of how leaders strengthen subordinates, see James Kouzes and Barry Posner, *The Leadership Challenge*, Josey-Bass, San Francisco, 1987, Chap. 8.

durance. After the opposition had grown weary with debate, the Communists were still insisting, still pushing, and still alert to every nuance of a meeting. The result was that they could gradually take over liberal organizations. On quite a different level, the harried mother often loses the battle with her child over cleaning up or finishing homework because she grows weary of insisting (and has both more critical and more attractive alternative uses of her time), while the child seemingly has little else to do but resist and malinger.

In both cases, a simple, yet critical, prescription for legitimating one's position is simply persistence—not giving up, insisting that one's legitimate demands be met. By persistence we mean simply repetition, clarity of command, self-confident *dominance*—being able to keep asking, talking, explaining. This very physical insistence may carry the day.

Persistence also means that orders and commands are given self-confidently. Would-be leaders who whine, who scold, who plead are communicating their presumption that subordinates will not do what is being asked—because they either are "worthless" or have failed before, or perhaps because the instruction itself is not worthy or legitimate. In any event, the leaders are expressing doubts. Whether the doubts are of self or of other, they get communicated by orders that are half-hearted, accusatory, or apologetic:

"I wish someone would take the responsibility of getting this place cleaned up."

"Now why can't you do this without my asking? I just know you're going to forget."

The plaintive, exasperated tone, the elevated pitch, the apologetic or excessive rationalization—all serve to say, "You have disappointed me before," or, "I don't expect that you will do this either," and these become, more often than not, self-fulfilling prophecies.

Practicing Power

Leaders gain their status and responsiveness by getting subordinates used to following their directions. To be sure, excessive initiations are destructive; they're resented as oppressive management. But the converse—the fewer the better—is not true. One establishes the role of the leader by actually initiating orders.

This is accomplished by gradations: moving from very few to the proper level (or frequency) and moving from the most obvious, easily accepted areas to the more ambiguous and potentially controversial.

Thus new leaders are cautious, not wanting to be confronted by refusal or to be challenged before their position is established firmly. The earliest orders are in areas where there are reasonable assurances that subordinates are willing, ready, and able. Also, the number of orders is small, but the frequency builds up as subordinates get used to this new source of instructions and, most importantly, can view their colleagues being responsive to and accepting the leadership.

There is a relevant analogy in the theater and in public speaking. The early lines often carry broad, obvious humor or symbols that the audience can and will respond to almost automatically. As members of the audience "warm up"—get used to the presentation and hear others vigorously and openly responding—they are made ready for more obscure and more subtle ideas.

Maintaining Momentum

To be sure, subordinates don't want mindless or needless orders from managers who relish demonstrating their authority by commanding deference. As we shall see, employees want reasonable autonomy, consultation, and all the rest—but they also want managers who take action, who bestir themselves to introduce, with appropriate periodicity, the decision sets we have earlier described.

This can best be observed in its absence. Then employees report that management is passive, indifferent, or just lazy. "No real decisions have been made in months (or years)." "We're stagnating." "Look at problems X, Y, and Z and opportunities A, B, and C . . . they're all ignored!" Absent is a sense of movement and dynamism.

Subordinates do recognize that their organizations require active leadership and that they are impotent without a leader, although they may be loath to admit this:

Faculties are prime examples of this. As "autonomous" professionals, they resent pushy, active deans because their actions frequently violate one or another faculty norm. On the other hand, when a passive dean appears there will shortly be complaints. There is no leadership here; obvious problems are not being dealt with; there is no one to take the initiative in getting "action." While every faculty member has his or her pet solution not unrelated to personal interest, even energetic and persuasive faculty members are stymied without the contribution of a formal leader.

HANDLING CONFRONTATION AND NONRESPONSE

In seeking to legitimate their position, in handling what we have called "sets" to maintain the momentum of the organization and to solve problems, and in performing as representatives or advocates of the group to obtain needed resources and concessions from outsiders, leaders must be able to confront and persuade reluctant others. Subordinates, superiors, and others with whom the leader must relate obviously have both their own interests—different from the manager's—and their own views of situational needs. Either or both may cause them to refuse the order or request. Such a refusal can both embarrass and handicap the leader seeking credibility and support. How do leaders confront the naysayer, the reluctant subordinate? (We shall concentrate here on dealing with subordinates, but the approach has broader applicability to organizational tactics.)

The "no" may be a refusal to accept a change in methods, a new procedure, or a new activity; to finish an assignment in the face of an obstacle; to redo an assignment; to help a colleague; or a hundred other possibilities in which the manager's perception of what is needed differs from the subordinates' view of what is equitable or desirable. And in the modern organization, there will always be good and sufficient reasons why something can't be done: lack of time or of resources; another department's having failed to fulfill a commitment; a contrary policy; conflicting rules, etc. Whatever the source and whether it's due to simple recalcitrance, a misunderstanding, or a desire to challenge the boss, it can become a crucial test of the leader's status and skills. Leaders who aren't followed soon lose whatever status they had and, in classical domino fashion, the refusal of one is quickly followed by the abandonment of all. Experienced leaders know they can ill afford many such losses, and they prize their persuasive skills.

The management literature—when it deals with the problem at all—usually presents simple choices:

Discipline versus reward
Participation versus unilateral decision making

Thus the solution is seen not as a process or a behavior but as a decision as to who's right or as to whether the supervisor should seek consensus or should make a unilateral decision. Obviously, most problems don't get solved that way.

Reviewing the literature suggests there there are really two primary abilities that are often lumped together under "persuasion." One might well be called charisma, and the other is a more practiced and mundane complex of human relations abilities.

Charisma

Many of us have observed articulate, persuasive leaders, proverbial "salespeople" who can talk reluctant others into accepting their proposals. Their technique is best suited to outsiders, not subordinates, because it quickly loses its potency and depends for its efficacy on infrequent contact. Further, subordinates who are overwhelmed by the "treatment" come to resent their inability to express their own needs and viewpoints, to swim upstream against the irresistible tide.

In fact, one of the elements most responsible for entrepreneurial success is the ability to convince financial sources and potential partners, key subordinates and stock purchasers that one has a winner. The business press is filled with stories of the "wunderkind" who can gather supporters for almost any project, any technical or marketing innovation. Even when previous ventures have faltered, their contagious enthusiasm and ability to counter any criticisms with a seemingly fact-filled set of assurances provide them with a never-ending source of "grubstaking" and supporters.[9]

Politicians obviously, like the late President Johnson, often reach the pinnacle of success by their persuasive abilities. Those

---

[9] For an explanation of this capability, see Chap. 11.

who knew Johnson often recounted his ability to decimate opposition by a withering, nonstop series of compliments and pleas and an almost physical insistence that agreement be forthcoming.

The business press frequently credits a particular CEO's effectiveness to a certain "charisma." The typical description usually goes something like this:

> He can be very critical and make you feel inadequate. But then later there is that big smile, the warm, engaging voice and encouraging conversation. You get the feeling he is focusing on you, is interested in you, will support you. And you forget those sharp, negative comments as you bathe in his attention.

This ability to focus on individuals and give them attention and warmth contrasts sharply with the characteristics of the aloof executive who considers only the "numbers."

Constructive Persuasion

Leaving charisma aside, most managers must rely on more mundane behavioral skills for gaining consent. To describe this process, it will be helpful to utilize a case not unlike any of those a typical manager faces. The case involves a subordinate's rejection of a supervisor's request for extra performance: a request to work overtime on a critical project. Since overtime is somewhat ambiguous (as to whether or not it can be required) and the situation we shall be describing has other ambiguities, the subordinate has a good "case" for being negative. But the "solution" is not a function of who can be proven "right," manager or employee, nor is it one of how the request can be phrased—as flattery, threat, or promise. Rather, it is a problem of designing a consent-gaining interchange, one that will move from rejection of the boss's request (and by indirection, of his authority) to acceptance. Further, as in real life, the object must also be to accomplish this turnabout without sacrificing the relationship or future cooperation. Here is the problem.

CASE: The Recalcitrant Designer

Late on Friday afternoon, Jake Palmer, head of engineering, receives a rush assignment. Some difficult preliminary engineering sketches need to be completed as soon as possible so that the model shop can begin construction of a new device to impress a valued customer. The only designer Jake feels can do this complex task—and do it so there will be no likelihood of problems—is Phil Firenzi, his most senior, experienced employee. He knows Firenzi is somewhat of a prima donna, smug in his competence, independent, and outspoken. He knows too that the job will require at least five hours of work and, since it's almost 3 P.M., that means three hours of overtime. A problem looms: overtime is not compulsory, and Friday overtime is especially unappealing to someone like Firenzi. He will likely be outraged. Rather than seeing it as a reward for being the most able and most senior employee, Firenzi will no doubt see the request as a "damn curse."

Palmer can even anticipate his response:

> This crazy company and inefficient middle management are so poor at planning that they are always late, always coming up with emergencies and crises that can't wait. The last thing I want is more overtime just before a weekend—and particularly this weekend. I've promised my wife to be home early to go to our daughter's wedding rehearsal. I'm sick and tired of being asked, "for the good of the company," to sacrifice my personal life for job requirements—and unnecessary ones at that. The company just isn't managed sensibly. You haven't even taken the time or had the foresight to train someone else to handle the complex drawings. The company's either too cheap to invest in training or too foolish to care.

Solution Scenarios

With this background, one doesn't need a great imagination to infer the problem Palmer faces. He must seek to get a subordinate to do something which is, in part at least, "above and beyond the explicit duties of the job." Further, he's dealing with an employee who is already in a negative frame of mind (although the manager would not normally know this).

What are the usual and almost predictable scenarios?

1   Palmer can make the request, get refused, and then be upset by the threat to his own position ("What will my boss say if I don't get this out after having been told how critical the job is?") and by Firenzi's gall. Palmer can then seek to pressure conformance by offering:

• *Threats.* "Remember how much I've done for you—extra time off when you wanted it, merit increases. Is this how you pay me back? How much do you think I'll feel like asking for another raise or giving you your way when *you* want something?"

• *Rewards.* "I know this is rough on you, but do a good job and I'll use this when I talk with the superintendent to get you a much bigger raise than you expected at salary review time," and/or, I'll try to get you" one or another goodies—better vacation time, new office space, or one of a dozen things—perhaps even a bribe: double time instead of time-and-a-half.

Note. While it's traditional to distinguish between rewards and punishments, they really come down to the same thing. From Firenzi's point of view, to be offered a benefit is also to be threatened with a "no-gift-if-no-conform" situation. So there is really no difference; both emphasize the power of the boss to give or withhold job benefits and the impotence of the subordinate: defer to requests, reasonable or unreasonable, or be punished.

2 Dominance is the other likely scenario. Detecting the un-willingness of his subordinate, Palmer can launch into a long speech about the importance of the drafting assignment:

• "It will show your skill—only you are good enough to do it and that's why I turn to you."

• "It's for the good of the company; it could mean an important new order, lots of new jobs, more job security for everyone."

In fact, if Firenzi continues to balk, Palmer may even side with him, sneering at upper management's inefficiencies (for which they both must suffer). There may even be a suggestion of a conspiracy: "It's you and me against them," or "I'm your friend—do it for me. Do it for your buddies, for the honor of our department, etc., etc."

Problems Created

The problems with either of these approaches are almost too obvi-ous to specify.

1 Firenzi is almost certain to be frustrated. He is being placed in a position where he is torn between his own sense of equity—what he wants to do and feels is his "right"—and the pressures of the boss. If he gives in, there will be resentment; if he doesn't, the relationship has been injured. Even if he changes his mind, there is bound to be anger and the feeling that Palmer, the all-powerful boss, has manipulated him—and positive manipulation is no better than negative. The sense of dependency is increased.

2 Palmer may spend a lot of time seeking to influence Firenzi based on what he assumes his needs to be—money, admiration, pride, a good relationship with supervisor. He may never uncover and assess what Firenzi may really need—for example, assurance that this problem will be solved by an investment in training another designer.

3 There is little opportunity or likelihood of developing a constructive solution to the impasse, which might solve Palmer's needs *and* Firenzi's.

4 Therefore Firenzi receives no input that would suggest that Palmer cares about him, except as an object through whom he can accomplish his self-important goals of looking good to his boss. So he feels exploited.

5 And Palmer will probably end up further distrusting his unresponsive, too-independent subordinate.

Conceptual Approaches to Persuasion

Field Theory Many years ago, the distinguished social psychologist Kurt Lewin developed a number of concepts called "field theory." Let us apply field theory to the case above. For Lewin, an individual's behavior is a product of the force fields acting upon him or her. There are "driving forces" and "restraining forces." Managers are most typically tempted to appeal to or to manipulate only the former by offering benefits or threats to the individual's goals.

The result of these inducements and coercions is increased pressure and tension; the individual is left frustrated. The subordinate is caught between the pressure to conform and the undiminished restraining forces. (In the case above, restraining forces are Firenzi's need for personal time, his reluctance to appear a "patsy," and his desire for reasonable autonomy.)

Lewin argued that it is often psychologically healthier and more productive to reduce the restraining forces—and thus theresistance and the frustration—in contrast to upping the pressure for conformity.[10]

---

[10] For a more complete view of Lewinian theory, see Dorwin Cartright (ed.), *Field Theory in Social Science*, Harper, New York, 1951.

More importantly, Lewin's field theory told managers (or anyone seeking to exercise influence) to explore fully the "life space" of the other individuals, the forces acting upon them, what they were seeking and avoiding. Only when they knew this constellation of forces would they be in a position to influence the direction in which the other persons moved. They would do this, of course, by being responsive to those forces.

McGregor's Means Control   Douglas McGregor, the famous industrial psychologist (who knew Lewin when they were both at MIT), popularized field theory under the term "means control." McGregor urged students of management to explore the "life space" of subordinates (as well as their own); he called it the "perceptual field" of the other persons.

In behavioral terms, this meant that, rather than starting with persuasion when resistance is first detected, managers should start with inquiry—through interviewing. Through a process of give-and-take, managers should seek to learn the needs and objectives of subordinates as they relate to the refusal to respond to a request. (Palmer, the supervisor in the case above, simply assumed he knew these things.)

Reflecting on the needs of both the employee (in this case the designer, Phil Firenzi) and the supervisor, one can chart their goals:

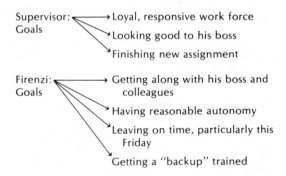

Supervisor: Goals → Loyal, responsive work force
→ Looking good to his boss
→ Finishing new assignment

Firenzi: Goals → Getting along with his boss and colleagues
→ Having reasonable autonomy
→ Leaving on time, particularly this Friday
→ Getting a "backup" trained

Next, supervisors must choose how they will work with these needs and goals. Among the choices in this case are the following:

1 Cut off the subordinate's access, i.e., his means.
  a "I won't help you when you make requests of me."
  b "I'll make it harder for you to get along."
2 Directly threaten his goals.
  a "I can take your job away."
  b "I can give you less interesting work."
3 Provide direct benefits.
  a "I'll give you a raise."
  b "I'll give you more time off."
4 Provide means for subordinate to gain his goals himself.
  a "I'll help you get into a less pressured situation."
  b "I'll help you get a 'backup' trained to take pressure off yourself."

The problems with (1) and (2) are obvious: threats, frustrations, and the like lead to aggressive rebuttals. Even if the employee "comes to heel" and conforms, over time his willing cooperation and responsiveness are likely to suffer. The problem with (3) as a tactic is both more interesting and more complicated.

As we've already said, offering rewards—what cynics would even call "bribes"—is fraught with difficulty. Every such offer is implicitly a threat. "Don't do what I want and you get nothing from me" is the message being communicated. Further, as will be discussed in Chapter 4, all managers have difficulty in devising rewards that will be perceived as equitable. Rewards tend to "wear out"; there may even be a point of saturation for subordinates. And whatever the size of a reward, the next one offered may have to be larger to make any impact.[11] And, of course, there are real economic ceilings as to how much can be given.

As McGregor also would have said, promising people things, even when there's no implicit threat to withhold, is demeaning; it keeps subordinates as dependent children. ("Big Daddy" gives you something if you behave.)

More psychologically healthy *and* more durable is a superior-subordinate relationship in which managers provide the *means* for or facilitate the subordinates' attainment of their own

---

[11] This is analogous to the Weber-Flechner law in psychology, which, simply stated, is that the distinguishable differential depends on the magnitude of the original stimulus to which it was added. As overall benefit levels increase, the least detectable differential will have to get larger and larger.

goals—*not* the goals themselves. Thus supervisors do control or can influence the *means* to satisfaction, and these are both the most useful and the healthiest to manipulate. Supervisors, as Lewin argued, can aid in modifying restraining forces which have prevented employees from reaching desired goals.

We can now summarize the elements that appear to compose a successful dispute settlement process and that go substantially beyond the simplistic notions of "participation" or "reward."

Summarizing the Elements of Persuasive Behavior

Whenever superiors and subordinates disagree and concurrence is necessary, and the matter does not lend itself to a simple directive, superiors should:

1 Seek to establish through mutual give-and-take a common understanding of the nature of the problem and the surrounding constraints. This does not mean both will have the same values, but agreement that there is a problem is an absolute prerequisite to motivating the search for a solution.

2 Seek to understand the subordinates' values, interests, anxieties, and desires. Superiors should gain this understanding by "interviewing," that is, letting subordinates talk and explain, a process which communicates to the subordinates that the boss is understanding, responsive, and interested in their needs. (*Note:* This doesn't mean agreeing with all of the subordinates' views, or even placing any particular weight on them other than accepting the obvious fact that they are "constraints" which contribute to the "problem.")

3 Seek to redefine the problem in such a way that it is possible for the employees to have some opportunity to contribute to its solution. The contribution may be a minor adjustment of how something will be done or a major shaping of what will be done; the important element is getting the employees' initiations.

The "solution," then, if it can be called that, becomes the result of the superiors' ability to restructure the problem and to encourage a comparable restructuring of the employees' mindset. Both loosen up their predilections, rethink their constraints, and seek to meet each other's goals.

Note how it becomes unnecessary to ask who made the decision (boss or subordinate) or how much participation was there. In fact, such questions are often the sign of naiveté about organizational matters. It becomes quite artificial to distinguish, as do so many management "experts," the "degree" of participation, i.e., to categorize solutions as to:

Decisions made by subordinates
Decisions made by subordinates, but only if approved by boss
Decisions made by boss and subordinates
Decisions made by boss after consulting subordinates

The joint problem-solving decision is made as a result of a *process* in which both boss and subordinate have useful roles to play; who has the greater balance of input will vary from situation to situation and usually cannot be predetermined.

NOTES ON MASLOW AND HERZBERG

The Classic View

Many managers have become acquainted with Herzberg's restatement of the famous Maslow "need hierarchy."[12] In brief, the theory holds that needs already satisfied (usually "lower-order" needs) can't provide motivation. Thus Herzberg has said that in the typical modern organization, giving employees what he calls more "hygienic" need satisfaction doesn't result in greater motivation because in these areas they are close to satiety. (Of course, such contentions are quite debatable.) The area that is relatively unsatisfied, and is thus the prime motivating factor, is the psychic one: the need to feel accomplished and to have a sense of achievement—here no satiety is likely.

These "higher-order" needs can only be obtained through the job, as a function of the *intrinsic* nature of the job. The lower-order needs come from elements *extrinsic* to the job: payment plans, fringe benefits, working conditions. Presumably, the higher-order are never fully satisfied, while lower-order needs can be fulfilled.

---

[12] A. H. Maslow, *Motivation and Personality*, Harper, New York, 1954, pp. 80–106.

An Alternative View

Now we would place a different interpretation on all of this. Intrinsic job satisfaction can only be obtained by the employees themselves. It can't be handed out on a platter (even by a job-enrichment specialist). The employee must find challenges, seek accomplishment, and sense achievement. In sharp contrast, the extrinsic needs, for the most part, have to be given out by a beneficent management. Thus management provides the most long-lived, psychologically healthy atmosphere when it creates a situation in which employees can obtain their need satisfactions for themselves. These are situations where the possibilities for satisfaction are expansive, not limited by economic conditions, parity, or coercive comparisons.[13]

So-called higher-order needs, then, are simply those to which individuals themselves control access. The supervisor's relation to these is one of facilitator: aiding subordinates to reach their personal goals in an organizational context.

The Ideal Incentive

Social scientists have found that employees are most responsive to incentives that don't depend on a powerful boss's bestowing them on dependent subordinates. Thus annual wage increases, even merit raises, better working conditions, and improved pensions and vacations may be appreciated, but they don't motivate better performance. (Don't be fooled: the reason is *not* that these are not higher-order satisfactions—as Herzberg keeps repeating—but that they are at the discretion of management.)

The ideal motivator is one that the employees control. Thus many managers are highly motivated and do everything they can to improve the visibility and effectiveness of their operation because they directly benefit. Long hours and dedication pay off in a more important, interesting—and usually better-paid—job. Thus putting the employees on a job where they directly benefit in proportion to how effectively they work is the ideal incentive. Obviously, blue-collar workers have their piece-rate

---

[13] Of course, pay-for-perfomance compensation plans may provide the same through-the-job achievement satisfactions, even as they provide income.

systems, but white-collar workers, staff, and managers can also have built-in reward systems.

Managers need to leave some of the definition of the job open:

> Look, you can make this as important as you like. If you can build support for this new function, justify increased budget, really show results, we'll keep feeding you more resources, and your job (or department) will grow and you'll grow with it. If you just provide average effort, you'll get the normal cost-of-living increases, the job won't become more interesting, and you won't become more important to the organization.

Many people flourish under this kind of scheme. They want to be in a position where they can get more and more responsibility—and the psychic and dollar rewards that go with it. But many others don't want it; they want clear lines of demarcation, little responsibility, and the need for as little initiative as possible.

CONCLUSIONS

Many managers may be loath to exercise definitive leadership, having absorbed a good many of the prohibitions against structure and control that our culture has provided. While we may be undergoing another swing of the pendulum, for the formative years of most of today's executives, permissiveness in the home and office was the ideal. It was assumed that employees and children alike are thwarted by authority, and there is a basic contradiction between efforts to improve the human relations climate of a situation and efforts to get work done.

Active leaders are needed to exercise initiative and to provide structure. There are no studies that show people in some Edenlike status of complete independence. In its most primitive state and throughout recorded history, the human race has sought, and flourished in, tribes and clans, communities, and associations. If a half-dozen people are placed in a room with a common task, we can predict they will quickly evolve common routines of behavior and a self-imposed organizational structure. The latter will include leadership to initiate instructions, and the group will penalize deviations from approved standards of behavior. Conformity will be expected, and dependence will be readily forthcoming. (Let it be noted that the street-corner gang, like the office clique, makes demands for conformity in thought and action that make the authority of the organization pale by comparison.)

People apparently neither want nor have experienced a state of complete autonomy. With few exceptions, men and women depend on human relationships, some fixity of structure, routine, and habit to survive psychologically. Although we do not like to admit it, most of us flee from an absence of structured relationships. Students of business organization know well that one of management's basic problems is to fill that void with leaders who will take initiative and accept responsibility.

And this scenario, as we have seen, of course involves active give-and-take between leaders and subordinates. Subordinates want assistance in reaching their goals from someone who can establish structure and "make things happen." They need interactional contact with superiors to assure them of acceptance and to obtain periodic relief from the one-way pressures and constraints flowing down the hierarchy. Most individuals also require an outlet for pent-up interactional needs, and these subordinate needs are complemented by the needs of leaders who can build commitment and support only by active contact. Real communication takes place by direct face-to-face contact.

Leadership must be active, not passive; authority must be exercised to be accepted. The strong, distant, placid, and silent types idealized in fiction are not the leaders of the real world.

CHAPTER 4

BUILDING COMMITMENT AND MOTIVATION

In Chapter 3 we sought to explore how leaders exercise authority. We suggested that providing satisfactions was a secondary rather than a primary concern of managers. But this doesn't mean that managers can neglect motivational factors. Commitment, morale, and loyalty are of substantial consequence in organizational affairs. A great deal of performance depends upon what subordinates do when supervisors are not present and when they are not responding to specific instructions. As we shall see when we discuss controls, the critical job dimensions (beyond the simplest tasks) are those involving taking initiative and making sensible trade-offs which go well beyond what can be ordered, mandated, or specified.

Often leaders have been conceived as having a relatively passive role in shaping employee motivation and commitment. Motivation was presumed to flow from the relation of employee to job, and as long as the boss was neither a bore nor a bully, a "good" job would provide "good" motivation.

Reviewing the literature on employee motivation and job satisfaction suggests that there are at least three components directly controlled by managers:

65

1   The potential payoff perceived by subordinates for improved performance
2   The degree of acceptance and security perceived by subordinates
3   The effective "management" of interaction patterns

SHAPING PAYOFF EXPECTATIONS

A very popular approach to employee motivation in the field of
organizational behavior is called, somewhat abstrusely, "expectancy" or "path-goal" theory.[1] It reverses the long-standing assumption of most managers that satisfied employees will be more
productive. Instead, the theory persuasively argues that employees must perceive productivity and performance as necessary
steps along *their* path to satisfying *their* own goals. And, as we
shall see, managers have a great deal to do to "engineer" those
perceptions. They must do much more than merely offer a
reward for a job well done. There are many links in the chain
and, for employees to be motivated, each of the links of the
extended chain must be carefully forged. Employees must
believe that:

1   They have the capacity (based on past experience and
self-confidence) to improve performance.
2   This improved performance will not be excessively costly
in terms of energy, friendships, or other personal sacrifices, including future obligations and commitments (i.e., what will be
expected "next time 'round").
3   This improved performance will result in demonstrably
good results, that is, something that others can measure, assess, or perceive—some significant difference from the situation
before.
4   These results will be appraised as commendatory, as a
positive contribution.
5   These results will be rewarded.
6   The reward will be equitable

[1] For a good description of its more academic elements and antecedents, see
Edward Lawler, *Motivation in Work Organizations*, Wadsworth, Brooks/Cole,
Belmont, Calif., 1973. This is also an application of Lewin's field theory as dis-
cussed in Chap. 3.

The Meaning of Equity

Equity has its own body of theory, which is a distraction for us here. But it's worth noting one frequently used expression of the perception of equity. Subordinates view rewards as equitable when:

$$\frac{\text{Rewards received by them}}{\text{Their inputs (effort, previous training, skill level, personal characteristics)}} = \frac{\text{rewards received by others}}{\text{others' inputs}}$$

Thus the more experience and status the individuals have, the greater must be their perceived reward to be considered equitable. Equity is always relative, not an absolute—rewards are compared with what relevant others are receiving.

Manager as Facilitator

Just looking at the long sequence that must be satisfied suggests how much work there is for the managers as facilitators of the linkages.

A great deal of interaction with subordinates to explain, reassure, and aid—and a great deal of outside facilitation (with other employees, other departments, etc.)—will be necessary to both encourage employees and translate their contribution into satisfying results. In addition, there is the obvious need to be sure credit is given and that the credit is underscored with reasonable recognition.

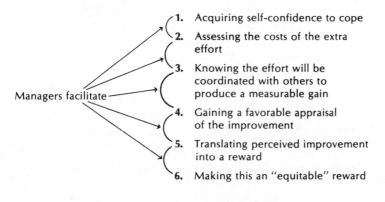

Managers facilitate

1. Acquiring self-confidence to cope
2. Assessing the costs of the extra effort
3. Knowing the effort will be coordinated with others to produce a measurable gain
4. Gaining a favorable appraisal of the improvement
5. Translating perceived improvement into a reward
6. Making this an "equitable" reward

Supervisors, when leaders, are facilitators, aiding subordinates and adapting the organizational situation to allow "bridges" to be built. Leaders will:

1 Aid in providing training and experience
2 Help redesign the job and the division of labor so that extra efforts are not excessively costly to produce improved individual performance
3 Make certain that these efforts are complemented and not dissipated by the efforts of others
4 Be positively responsive to improved performance
5 Facilitate obtaining of fair compensation for this improvement
6 Adjust the reward to make it equitable compared to what others receive

GIVING SECURITY AND RESPECT

As many studies of job satisfaction have shown, employees at all levels—from vice president to sweeper—want a considerate, understanding, and appreciative boss. Their own personal security is dependent on this since managers hold power over them. Further, it is difficult to gain a sense of accomplishment when one of the critical measures—the managers' appraisal—is negative. And, of course, everyday peace of mind and easy working relationships require a considerate boss.

Furthermore, given all the ambiguities of the modern organizational world—the opportunity to discriminate, sabotage, or undercut—subordinates need to know that their boss is a trustworthy person, fair and well balanced.

> The nature of organizations is that they encompass diverging interests. Those interests have differing priorities for different members of the organization. There are differing perceptions of the consequences of a given action. The infinite richness of the tradeoffs between effects, beneficiaries and consequences often leaves *perception of motives* as the cardinal frame of reference.
>
> So trust in the organizational sense becomes a critical factor in obtaining cooperation and the required coordination, because *trust determines whether leadership can be exercised.*[2]

[2] Bruce Henderson, *Trust*, Boston Consulting Group, Perspectives, Boston, 1977, n.p.

Nearly all managers know this. Most—at least those who are performing effectively—want to communicate this fairness and acceptance to their subordinates. However, there is sometimes a major discrepancy between the manager's feeling and what gets communicated.

Communicating Fairness

The naive managers say they will communicate their "fairness" and respect for employees by always making "fair" decisions, but we know that there is no way of consistently doing things that the other person will agree with. Inevitably, managers have to say and do things that will be misperceived, disliked, and considered inequitable or unfair by one or more subordinates. (In fact, managers who set a goal of never doing anything people will dislike are both naive and ineffective.) Thus assurance that the power difference will not be misused must be communicated differently.

Reviewing the leadership literature suggests that leaders communicate this trust by behavior more than by words. In turn, the employees' sense of security arises out of perceiving this behavior as distinct from hearing the right soothing words. The requisite behavior is a balancing of dominance and responsiveness, of control and being controlled, of initiating and responding. Various researchers have in fact identified this need for balancing, although they have used diverse terminology.[3]

In the past, some students of leadership have sought to prove that managers have to make a choice between work and people; between task and feelings.

In the political world, we are all familiar with the European tradition of separating the head of state from the first, or prime, minister or premier. The head of state, symbolizing national unity, engages in a variety of supportive, responsive activities—doing good and appearing gracious—to maintain national esprit. The premier or prime minister faces the more difficult job of making unpleasant, often constraining, decisions and requiring, at times, sacrifice.

---

[3] Terms like "task" versus "socioemotional," "initiating" versus "consideration," and "production" versus "people" have all been utilized.

But more contemporary views of leaders recognize the duality of the role: managers must assert authority *and* demonstrate concern for subordinates. It is the proper balancing of the two that provides a sense of security and confidence in the supportiveness of the boss.

Reaping the Benefits

Most subordinates are surprisingly good at distinguishing exploitative from supportive bosses. The former put their own careers and rewards first, every time. They will not take risks or even expend much precious time and energy to win benefits for or to protect their subordinates. In sharp contrast, the manager who puts the interests of subordinates first in priority derives extraordinary loyalty. In the military, from the time of the Romans, generals who first made sure that their troops had adequate food and shelter, even before they made provision for their own comforts, earned the kind of dedication that won tough battles. Obviously, it's easy for high-status executives to presume that those below them should "settle for less." But experienced leaders are aware of a certain not-so-vicious circle:

> Loyal subordinates who perceive the leader as concerned with their welfare will perform more responsively. Often such responsiveness will enable the leader to be more successful (in meeting goals, finishing projects, etc.). This success enables the leader to be more influential in the organization, which means better compensation and "perks" for subordinates. Sensing they are well treated, the subordinates perform more loyally, which leads to more successes for their boss.

USING INTERACTION TO MOTIVATE

The physical dimensions of the give-and-take, the social interactions between superior and subordinate, have a significant effect on motivation. By "give-and-take" we mean the dimensions of *whom* the managers talk with *when*, and the balance in the discussion between talking and listening—in contrast to the words used and the subjects discussed. The formula for developing good subordinate relationships using interaction is almost so simple that it may appear either naive or obvious.

Relationships are almost entirely dependent on contact. Strangers, those infrequently seen, those known only by reputation or imagining, are usually distrusted or disliked. Assuming that the contact can be well handled (see below), the degree of friendship and trust is almost entirely dependent on having been established through frequent contact.[4] To accomplish this quantity of interaction, managers must anticipate spending from half to three-fourths of their day in talking with others.

Those contacts that are with subordinates must be reasonably evenly distributed. The usual barriers to this are mistaken beliefs and the discomfort of dealing with "less pleasant" subordinates.

1 Many managers foolishly allow their contacts to be determined for them by the relative aggressiveness of their subordinates. Those who seek out the managers and take the initiative get too high a proportion. Those who are more passive or less readily available (physically removed or more taciturn) get ignored.

2 Some managers are even more foolish; they almost echo the old refrain about absence causing fondness to flourish. What they really say, however, is more likely to be something like this:

> Jones knows that if I was dissatisfied with what she was doing I would say so. When I say nothing, that means she's doing a fine job; like they say, no news is good news!

3 Managers sometimes mistake timidity or reticence on the part of subordinates for a wish to be left alone. To be sure, a few individuals resist contacts with supervisors, but most need to be encouraged to "open up."

These contacts should be well distributed over a broad range of durations. A few should be long, perhaps lasting on occasion more than ten minutes; many should be less than a minute. (On occasion, there may be the need for contact of up to an hour, but that's rare.)

---

[4] George Homans was one of the social scientists to draw this observation from a review of a wide variety of human studies. He showed that increased interaction led to more favorable sentiments (toward one another), which in turn generated a host of new mutual activities—which provided more interaction and still more favorable sentiments. See Homans' *The Human Group*, Harcourt, New York, 1950.

Counting Interactions

The degree of specificity that can be provided for interaction patterns is well illustrated in a little known but critically important study of managerial effectiveness in a large R&D lab that was part of a major industrial corporation.[5] Richardson, the researcher, found that there were distinct differences in the interaction patterns of managers who were clearly superior and those who were ranked as inferior. (Interestingly, the superior managers tended to have patterns which avoided the extremes and were roughly in the middle of the contact distributions.) These managers typically had 300 to 500 contacts per month with forty to sixty people who were distributed over five organizational levels. The following observations were made in the study.

1 Superior managers spent between four and six hours each day interacting with other people. Ineffective managers spend less time (therefore ignoring people) or too much time (ignoring the need to read, plan, and do paperwork).

2 Superior managers tended to distribute these contacts widely; ineffective managers favored some employees and ignored others.

3 More effective managers contacted their own bosses from two to five times more frequently than they contacted their subordinates. Ineffective managers spent even more time with superiors, becoming "too out of touch" with the engineers and too dependent on supervisor-filtered information. Too much contact with subordinates also reflected a failure to delegate.

4 Effectiveness also correlated with the ability and willingness to initiate these contacts. The better managers initiated from 35 to 80 percent of their contacts. Those who had higher percentages discouraged subordinates from taking the initiative, and those who were below this range apparently lost control.

5 Excessively short contacts (in one case over fifty an hour) reflected either understaffing or poor delegation Excessively

---

[5] The study was conducted by F. L. W. Richardson, Jr., and is reported, in part, in F. Richardson and S. Zimmerman, "Comprehending the Process of Organizational Improvement," *Management of Personnel Quarterly*, vol. 4, no. 1, 1965, pp. 14ff. More complete statistical data are provided in Richardson's "Executive Interaction and Avoidance of Counter-reactions," *American Documentation Institute*, Library of Congress, Auxiliary Publication Project, Document No. 8426, 1965.

long contacts was evidence of overstaffing or the desire to get too much detail and to overwhelm the subordinate. Richardson concludes, "The better managers were those who varied their contact rhythm to suit the needs of the situation. They were equally at ease conversing briefly or at great length."[6] He contrasts these with others, less flexible, who were either always curt or long-winded.

6 The better managers knew when to bring people together in groups in contrast to dealing with them individually. Poorer managers either never had meetings or used them as their primary source of contact with their people. Of interest is the fact that effective managers spend from 44 to 65 percent of their time in contact with individuals in contrast to groups.

Synchronization

Almost as important as duration and frequency is synchronization: the ability of managers to adjust their give-and-take to that of the subordinates so that there will be neither discomforting pauses (where neither speaks) nor excessive interruptions and dominance where the managers talk down the subordinates. The simplest approach to this is to be sure there is variety in your interaction pattern: the ability to speak consecutively for more than a couple of seconds and the ability to be silent and listen. Individuals differ in the length of their typical burst of words and in the duration of their periods of silence, when they're willing to listen while preparing the next rejoinder. While friends learn one another's desired patterns, managers have the responsibility of seeking to fit, to synchronize their interactions with those of subordinates.

Both excessively curt and mononloguelike responses are likely to be destructive of comfortable give-and-take. Inept managers, with their higher status and self-confidence, are likely to silence employees either with a torrent of words or with curt, laconic monosyllables. Their impatience can also communicate an unwillingness to listen.

The product of well-synchronized interaction is very easy to observe. There is a physical release, an obvious brightening and

---

[6] Richardson, "Executive Interaction and Avoidance of Counter-reactions," p. 23.

enlivening that occurs when someone is talking within a well-adjusted interaction pattern. Otherwise dour, discouraged, or apathetic individuals literally come alive when interaction is reinforced by the proper conversational complement. These verbal strokings, this mutual adaptation, appeal to our basic animal nature that calls for rhythmical social give-and-take.

Not only does this provide satisfaction—the sense of physical and psychological well-being—it brings other benefits as well. The subordinates who are "adapted to" in this fashion are both more willing and more able to provide information and insight to their bosses. The real problems that have been worrying them, the embedded anxieties and criticisms, all the things that managers need to know, come forth as an employee subconsciously senses this acceptance by the boss and the implied affirmative sentiment. When managers are able to do this, subordinates react enthusiastically:

"When we get together to discuss the progress of my unit, she [my supervisor] is so open that it's difficult to withhold information."

"His expression of faith and support—in the way he talks with me—is so great you naturally do all you can to merit it."

Managers are aware of how important it is to gain this trust, this good feeling, *before* moving into controversial or pressure-filled topics. Like salespeople or wary subordinates, managers first seek to build an easy give-and-take in a meeting as a base or foundation for talking about tough questions. Note that this doesn't mean "sandwiching in" the negative with a positive (i.e., complimentary) introduction and closing. The base consists of mutual responsiveness—well-synchronized interaction, in the sense of true interaction—not praise or phony "small talk."

Where Interaction Is Destructive

Managers have greater difficulties gaining commitment from peers when they seek aid or support in their "lateral" relationships, the subject of Chapter 5. If we utilize the perspective of interaction, we are in a better position to understand why those relationships are more laden with conflict.

Intergroup relations differ from intragroup relations in that intergroup relations (1) are much less frequent, (2) are more likely to take place when either or both parties are upset, and (3) have a tendency to deteriorate rather than improve.

Unless managers push themselves to build a network of supportive relationships throughout the organization, they are likely to see the manager of another group only when there is a problem (for example, they haven't gotten the data or materials they need or the other department is failing to approve some needed action). Without prior frequent, easy give-and-take around nondivisive issues, the interaction prompted by a problem is likely to be tension-provoking. Each party interrupts the other, talks him or her "down"; there is likely to be little sense that the other is listening and is responsive, that the other even perceives the problem accurately. The sense of injustice is heightened on each side and the "interaction" quickly escalates into a shouting match.

To avoid this destructive result, experienced managers seek to initiate contact with a wide spectrum of "outsiders" at times when there are no outstanding problems and therefore no anxieties and suspicions. On these more "social" occasions, they engage in responsive banter and small talk.[7] Astute managers also seek to build up "credits" with their peers. In terms of interaction, this means that they seek to be responsive to the other's request for aid. When one person views another as "pleasant," "credible," "helpful," based on past contact, then the first response to a problem posed by that other is likely to be positive and nonconfrontational. In turn, that positive response makes it more likely that the retort will be positive, and more likely that the effort to find a mutually satisfactory answer will be successful.

Watching Interaction in Practice

The process of metering interaction inevitably sounds more complex and demanding than it is. The essentials, once learned, are almost childishly simple. As we have said, their very simplicity may make them suspect. The typical managers

---

[7] For an excellent study of the importance of having a broad network of supporters throughout the organization, see John Kotter, *The General Managers*, Free Press, New York, 1982.

ask, "How can balancing physical contacts be so important?" The answer, of course, is that the essence of being human is the need for social intercourse: the chance to express yourself and be listened to, and yet know that others care enough to tell you what they think and to take time to exchange verbal pleasantries and information with you.

While at times this balancing of interaction requires special contacts—calling someone in to your office or making a purposeful visit to their work location—it can often be embodied in the day-to-day work routine. The following excerpt describes a supervisor in a high-pressure factory (food processing) in which constant surveillance is necessary to maintain productivity. Watch how he combines managerial control with good interaction:

> [At the beginning of the shift supervisor C] pauses briefly to tell each worker how the department as a whole performed last night. . . . Then he grins and thrusts out his hand for a quick congratulatory shake [where the quota was reached]. . . . C patrols continually up and down the line. . . . C's contacts are brief . . . they are also easy, with a touch of banter. For example, he seems to have a standing joke with one operator, a lady older than he is. She "won't permit him" to inspect more than one pack at a time; otherwise she threatens to "slap his hand." Naturally he pretends to grab . . . and she pretends to slap; they both giggle. . . . If his contacts are brief, they are also frequent. C is constantly on the move. . . . They see a lot of him without ever having to endure a concentrated dose of scrutiny. . . .
>
> [When a machine breaks down and it's necessary to get a labor pool employee to hand feed for the machine operator, he spends considerable time with the operator.] "Don't you worry, Lester," says C about lost production. . . . Lester doesn't seem convinced, but C keeps on reassuring him through the next few hours. . . . [8]

In contrast, in the plant studied by the researcher, less effective supervisors hovered over people, didn't keep moving around, often failed to comment for fear it might be resented, had no small talk, and were easily distracted from maintaining relationships with the total system by getting absorbed in individual trouble spots.

[8] Saul Gellerman, *Managers and Subordinates*, Holt, New York, 1976, pp. 36–39.

To summarize, supervisors can effect security-giving, satisfaction-giving interaction only by:

1   Spending a majority of their time talking with people in the organization—at a high interactional energy level which can be maintained day after day

2   Giving roughly equal time to all—those that don't seem to want (or need) it, as well as those they find easiest to be with

3   Striking good balance between short and long contacts, with higher frequencies of the brief "howdy" or bantering type

4   Being flexible in length of speaking and silence periods, which allows them to synchronize their interaction pattern with those of a wide range of others

5   Encouraging subordinates to initiate discussions as much as they do

USING STATUS TO MOTIVATE

Considerable leverage may be obtained by use of contacts to communicate status and recognition. Suppose, for example, that some procedural or technical change is being contemplated and a relatively senior, key employee is asked early in the planning process to express reactions to the plan. That indication of importance or relevant knowledge usually produces substantial gratification for the worker who has been consulted. Similarly, at a meeting when the manager turns to Jan and asks for her reaction, Jan feels that her importance is being recognized and reinforced because everyone sees the boss seeking out her opinions. The opposite produces a great loss of motivation when some experienced worker is not consulted early in the planning process.

Managers need to sensitize themselves to how closely employees watch how often each is contacted and in what sequence. If a higher-level manager joins a meeting being run by a subordinate supervisor, normally all conversation would be directed to the manager. Their subordinates react to the high status of the senior manager, and quickly the supervisor feels upstaged. If the manager turns questions or comments back to the supervisor—"Jim, what do you think of that suggestion Al has just made; could it be implemented?"—his spirits rise quickly.

Observing by noting the actual behavior of superiors—the *who* gets contacted *when*—is a source of either very real motivation or, the reverse, a sense of discouragement. By carefully monitoring, directing, and redirecting contacts, managers quite simply and easily can have powerful effect on the motivation of key subordinates.

Below is another case from our research files. Note the changes in interaction. It was these relatively minor shifts in the pattern of give-and-take between the supervisor and her subordinate that had a profound effect. Consider how the loss could have been averted had the manager been sensitive to the situation.

CASE: The Employee Who Was Left Behind

Mike had worked as production editor for Allen Publications for about five years, having been promoted from copy editor. His direct supervisor was the managing editor, Jane King. King was considered a top editor, and while she worked her people very hard, they respected her editorial skills and her reputation in the industry.

In some ways Mike was an unattractive, almost "mousy" man. His job probably suited him quite well, handling the detailed work of putting the issue together, checking and double-checking things. He was unlikely to notice big problems that required some imagination and flair. He had a pleasant working relationship with King and liked the fact that she complimented him when "makeup" went smoothly. He also enjoyed their occasional chats about some of the more interesting stories in the magazine—their little gossip sessions about top management's sins of omission and commission. Basically, Mike was very useful, and King depended on him.

The publication had recently hired a special-projects person, very junior to Mike, who was supposed to help him and King handle some of the messier work flow problems of the production cycle and fill in for Mike when he was overloaded. Hanes was 23, less than half Mike's age, but quite bright and certainly much more articulate than Mike. While Mike rarely spoke at informal staff meetings, Hanes talked frequently; he seemed to have a lot of ideas about minor improvements in procedure, and King often commented that he was learning the business "very fast."

When it came time to install some new computer-driven type-setting equipment, King and Hanes began spending a lot of time on the minor "bugs" associated with getting it operational. In fact, Mike noticed that King hardly had time anymore to talk with him, although she had nothing negative to say either.

Then rumors began to circulate that this new equipment was just the beginning of a companywide conversion to computerization. In time, there would probably be an excess of personnel in the editorial function. Up until this time Mike had assumed that he had a job for life, so to speak, at Allen. He had even aspired to some day moving up to being production editor on one of Allen's larger publications. But as he began to think about what was happening with Hanes—who seemed to have many interpersonal skills he lacked and who had obviously caught King's eye—Mike wondered how realistic he had been, both in his career expectations and in his sense of job security.

Each time he saw Hanes go into King's office now he winced. He imagined it would soon be announced that Hanes was to get his job and he would be shifted to some "off-line" staff job. His natural timidity and fearfulness took over, and he began to exaggerate every slight. The real blow was dealt when he went in to see King on the pretext of needing her judgment on something. When she said that she didn't have the time to deal with the problem, that it was something he could handle himself or perhaps get Hanes's help on, he was crushed. He had hoped for one of their little gossip sessions.

In the "Help Wanted" section of the next Sunday paper, Mike happened to see an advertisement for a production editor on a small newsletter being published in New Jersey. He applied for the job. After a personal interview he was offered the position at a salary comparable to what he had been earning, though there would be extra commuting costs. On that Monday morning, Mike quit his job at Allen.

Though King was shocked, she later covered herself nicely: "I suppose Mike wanted me to baby him, but I don't really have time for coddling people. This is a tough world, and I don't think people like Mike have a future in this organization."

Managers face difficult problems once a vicious circle is in motion. A typical one has several aspects:

The employee feels unappreciated and senses a lack of responsiveness in the boss.

In turn, the employee becomes less effective or, at least, appears less enthusiastic.

The manager interprets this change as negative and, in turn, shows less positive response and gives less positive reinforcement to the subordinate.

This creates still more apprehensiveness in the employee, leading to poorer performance and less predictable behavior.

All of which brings further negative response from the manager.

Being aware of the possibility of such a destructive spiral is only the first step in learning how to cope with a tenuous situation in a constructive fashion.

CONCLUSIONS

Managers and students of management are confronted by an abstruse vocabulary and abstract, vague goals like motivation and job satisfaction. Managers are told to provide these things—in order to create a responsive, effective work force—but all of them seem to have endless antecedents. More realistically, a subordinate's motivation and satisfaction and a leader's own perceived charisma are the end results of a great deal of superior-subordinate interaction. One cannot directly provide "motivation" or satisfaction.

Therefore we sought to examine the details, the fine-grain behavioral elements that together compose the leadership style that results in subordinate esprit.

Managers need subordinates who, beyond responding to directives, reacting responsively and responsibly to supervisory inputs, will maintain their commitment. For this commitment to be obtained, the rewards of being a subordinate (to a particular manager) must outweigh the costs—the constraints and unpleasantness. A great deal of research on job satisfaction, if summarized, suggests that employees seek general sources of fulfillment or satisfaction: predictable and equitable rewards in proportion to effort, security, and acceptance. When these are adequate (compared to the "costs" of working), there is loyalty and commitment.

Lost in a maze of theories on supervision, most managers lose sight of the purely physical dimensions of managing. Some significant share of supervising consists, simply enough, of initiating contacts; making the other person comfortable; providing a sense of acceptance; and developing decent, reassuring, conversational give-and-take. Well-established interaction theory tells us that comfortable, reasonably satisfying relationships involve one's ability to meter out the actual physical give-and-take with another person.

CHAPTER 5

INTEGRATING MANAGERIAL JOBS: HANDLING LATERAL RELATIONS

Managerial work is usually conceived in static terms. Managers presumably spend a great deal of time on analysis and decision making, planning and optimizing. The action component is the interface between superiors and subordinates. Problems are conceptualized as irrationalities in decision making (e.g., over-optimism or stupid calculations), unrealistic expectations of bosses or subordinates, or poor communications between levels.

But, of course, reality is far different. Empirical studies show managers spending the majority of their time outside the simple vertical channel prescribed by the hierarchy. We shall want to explain the significance of these lateral relationships and then seek to ascertain why they pose difficulties in execution and how they can be improved.

If one looks at an organization chart or listens to the standard management principles, a most sensible, logical, rational system appears. The head of the institution parcels out (delegates, in more formal terms) jurisdictions (authority, as it's usually called). The sum total of these adds up to the total mission of the organization. Each group is responsible for delivering its share of the mission and is therefore provided with resources equal to the task. There are also some "staff" managers who have a variety of supplementary functions, but these staff executives are presumed to be rather secondary as far as the manager's tasks are concerned. If the managers, line or staff, have to get together very often, it might appear from the organization chart that this is the result of miscommunication, laziness, or someone's illicitly crossing a jurisdictional line, poaching on someone else's turf.

WHY SO MANY LATERAL RELATIONS?

As soon as management differentiates (specializes, introduces a division of labor), there is a need for human transactions to put the organization (or the work or operation) back together again. Sometimes new managers get fooled by this; they assume that if all workers do their jobs according to some master plan or direction, there will be no need for contact or human intervention. This is very unlikely. Except where jobs are extraordinarily simple, it is likely that getting jobs to intermesh will require discussion and communication. (Shortly, we shall examine more closely the source of these interactions.)

The transactions are to facilitate coordination, to assure that A's work won't be done by B and that B will do things consistent with what A is doing so that the parts of the total task will fit together. By coordination then we mean individual tasks will be done such that:

1   There is consistency and complementarity.
2   The organization makes sensible use of all its resources, and reasonable allocations and priorities are assigned.

Thus managers have to check with other managers to be sure, for example, that the vendor they are dealing with is the "best" from an overall company point of view, and the terms agreed to do not make it difficult for other departments to get "good" contracts.

No matter how the agency or company is organized—by product, service, function, region, customer—there will always be important information and coordination requirements outside the work group that require managers to work with people who are not subordinates or bosses.

This coordination can't be handled solely by programming—that is, advance plans and procedures—nor simply by the hierarchy: appealing up the hierarchy to some high-level boss with a broad enough perspective to make a judicious, organizationwide decision. There are two reasons for this. The most obvious is, of course, that there aren't enough bosses or hours in the day. There are hundreds of these transactions every day in even the smallest of organizations. And, in addition, higher managers wouldn't necessarily have the specific knowledge needed to resolve the question. It's other managers on your level who know, for example, whether or not their work schedule will be decimated by your delay, what a "good" price is for purchasing computer services, and whether or not it's a violation of antidiscrimination laws to use a specific selection test.

Given the amount of specialization within management, this dynamic give-and-take is essential. No amount of sticking to a programmed plan, doing your own department's job "correctly," will suffice. Let's look for a moment at these interdependencies in a case example.

CASE: Working the Total Management System

Nancy Pfizer is the manager in charge of small fan production. Her production costs have far exceeded budget because a shortage of plastic blades is causing stops and starts in production. In calling her counterpart in parts fabrication, she learns that they have in stock a large supply of discontinued metal blades from a previous model fan. Nancy calls her boss, vice president for manufacturing, to inquire whether she can make use of these substitute fan blades.

The VP–manufacturing, Hal Cohen, says he'll have to check this out. He contacts the head of engineering to ask whether he'll approve this change. The engineering manager says he'll have to call his technical subordinate who knows that equipment firsthand. "He'll be able to assess whether performance or user safety could be affected." Cohen then calls the sales office responsible for getting these fans to distributors to tell them of the likely change. They must also approve. Their reaction is one of great anxiety. The sales manager says she can't approve this without the OK of her boss, the VP of sales, and they may want market research to run some tests on whether consumers will be loath to buy metal- versus plastic-bladed fans (which would, of course, hurt her sales targets for the coming months).

When the sales manager reaches her VP, she is told that the substitute is acceptable only if manufacturing agrees that no metal-bladed fans will be produced for delivery after June 15, because that is when advertising will be distributing a new catalog and magazine advertisements for the company's fans.

The sales manager negotiates that concession from Cohen, and then Cohen is told by engineering to go ahead as long as an extra lock washer is placed on the blade guard to make it unlikely that the guard would accidentally fall off and expose rotating metal blades. Cohen then calls Pfizer and tells her to add the lock washers to the manufacturing procedures and to be sure to finish production of metal-bladed fans by June 1.

Now let's recapitulate what happened. Perhaps a dozen or more contacts were necessary to answer Pfizer's problem of how to cope with a supply problem. Upper levels of functional groups who had a broader purview had to get involved to authorize the departure from previously agreed-to plans (e.g., the sales VP knew about the advertising campaign, and the sales manager for fans did not). Lower levels were contracted for their specific technical information based on their ongoing work experience (e.g., an engineer who had worked with small fans had to be consulted by the VP–engineering before the latter could decide how to respond to the request from manufacturing). There was no "buck-passing" or needless complicating of the problem by difficult personalities, although in many organizations there could be. For instance, the head of engineering could have said that without a ruling from the legal department he could not approve the use of potentially hazardous blades. Similarly, sales could have resisted any accommodation on the grounds that their customers didn't want change.

WHY LATERAL RELATIONS ARE DIFFICULT

Of course, one reason these are difficult patterns of behavior to learn is, as we observed in Chapter 1, the number—and the importance—of lateral relationships is simply underestimated. In fact, to many managers, the need to spend a majority of their time coordinating with other managers suggests that the organization is somehow misshaped, that someone is acting illicitly or is not a "team player."

But there are more sensible reasons why this core of managerial work represents such a difficult challenge.

Intragroup versus Intergroup Contacts

Essentially, the problems of lateral relations are the problems of moving from intragroup to intergroup relationships. Let's imagine two section heads who work in the same department and who have developed a close working relationship. Mary asks Henry to give her group another few days to finish the analysis Henry needs to include in the report he is preparing for top management. Henry is likely to say, "Sure, but I hope it won't be delayed any longer than that because that's the latest I can get it and still finish my end on time." And the deal will be consummated with that simple, almost automatic, exchange—because the parties have built a foundation of goodwill that provides them with optimistic expectations based on certain factors:[1]

1   *Integrity.* Since Mary and Henry are working closely together, it is reasonable to assume that Mary isn't asking for something that would be a violation of Henry's professional norms or group values. She would know and likely share these. She would ask for concessions or modifications consistent with the standards, norms, and values she and Henry share.

2   *Image and precedent.* Henry would not be concerned that his concession places him in a lower status, symbolizing a more deferential role that will only encourage more oppressive demands and more interference with the routines necessary for efficiency.

3   *Interests.* Henry would not be anxious about whether this demand was simply a tactic on the part of Mary to delay completion (e.g., because the report will injure her interests and a delay will mitigate the damage) and gain some strategic advantage to the detriment of Henry's section. Again, they share strategic goals; they are not competitive.

4   *Interpersonal understanding.* Mary won't use behavior or approaches that antagonize Henry. They would have learned to fit their interactions together to minimize stress on one another.

---

[1] These categories were suggested by John O'Shaughnessy in his working paper "Industrial Buying Behavior," Columbia University Graduate School of Business, New York, 1976. (Mimeographed.)

Repeated exchanges like this one would have been perfected in give-and-take in the context of a common group.

A great deal of interaction and long experience with give-and-take allow for fitting personalities and jobs together, as outlined in the example above. Without that, there is little likelihood that such demands can be made without creating tension. Further, intergroup demands almost by definition involve conflicts of interest simply because there aren't shared goals.

These are the factors that make in-group relationships simpler, more automatic, and easier for managers than interacting with outsiders.

Irregularity

We have large numbers of studies showing how in-group work flow relationships become regularized. At any level of the organization, as long as individuals are interacting with great regularity, they will typically evolve easy and simple methods of transacting their business. With the exception of the occasional personality conflict, members of organizations who work together learn to adopt comfortable routines of give-and-take to exchange ideas and help. The comfortable perfection of this reaches its zenith in the hospital operating room or on the flight deck of an airliner in an emergency. Hardly a full sentence is spoken to obtain coordination; just a glance, a muttered word, or a wink communicates all the other persons need to know to adjust their behavior to each other. It is only when people are irregular in their contacts that they must explain and expound in lengthy and often discomforting detail. One could almost say that words are for strangers, body language for colleagues.

Interference with Routines and Subgoals

Not only is there this unanticipated quality about these managerial contacts, they also represent a threat in most cases. As "work" crosses departmental boundaries, there is an inevitable difference in values that affects what is done how and when. The clinic sending patients to a centralized test/analysis facility has an internal schedule based on its own routines and its evaluation of how pressing the patient's problem is. The test facility, on the other hand, is seeking to routinize its own work, and certain tests can be done best together (assuming the equipment requires no readjustment) or at special times of the day. It is not difficult to understand why there will be differences to resolve over the flow of patients moving from clinic to testing.

The classic controversies between development and manufacturing are legion. The development engineers conceive the new project in terms consistent with their own professional standards, perhaps involving technical breakthroughs and complexities worthy of a major product innovation. The hardheaded manufacturing managers are sensitive to the difficulty of translating sophistication in design into mundane, low-cost, routinized production. There can be vituperative exchanges as each doubts the other's willingness to extend themselves to facilitate the adjacent function.

While management and economic formulas abound, when services and products have to be priced, there are inevitable ambiguities to be exploited by the distinctive interests involved. Finance wants a price to shorten the payback period for the new investment; engineering wants a price to justify unanticipated development costs; and marketing wants a price sensitive to competitive conditions in the market.

The Large Numbers Involved

Witness, in the Nancy Pfizer case, how many people had to be contacted (and how many times) to get a rather simple change approved. Multiply this by the number of questions and problems that occur in any typical day and one has some idea of why managers are so busy and so interactive.

Unstable Equilibrium

What most executives do not appreciate is that these managerial relationships are not in stable equilibrium; that is, small problems cause major dislocations. The reason is not difficult to fathom, although it is interesting how rarely this has been perceived. The source is the very number of interrelationships that are built into the organization by the technical mutual dependencies. For instance, in the fan case above, a great many people had tasks that were technically interdependent. On paper it looked as though no outside contact would be necessary, and indeed it wasn't, as long as everything worked perfectly. But that nirvana never exists for long; the minute some unanticipated event arises, requiring approval and consensus, there is a mushrooming of interrelationships—a sort of domino effect. To restore the stability and equilibrium may take literally a hundred phone calls and meetings.

In the case above we've probably understated the number of actual communications and negotiations involved. A simple diagram will explain how quickly they multiply. Assume that manager A works closely with managers B, C, and D. A wants something from B: an approval, a change in schedule, some aid—it doesn't matter. But A's request (and B's offer—generous or niggardly) will likely affect A's relationship and work with C and D, and each of those with all the others:

Thus we have these additional contacts:

AB   BC   CD
AC   BD
AD

But we've left out something. B (and C and D, for that matter) are related to other parts of the organization as well; that is, they have commitments and responsibilities of their own:

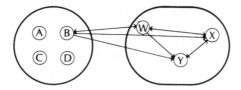

So we also have

BW   WX   XY
BX   WY
BY

And this works similarly for C and D.

Thus, if there is any quantity of interdependencies in the system, the numbers of lateral contacts grow enormously to cope with any changes that occur.

Iteration

These relationships quickly multiply in quantity because most requests don't allow for "yes" or "no" answers. It's typically, "It all depends," and thus the contact must be repeated:

"I can do what you ask if I can get some relief from. . . . "
"We'll agree to that if our tests show. . . . "
"Unless you can modify that specification, I won't be able. . . . "
"If I can get someone else to take over, then we'll be able. . . . "

Each concession creates problems for others. We see that the manager must go back again and again or follow up by seeing others who control access or releases. The failure to follow up ensures nonresponse since most other executives will have every reason to avoid change and to maintain the status quo. Almost any change will require a good deal of extra effort for all concerned—more seeking of information, more persuasion of subordinates to change their procedures, more replanning and rescheduling. Each full circle of contacts brings some new concessions and some new problems to be worked through.

Ambiguity

While there may be some room for misinterpretation and some grounds for questioning their legitimacy, most relationships between boss and subordinate are relatively clear-cut. Only occasionally does anyone have much doubt about who is asking for what and about the probable legitimacy of the request. This is not true of many of the lateral managerial relationships we are talking about. Look, for a moment, at this example:

A new product department calls on the research division for some help with the design of a new product. Somewhere, sometime, upper management has decreed that RD should aid and assist NPD in its efforts to spawn commercially viable products. But how much help, at what "price," and with what time priority are left unspecified. Similarly, it will make a substantial difference if NPD defines the problem very narrowly and wants a highly specific technical answer—involving a kind of testing service—or whether they want high-level professional counsel on a much more general problem. The RD wants challenging, general problems, and it's likely that NPD wants specific service work.

Further, both because of the ambiguities and because the future status of an executive or a whole department depends on the relationship which emerges from these negotiations, they are made even more difficult. In other words, in the case above, NPD and RD aren't simply concerned with spelling out the meaning of a specific request for assistance. How this gets interpreted may well affect the relationship of RD to many other parts of the organization. It's not difficult to predict that RD is worried about becoming a pure service activity, jumping to the "becks" and "calls" of other departments and unable to shape broad, professional-stature problems for itself. We shall want to look closely at just how managers can shift the power and status of a department and themselves by knowing how to manipulate these lateral relationships. (See Chapter 6.)

Influence through Negotiation

Whether they realize it or not, managers spend a significant share of their working day negotiating with other managers. Negotiations are necessary when there is no obvious answer, no obvious decision. Managers often have to ask other departments to change their priorities or do things differently. Because they frequently deal with peers they cannot order around, and because internal routines and objectives may differ, most managers are forced to *negotiate* for the resources they need.

Many managers just assume that most of their business day will involve dealing with bosses or subordinates, and needing to influence peers comes as a shock. More upsetting still is the reality that their boss will demand things from them that will require critical resources from another department, responding with delay or outright refusal. It seems so unfair that they should be held responsible for finishing a project by a deadline when another department can't or won't deliver needed information or materials on time.

A typical reaction is indignation, even outrage. Seeing the other department's head as an obstacle, a manager may seek to bully him into submission. Of course, such high pressure usually produces an equal and opposite force that fails to get the need satisfied.

An equally ineffective reply to apparent noncooperation is to accuse management staff in the other department of not having the company's interest at heart, or of being inefficient or incompetent. This, too, usually produces friction rather than positive results.

Another typical reaction to not getting the needed resources or aid is to make one of two assumptions:

"It's just a misunderstanding, a communication problem. When the situation is 'clarified,' cooperation will be forthcoming."

"There must be a clever way of 'fooling' the other party and overcoming his resistance."

The first assumption is wrong because it supposes that the organization is really one big happy family and everyone has the same interests and goals. *Not so.* Other departments usually have different interests and get rewarded for doing things that may not be consistent with the manager's needs. Most conflicts over what should be done are not simply misunderstandings: they are often real conflicts over goals and tactics.

The second assumption, the "one-upmanship" approach, is doomed to fail—if not immediately, surely in the long run—because it assumes never having to deal with that department head again. And, of course, in organizations, effective managers build long-term relationships and count on friendship or, at least, mutual respect to win them the assistance they need.

Since managers cannot order cooperation or get it by trickery or threat, at least not without costly reprisals, they must *negotiate* to gain acquiescence from reluctant sources of aid or supply. Negotiation simply means give-and-take. As managers explain their needs, they learn about the constraints the other person is facing. Some of the constraints are easy to alleviate by modifying a request. Example:

> If you can't get the project to us on time, what if we get partial specs to you tomorrow and then you'll have three weeks to work on those? When we finish our part of the job, we could contract out the more time-consuming parts and the people in your department would only have to look over the total package when it's done.

If the manager has built up some credibility and demonstrated flexibility, the other side is likely to show some flexibility, too. Example:

> There is no way I can get Harry to work on that, even though he is the one you want and could do it best. But I could get Harry to look over Bill and Jane's work, to be sure it's consistent with the way you like things done.

Negotiations are time-consuming and can be destroyed by emotional blame fixing or threats. If one party in the negotiations becomes indignant, he will be unable to engage in a give-and-take in which the other party thinks he is credible and worth helping. Negotiations assume that both parties want to build or continue a relationship, not just solve the problem.

The Steady Stream of New Managerial Roles

Lateral relationships are made more open-ended and less stable and predictable because they are vulnerable to power seeking and to the insensitivity of top management. Most organizations are constantly introducing new functional requirements—e.g., a manager to cope with the burgeoning consumer movement—without taking into account the consequences for the jobs of other managers.

Thus management appoints Ann Hacz as its consumer specialist. What is her job? She's told that she is responsible for assisting the corporation in being more alert, and more responsive, to consumerism, consumer complaints, and the growing sensitivities of the customer.

Does she now evaluate and criticize what divisions and managers are doing? Can she stop production if word reaches her that a potentially serious product safety and liability question surrounds one of the company's products? Whom does she collaborate with and how, and how does she get information, criticism, and assistance into the hands of operating managers?

Corporations today are seeing a constant stream of new managerial specialists introduced—to handle risk management, quality, productivity—usually without an evaluation of the hundreds of new interrelationships these positions will entail. In the case below, imagine the distress of the manager of the research group of Data Services when top management introduced the new expert! What was required now? How much time and effort were going to be involved in integrating the staff expert into the new hardware program?

CASE: A New Expert Joins the Fray

Data Services provided a variety of information—including economic trends, credit ratings, and demographic data on various communities—to a wide range of commercial customers who paid high annual fees for these databank services and expected prompt, accurate reporting.

On occasion mistakes were made because of clerical errors, software problems, or simply delays resulting from computer downtime. Research, a small section within Data Services who handled complaint correspondence, was in the process of installing a new minicomputer, which would radically change their data retrieval procedures and their procedures in responding to customer complaints. For months the supervisor of research had met with other work groups within Data Services that were also installing new technology and new procedures. Initially there had been a number of disputes over the division of labor between research and other groups that handled customer requests, over the new work procedures, and even over the type of terminal to buy.

And there were other considerations. At the same time that research and the other groups were installing the new minicomputers, the company itself was introducing a new software system—LAN (local area network). In anticipation of that move, a new "player" had appeared on the scene—Jeff Egan, who had been hired by top management to help the company cope with the LAN technology.

In looking over the company's plan for conversion to the new system, Egan was most critical. He said the cabling that was specified was not adequate for future expansion. Nor were the terminals (which were the first choice of research and for which they had "paid in blood") the best from a LAN point of view.

The research group was now in a tenuous position. Was it possible that Egan's criticisms and proposals would be taken so seriously by senior management as to negate the months of negotiation and delay the delicate conversion? Those same managers had insisted that the conversion go into effect in thirty days, and even understanding the implications of Egan's critique would take several months. Where was he when the issues were being debated? If LAN considerations were so important, why hadn't he or someone like him been hired earlier?

To summarize, lateral relations pose distinctive challenges for the manager because:

1　They involve intergroup relationships.
2　They are irregular.
3　They interfere with routines.
4　Their numbers are so great.
5　They mushroom in quantity quickly because of unstable equilibria and the need for iteration.
6　The required relationships are often ambiguous.
7　Management keeps adding new specialists.

HOW TO MANAGE LATERAL RELATIONS

We have explicitly described the behavioral components of dealing with subordinates. What are the analogous elements of lateral relationships? As we've implied, managerial jobs intertwine in quite complex patterns of interrelationship. It is not adequate to say that Egan and research should periodically exchange information or that Nancy Pfizer has numerous external contacts. Managers want to know when and how: do they call up and notify a colleague that a batch is spoiled, or rather do they ask what they can do to compensate for the spoiled material? From whom, if anyone, must they get permission before changing specification? How seriously do they take criticism from other managers that their reports are faulty?

We now know that when new managers are told (and job descriptions hint) that they must coordinate with, check with, consult, inform, meet the standards of—and countless other phrases suggesting lateral contacts—these are usually understatements. A good share of their managerial life will involve working with other people in a non–superior-subordinate relationship. We ought to be able to go further than saying what they are not, go beyond simply calling them "lateral" relationships.

Watching managers engage in this kind of "managerial work" discloses a number of distinguishable *patterns* of relationships. And the distinctions between these patterns become critical for the managers. Some relationships require a good deal of deference; realistic expectations must be that these will be more stressful. Others give real power—easy to abuse but also exhilarating. And still others involve rather subtle give-and-take with one's counterparts. So while instructions and procedures will use vague terms like "coordinate," managers must learn to interpret and distinguish between many types. What is called "lateral" is a variety of managerial relationships that must be distinguished and mastered if the division of labor contemplated by the organizational structure is to work. The alternative is constant arguments about who is overstepping their "authority" or not holding up their end of things. What is often called a "personality" or "communications" problem or just a poor match between a managerial job and its incumbent may simply be the failure to comprehend what's required and what can be expected from others.

But all of this is too abstract; let's move to an example to illustrate these lateral types. We shall take the case of a manager of a centralized analytical-diagnostic laboratory in a medical center operated by a commercial organization. The laboratory processes a variety of tests for various clinics, as well as for the medical and surgery departments of the hospital.

Work Flow Relationships

A given manager's department will be processing ideas, papers, or materials, some elements of which have come from other departments. Usually the finished work also must move to another department for further processing or use. While plans and procedures specify what, how, and why these three departments (in our case, before A-D, A-D, and after A-D) "coordinate," the process rarely will work out perfectly. For one of countless reasons, the demand or supply at various points in the work flow will be too little or great, or the work will be performed in a manner that is suitable for one unit but not for another.

Managers, since they have the status and freedom to move around, are expected to defend their work group's need for predictability and to respond to other managers' requests for predictability:

> In our case, the A-D lab manager will have to call departments that send specimens packaged poorly, bunched together rather than spread over the working day, or otherwise difficult to process. When equipment is malfunctioning or other delays are experienced, the manager will have to alert the "receiving" departments that analyses will be late, perhaps request new priorities, and otherwise assist in compensating for the delays. Frequently, requests for faster or special service from a number of customers will have to be parried and compromised. Departments receiving analyses and reports may want a different schedule, more or less detail than is now provided, or a changed format.

If we look at these exchanges between work flow stages we should be able to distinguish four types:[2]

1 Mandated contacts that are reasonably predictable: e.g., "When changing solutions or standard materials against which test materials are 'run,' call all receiving departments to alert them to the possibility that test results may have greater variability."

2 Mandated contacts that are not predictable: e.g., "Should unforeseen contingencies require the laboratory to delay test results for more than two hours from the normal schedule, receiving departments should be alerted and discussions undertaken as to what are the most critical priorities."

3 Negotiations and explorations to reduce uncertainty that are not prescribed: e.g., "Given the frequency with which it's been necessary to complain to one of the surgical wards, the lab

---

[2] These same four types exist in other lateral relationships we shall be describing.

manager may seek an agreement with that ward that one nurse be trained to work with the laboratory, as distinct from making it almost a random assignment."

4   Power plays: e.g., efforts on the part of other managers to gain the right to veto any changes in the laboratory's work schedule (what we shall call a new "stabilization relationship").

Obviously, the last type of contact represents what most people call organizational politics; the other three types are desirable and arise out of the division of labor. From a given manager's point of view, in responding to a request from outside there is the need to distinguish what is being asked: a type 1 contact probably yields the easiest and quickest response; types 2 and 3 are a little more difficult, even assuming there is a desire to build good working relationships; a type 4 contact is invariably going to be difficult and resisted. Astute managers learn the importance of distinguishing type 3 from 4; naive ones never learn!

Based on a number of studies of work flow relationships, we can predict that the A-D lab manager will be handling this interactional part of the job effectively when the number of requests initiated *from* the lab *to* each of the previous and succeeding stages in the flow about equal the number initiated *to* the lab manager *from* each of these work flow stages; that is to say, there is mutual reciprocity, roughly equal give-and-take.

Service Relationships

Work flow relationships involve managers who are sequentially placed. Any managers in the flow are likely to generate pressures on others roughly equal to the pressure they receive. Similar, but with an important difference, are service relationships. These are created when top management centralizes an activity—thus requiring a large number of organizational units to gain access in order to fulfill their own task requirements. In a sense, a monopoly is created to replace the independence of each unit in having its own captive source of this skill or activity. Typical examples are computational facilities, exotic professional analytical work, and activities requiring expensive capital equipment.

Managers controlling such resources can anticipate having to cope with conflicting, contradictory, and one-sided pressures, particularly whenever a hint of shortages or delay appears. It's an old-but-true axiom that there is no such thing as a "little shortage" in a service department's work. Overly vigilant managers rush in to claim priority and get their share "before the hoarders do"—leading inevitably to real scarcity. Thus these managers come under heavy interactional pressure.

> In addition to normal processing work, the A-D labs maintain equipment located throughout the hospital and in some of the satellite laboratories. The staff is on call for maintenance work. Many times these calls require more resources than are available, and technicians are harassed and implored to give higher priority to one "customer" than another.
>
> The manager must act as a buffer to defend the group from the inevitably pressuring demands of other groups whose work is stopped by inoperative equipment. Insofar as these repair skills become a critically scarce resource, it will take a great deal of time to work through priorities in such a way that customers believe their legitimate needs will be cared for. It will be tempting to fight back against those who apply pressure, and it will be difficult to be tactful when each phone call brings a new demand.

Advisory Relationships

Managers and their technically trained subordinates also serve in contingency relationships called "advisory." When other departments have problems that require more knowledge and experience than is internally present, they are expected to call upon centralized sources of expert knowledge who will then seek to aid the troubled department.

> Our laboratory manager receives a certain number of calls to assist in developing more trouble-free specimen collection procedures, more efficient methods in satellite labs, and better criteria for selecting lab personnel. Often he will see other problems, but to maintain the "advisory" relationship, he is expected to limit himself to the problem for which he is called, and *to wait to be called.*

Audit Relationships

Organizations expect to utilize the technical expertise of their management in evaluating existing methods and identifying where improvements can be made. The hierarchy has neither enough technical expertise nor enough time to appraise all the ongoing activities in terms of how well they meet the financial, personnel, technical, and legal standards desired by top management. In a sense these experts become the eyes and ears of upper management.

> Our A-D lab manager, being well trained in biology and related fields, periodically examines certain procedures and activities in various hospital departments to assess whether hygiene and sterility standards are being adequately maintained. He is expected to communicate his findings to department heads who, in turn, should take action when defects are shown. Some standards will be ambiguous, and the relevant department heads and the "auditor" will have to work through the appraisal together.

Stabilization Relationships

While this "auditing" is done after the fact, "stabilizing" has a much more powerful effect. Fearing that some serious problem will occur, management requires that, for some activities, managers must obtain clearance or permission *before* beginning or continuing their work activities. They must justify the appropriateness of the actions they intend to take in terms of the interests of the larger organization.

> In our case, hospital departments beginning research where contagion is a possibility are required to review their protection and decontamination procedures with the A-D laboratory manager and obtain his concurrence before initiating the studies. He becomes a check that they have taken all the necessary precautions to protect the entire facility and staff.

Liaison Relationships

Both inside and outside the organization, there will be a number of groups whose practices, language, or interests make them difficult to deal with. The modern organization must face community pressure groups, unions, the government, "long-haired" professionals, even the group down the hall; any or all of these special interest groups may pose problems in communication that can only be resolved in liaison relationships. Man-

agers who can establish such relationships and bridge the communications gap between specialists are asked to serve as
intermediaries: honest brokers. For instance:

> A project scientist, trained in biology, helps a university-based
> research team understand some of the FDA regulations that will
> affect the development of a new drug. The scientist also serves
> to relay the needs of the team (for funding, autonomy, etc.) back
> to the company that has established this research "outpost."
>
> A systems specialist working for operations helps that depart-
> ment become more realistic about what data processing can and
> cannot do for them; the specialist also represents their needs to
> data processing when operations foresees problems requiring
> changes.
>
> A company establishes a liaison office to assist visiting prod-
> uct managers from overseas in interfacing with their American
> counterparts and with the market research and manufacturing
> personnel with whom they will be working temporarily. The of-
> fice is staffed with people who "know their way around" the
> corporate head office.

Such liaison people speak the "languages" of several groups,
have the technical background that earns them respect and acceptance across boundaries, and have learned to communicate
cross-culturally, i.e., to act as "translators."

ASSESSING THE TOTAL JOB

All managers need to break down their activities into behavioral
patterns to understand what they are expected to do with
whom and how. In addition to providing a more realistic view
of their responsibilities and likely stresses, such an analysis allows them to see where others may be failing to perform and
where they are, consciously or not, "converting" one job pattern to another. The analytical procedure is simple:

Work Flow Relationships
1 From whom do you "receive"?
2 To whom do you "send"?

Service Relationships
1 To whom do you go to request centralized services?

2 From whom should you expect to receive demands for a service relationship?

Advisory Relationships

1 To whom do you go to gain aid on specific types of problems?

2 Who can call upon you for specific types of technical assistance?

Audit Relationships

1 What other managerial units does one "audit" for specific functional criteria?

2 What other managers will be "auditing" you?

Stabilization Relationships

1 What permissions, "sign-offs," and authorizations do you control and for whom?

2 To whom must you go for authorization to proceed for specific areas and activities?

Liaison Relationships

1 With whom do you "connect," that is, act as intermediary or broker for in maintaining communications and relationships?

2 Who will be seeking to act as an intermediary between you and others?

Obviously, managerial jobs differ in the "mix" of the relationships they contain. So-called line managers are likely to have rather little "service" work and a great deal of "work flow." Those called "staff" may do anything from the relatively passive and not very powerful "advisory" work to very powerful "stabilization" and "audit" patterns. However, even those managerial jobs which are largely one or another pattern will usually have some quantity of other "patterns" intermixed with the dominant role.

Explicitness becomes particularly important when new positions are talked about. The language of management is usually highly imprecise; for example, an organization that is expecting a new manager to emphasize service and advice may find that the manager prefers or believes the proper role is one of stabilization.

The product managers in a consumer goods company were surprised when the head of the new "consumer affairs" department sought to control their activities. The published descriptions of the job had emphasized how this new person would help interpret new legislation and act as a liaison with the growing consumer movement. Instead, the manager sought—rather successfully—to get the power to evaluate all existing products for safety and reliability.

But even existing managerial jobs are gradually shifted, transmuted, and stretched to fit the personality and predilections of the incumbent, often without anyone's approval or even tacit consent.[3] Since managerial work involves a rather subtle, complex division of labor, it is important in training and evaluation of managers to be able to make these required profiles explicit rather than implicit.

It becomes particularly important to distinguish between the patterns which are frequently transmuted.

Advisory becomes audit: "I tell you what is wrong so you'll take my advice."

Service becomes stabilization: "In order to reduce the pressure, I tell you what you require or will be permitted to have instead of responding to your requests."

Audit becomes stabilization: "Instead of waiting to appraise, I insist you have to get clearance in advance."

Work flow is ignored: "Rather than keeping you informed of changes I'll make or responding to your requests to make accommodative changes, I pretend to be autonomous."

Obviously, in appraising subordinate managers it becomes critical to know the explicit behavioral content of each manager's job—whom the manager should deal with, how, when, and how often. Most management appraisals fail—and the ensuing coaching and criticism are useless—because they are undertaken in a vacuum. There is no clear managerial job requirement standard against which performance is appraised. To be sure, there may be objectives and goals, but as we shall see in

---

[3] In Chap. 6 we describe how one can predict the direction of these changes. They will not be random patterns, but rather those that tend to move managerial jobs toward the more prestigious, powerful roles—work flow, stabilization, and audit—and away from the relatively weak and dependent patterns—service, advisory, and liaison.

Chapter 8, these often fail to provide effective standards for performance appraisal.

The case below gives a dynamic view of lateral relations and their problems for the manager. Note particularly the multiple and even contradictory relationships handled by the data systems group. Do you think the manager does about as well as could be expected or could she have coped better with these interfaces?

CASE: The Politics of New Equipment Acquisition

Fidelity Insurance had moved rapidly into the age of electronic data processing and computers. In addition to an imposing centralized group of mainframes, which maintained basic records of the company's policyholders, Fidelity used a variety of micros for everything from helping agents evaluate alternative financial-service packages for customers to doing accounting in their farflung operations. The mainframes and the various communications systems that interconnected many of the subsystems were controlled by Fidelity's data systems group, which was responsible for a large proportion of the computing operations, including purchase and maintenance of equipment and software development.

Over the years many departments had developed their own systems and hardware base, usually with—but occasionally without—DS's cooperation. In almost every case, these systems had to interface with one or more DS-maintained system, and DS charged an appropriate fee for providing the interconnections.

One hard-driving Fidelity marketing group, headed by an executive who had long been with the company and who had a superb reputation, had recently purchased an innovative terminal from a small hardware vendor. The terminal was relatively low cost and had a number of features that made it uniquely suited to that group's needs. Helene Graf, another marketing manager, who was involved with tax shelters in a totally different part of Fidelity, heard about these new Temple terminals and decided to evaluate them as an alternative to a terminal her group had been using for a number of years, a terminal endorsed by DS and manufactured by the same large corporation that furnished Fidelity's mainframes.

But Graf was relatively new on the job, and she decided to proceed slowly. She first had a meeting with Josh Stein, an analyst for the data systems people she had gotten to know in a previous job at Fidelity. Stein told Graf he had seen the Temple terminals operating and he thought they did an outstanding job; he confirmed that they had features no other vendor, including the prestigious mainframe manufacturer, could provide and that they were about half the cost.

To further test the comparisons, Graf arranged for Temple to install some of its machines in parallel with the existing equipment. During the test the Temple machines were clearly inferior. Graf, who had some substantial experience with various kinds of terminals, was struck by the anomalous discrepancy in performance and decided to see whether a problem in the microwave circuits might have contributed to the unexpectedly poor performance of the Temple. Although it was a clear violation of DS rules (and DS controlled all the microwave equipment and lines), Graf had one of her technicians shift the Temple terminals to the line connected to the mainframe manufacturer's terminals and vice versa. At that point the Temple equipment began to outperform the competition by a substantial margin.

When word got back to DS about the microwave line switching, Graf received a condemnatory letter from the head of DS (with a copy to her boss). She was also called to appear at a meeting at which her boss and a senior DS manager heard the charges repeated. When Graf argued that her own experience had led her to believe that one of the lines was not operating properly, her rebuttal was ignored.

Even so, Graf was persistent. In her capital budget requests for the upcoming year, she requested the purchase of twenty Temple terminals, a relatively minor item, and justified the request on the basis of a 50 percent savings in equipment costs and a 25 percent improvement in operator productivity. She asserted that the new terminals would, in fact, pay for themselves in eighteen months, and she included Stein's technical evaluation in her request.

Although the data seemed clear-cut, Graf's boss turned down that part of her budget request. Among the reasons he cited were DS opposition (as expressed in a formal memo), a DS decision to charge Graf's department with a $20,000 penalty for cancellation of the rental agreement on her existing terminals, and the extra charges assessed by DS to connect and maintain the Temple terminals. Graf fought vigorously for a reversal of the decision. The total cost of the Temple terminals was small and her department was faced with a number of productivity problems because of an expanded customer base. She questioned why DS would impose a cancellation penalty of that magnitude and why Temple terminals should bear higher line charges than the rental terminals they replaced. But her boss stood by his decision and warned her in no uncertain terms to stop being a troublemaker.

Weeks later Graf learned that her boss had authorized the rental of a hundred additional terminals, the old models, for another operation under his control. The decision was made after a strong recommendation by DS that they were "ideal for that application." By her own rough calculation Graf knew that sixty Temples would do the same job at about one-half the cost, and she was tempted to raise the issue again. New Temple terminals would greatly expedite the workload projected for the coming year. On the other hand, she was still new, and she felt her relations with her boss might be at risk if she continued to push for the Temples.

THE NEED TO "WORK" INTERFACES

Managers are used to considering the implications of the division of labor at the worker level. In fact, operating work has been studied minutely in terms of who should do what with whom and when. Ironically, the coordination problems of managerial work are much more difficult for the reasons we have cited. It's a hundredfold easier for a team of assemblers or tradespeople to work together than it is for a group of managers from a variety of departments with their diversity of goals and perceptions. Usually workers simply have, in our language, "work flow relations" to implement the coordination between jobs. But managers have a much broader and more ambiguous variety of relations—not to mention the sheer quantity required, the perseverance and stamina demanded.

Naive managers see these interfaces as either unnecessary (someone must be violating a rule or his or her responsibilities) or simply office politics. Academics dismiss them as "the informal organization" at work. But neither bureaucracy nor politics is an adequate explanation. What appears to the untutored eye as either stubbornness or a free-for-all is actually an orchestrated work process designed to pull together a large number of *legitimate* viewpoints and concerns. Management thus becomes in large part a process of working interfaces.

Lack of understanding in this area leads, at the very least, to frustration—and more likely to failure or needless additional complexity. For example, consider the problems that arise from neglecting to give information to another manager in the work flow or to check with a manager having stabilization functions or failing to be responsive in a service role. All such actions begin a series of countermoves that require many more interventions than would have been required had the process been done properly the first time.

Similarly, the failure of managers to comprehend and evaluate the administrative patterns of subordinates allows the latter to engage in power binges and critical omissions. Getting neither guidance nor reinforcement, subordinate managers feel free to interpret their jobs in ways most consistent with personal proclivities or just easy living. Critical interfaces are neglected or shifted (as we shall observe in Chapter 6), and the medicine then applied is likely to exacerbate the disease. In other words, the resulting so-called communications or personality problems often encourage the addition of new personnel as expediters and controllers, in turn complicating the organization's structure.

The Systems Manager

Given the strides made by operations and systems analysts to model organizational problems and computerize some decision making, managers are encouraged to adopt a "systems" point of view. But "systems" has multiple meanings.

The word "system" connotes interdependence. Managers must remember they don't live in a vacuum. Thus, the firm or the agency has to remember it has a marketplace, an environment, and a whole host of "outside" groups that impact its decision making. Analogously, production needs marketing needs research, etc. Decisions made or problems occurring in one unit are difficult to compartmentalize; they ramify throughout the organization.

A real systems approach seeks to explicate the actual dynamic functioning of the organization by looking at the behavioral interrelationships required by the division of labor that has been created. Thus a *systems view* asks who is expected and/or required to do what, with whom, when, and where.[4]

Comparisons to Family Life

The ambiguity of these intramanagement relationships may be compared to some of the tensions and problems found in modern family life. Anthropologists have noted the greater clarity of relationships in the traditional family. There were clearly established rights and duties among members of the extended family that were further clarified by terminology. While today we use the term "uncle" to refer to any parental brother, more traditional societies would have distinguished between the mother's brother and the father's. Similarly, a newly married couple would know what to expect in the way of demands from the wife's mother as compared to the husband's. Older and younger siblings had their relationships spelled out as well, including the distinctions to be made between male and female siblings and between different age levels. In contrast, our families today are vague about who owes what responsibility to whom. Any member is likely to feel unjustly treated or partially guilty about relationships with close relatives.

CONCLUSIONS

Some years ago, when *Managerial Behavior* was first published, it was somewhat shocking to say that managers spent most of their time conducting lateral relations, rather than giving and receiving orders.[5] Our field work had disclosed this quite clearly, although it contradicted what were then the major management texts. Even today, students of management are often surprised by this reality. Their casebook academic training has led them to think of problem solving as requiring very orderly, sequential actions that follow both the organization chart and the precepts of rational economic analysis. (After all, that is how they solved their case assignments!) Rough-and-tumble reality with its stops and starts and many cross-interrelationships

---

[4] In Chap. 8 we shall turn to the question of identifying the criteria for going into action, for initiating a relationship with other managers.

[5] Leonard Sayles, *Managerial Behavior*, McGraw-Hill, New York, 1964.

seems disorderly and political. But the number of specialized interests and constraints mandates this high quantity of lateral give-and-take. From the point of view of subordinates, managers who are respected—and followed—are those who can anticipate problems "in the system," get them the things they need, and protect them from unreasonable demands. To be effective at representation and buffering for subordinates, managers must comprehend correctly and be able to "work" the interfaces of their jobs.

CHAPTER 6

GAINING POWER IN
ANY ORGANIZATION

Among other things, the hierarchy in an organization specifies power: who outranks whom and who can expect deference from those below. But, as any experienced executive knows, that is only the tip of the power iceberg. Many individuals and groups have real power—meaning the ability to get others to comply with their wishes—far greater than their apparent formal status. Even when the organization chart shows a number of divisions or functions at the same level, this rarely means they have the same power.

In the federal government, Cabinet officers have the same rank, but everyone knows the secretaries of the Treasury and State have enormously more clout than those of Interior and Commerce.

Further, so-called staff groups often can emasculate a line department that challenges their "real" authority.

The consumer products division decided to build a new centralized warehouse. Accounting sought to initiate a study checking the return on investment, but the vice president of the product group said their own data were sufficient. When he continued to ignore requests for information from accounting, the head of that staff group announced a surprise audit of all consumer products facilities and records. He was able to produce enough questionable recordkeeping to discredit the data justifying the new warehouse—and the vice president. The latter soon learned not to challenge accounting's requests.

WHAT IS POWER?

Various studies have shown rather conclusively that members of organizations have no trouble identifying power differences within an organization. While formal title and rank may not show it, insiders know that department A and manager X have more power than do department B and manager Y. In turn, these differences show themselves in whose work carries greater weight in difficult managerial decisions, whose budgets are more likely to be approved, and who is perceived as someone "you need on your side" if you are going to get agreement for a proposal.

The existence of this power differential is a reflection of two characteristics of the modern organization. First, there are a number of different interest groups within an organization; it's a far cry from one big, happy family. Inevitably, what pleases (meets the goals of) one division or functional group is going to be inconsistent with the needs of another. Further, there will be, as one astute observer phrased it, "differing perceptions of the consequences of a given action."[1] In other words, it's not easy to tell whether the new warehouse, product, or policy is objectively better than what it will replace—at least in advance. When economists say that "the production function is unclear," they are saying you can't prove that adding x at a cost of y is better than doing nothing or than subtracting z at a saving of y'.

It is important to recognize that almost every decision made in an organization has power implications; few are neutral. One group gets favored, inevitably at the expense of another; a group's power is either validated (and enhanced) or discredited

---

[1] Bruce Henderson, *Trust*, Boston Consulting Group, Perspectives, Boston, 1977, n.p.

by any decision. For example, if a pricing decision on a new product results in a relatively higher price, this may favor engineering and manufacturing over marketing. Obviously, the arguments the managers make prior to the decision will stress the welfare of the total company, but it's never hard to identify small group goals with larger goals—if one has the motivation and experience. As one candid executive described it, "You give the groups that are important a lot of flexibility, and those that are less important you squeeze like hell."

Thus power differences, rather than calculations, are likely to be influential in whose requests, interests, and projects get supported and whose get rejected. Only naive managers assume that budgets get allocated and key decisions made solely on the basis of rational decision making. Managers use—they *must* use— power to get their department interests served. This leaves us with the important question of who gets power, how, and why.

GETTING POWER BY AVOIDING ROUTINIZATION

Research and observation suggest that the most important source of power is absence of routinization. From the production worker to the executive suite, the task that is routinizable, that is, highly predictable and regularizable, has less power. When you think about it, it's obvious. If your job can be minutely measured and regulated, there is no power there. Some years ago the programmers in a large computer company sought to improve their organizational power position:

> Top management thinks of us as highly predictable. They can lose time and budget on the hardware design and development and not worry because they figure they can make it up when it comes time to do the programming. They figure scheduling is simply a matter of telling us what to do, setting time and performance specifications and that's it. But programming isn't that kind of task; it's a real science—with creative ability and budget you might be able to make real breakthroughs. It can't be planned like an assembly line. We need lots of leeway and the opportunity to do our thing.

In other words, the programmers wanted top management to feel more dependent on their exotic skills and less sure of what they could tell the programmers.

In fact, if you watch any reasonably cohesive work group,

you'll see them seeking to make their external (as distinct from their internal) relationships unpredictable in order to increase their power. They don't want to be taken for granted, to be treated like a low-status service group that jumps to respond when asked to perform.

> We [an analysis group in an insurance company] often get requests from almost every department in the place for our studies. But we're careful not to accept the time budget or dollar cost they want to give us. In fact we sometimes even try to change the assignment to make it into something more exciting and professionally challenging. We don't want them to think of us as clerks that they can just order around.

Some years ago when we studied the National Aeronautics and Space Administration, we found that a small group of highly trained professionals doing basic studies for the agency had developed their own slogan—"We don't pump gas"—meaning they would seek to avoid research assignments for which they were not uniquely qualified and which gave predictable results.

Gaining Visibility

Thus far we have emphasized that absence of routinization involves demonstrating that one's work is unpredictable, not easy for the outsider (boss or other manager) to schedule, specify, or cost. There are other ways of accomplishing the same objective. This involves undertaking innovations. Obviously, the first time a new activity is undertaken, a function performed, or technology implemented, it will appear extraordinary and worthy of high status. As the new element in the system is perfected, that is, routinized, it becomes downgraded in the eyes of top management. As one astute observer remarked, after noting that "fast-track" people were attracted to newly created jobs, "It was almost paradoxical: the success of a function . . . made it less and less possible for people running it to seem successful as individuals."[2]

Ambitious managers therefore find that it pays to innovate,

---

[2] Rosabeth Moss Kanter, *The Men and Women of the Corporation*, Basic Books, New York, 1977.

to get approval for new projects, to sell customers on a new product they hope to be able to acquire or develop, to find a problem area that hasn't been attacked successfully. Then building new programs to cope with these accepted problems or opportunities accrues substantial power to the sponsor, particularly in comparison to those handling older, routinized activities. It is difficult to judge, therefore, whether innovative proposals are designed to increase the power of the sponsor or to further the larger goals of the institutions, and it may well be impossible to discriminate. For example, some bank loan operations, such as evaluating credit risks, can be handled by computer programs, and this downgrades the work of the loan officer while upgrading data processing.

Visibility and Critical Skills

New activities obviously provide visibility—the assurance the managers will be noticed. Visibility is also enhanced whenever one moves into departments classified by top management as *critical*. Often these are so-called boundary roles—monitoring or dealing with outside forces: government, key suppliers, and customers. This goes back to nonroutinability. At any one time, certain functions of the business are perceived as most critical to organizational success just because they're less predictable, less routinized. At one time, it may be finance, at another, manufacturing or marketing. Influence and power are direct functions of membership in the critical, as compared with the "taken-for-granted," departments.

One of the most influential groups in a French cigarette factory was the maintenance engineers. Management had personnel and production under control, but the elaborate and expensive automated machines were constantly breaking down. Since the machines were considered "temperamental" and unpredictable, the engineers who kept them operating were considered critical to the organization, and their voice was influential in a wide variety of decisions beyond their functional responsibilities.[3]

---

[3] Gerald R. Salancik and Jeffrey Pfeffer, "Who Gets Power—And How They Hold on to It," *Organizational Dynamics*, Winter 1977, p. 5.

Within a university, department heads who are most able to attract discretionary funds from government agencies and private donors are recognized as the most powerful within their peer groups.[4] In turn, this enables them to command greater budget out of general funds, quite aside from their ranking in terms of student demand for their courses or other criteria.[5] We have viewed the same potency when corporations made decisions as to what projects are to be financed or where new facilities are to be located. The units with power based on visible, critical skills will get more than their share. Obviously, the influence of specialists will rise and wane depending on environmental forces:

> One can observe this historically in the top executives of industrial firms in the United States. Up until the early 1950's many top corporations were headed by former production line managers or engineers who gained prominence because of their abilities to cope with the problems of production. Their success, however, only spelled their demise. As production became routinized and mechanized, the problem of most firms became one of selling all those goods they so efficiently produced. Marketing executives were more frequently found in corporate boardrooms. Success out-did itself again for keeping markets and production steady and stable requires the kind of control that can only come from acquiring competitors and suppliers. . . . During the 1960's, financial executives assumed the seats of power. . . . Edging over the horizon are legal experts, as regulation and antitrust are becoming more and more frequent. . . . [6]

The moral of the story for the power seeker is to move into critical functional areas, and then move out at the right time! But one doesn't have to wait for fate; it can be coaxed. For example, industrial engineering was a declining specialty as production became more routinized and time and motion studies played a less critical role. Astute heads of IE began to accrue skills in operations research which opened whole new arenas for study and policy recommendation to them.

Others have noted that some managers are induced to create

---

[4] Ibid., p. 11.
[5] Ibid., p. 13.
[6] Ibid., p. 16. See also Jeffrey Pfeffer, *Power in Organizations*, Pitman, Marshfield, Mass., 1981.

crises (presumably knowing the solution) in order to show their abilities to cope successfully. Others volunteer or seek out more truly risky situations (e.g., a losing operation) to show they can turn it around. Somewhat less dangerous is the finding of new projects (construction, reorganizations, new programs) that can be associated with their initiator.

SHIFTING THE STATUS OF THE DEPARTMENT

Managers seeking power look for the right launching platform by finding problematic jobs or creating them. But astute managers also have learned how to shift the power base provided by their own departments. Here the basic rule for accruing power is also a simple one: gradually adjust the duties and activities you perform so that you and your department are able to get others to defer to your initiations and minimize the frequency with which you have to defer to others.

Strategies to Increase Status

Here are some suggestions for shifting the basic power base within your department.

1 Seek to professionalize your work—meaning that only you and your colleagues (with special training and experience) understand a certain class of problems. Therefore, too-specific orders, requests for quick service, checks on your work by "laypeople"—that is, nonspecialists—are all inappropriate. Professionalization is associated with giving a technical mystique to the work you do, a special language, showing special educational requirements.

2 Rid your area of activities that are routinizable, "service work" that others will be making heavy demands upon to aid in getting their own work done. Shift these to someone else's jurisdiction as being irrelevant to your major thrust, requiring too much managerial time.

3 Add on to your department activities necessary to maintain the internal regularity of your work, so that it's no longer necessary to negotiate these from others. As with number 2, this will increase your autonomy and provide you with greater independence from other areas. Increased autonomy means more status.

4 Try to add functions that allow you to appraise the work of other departments (auditing relations) and that will also require your permission before certain other activities can proceed (stabilization relations). Point out that you need to be "checked with," your "sign-off" is necessary, and/or you need to be included in any decision meetings, because what is done there will severely affect your area or because you are in the best position to appraise the impact of that decision on the total organization.

5 Seek to shift the location of your department in any decision chain from the later stages to the earlier stages; do the same for all work flows in which you participate.

Some years ago our former colleague George Strauss studied a plant that manufactured portable television sets. When they were powerful, the circuit designers always made the earliest decisions regarding the design of a new model. As circuitry became more routinized, manufacturing methods and cost control departments took precedence, and the circuits people ended up in the position of responding to their initiations, rather than the reverse. The same thing could be observed in noting when labor relations managers were involved in contracting out decisions. If these decisions were made and then labor relations had to cope with the resulting internal union problems, one could be sure they had low status. When they were involved at the outset in helping to decide what could be contracted outside and when, they obviously had more power.

6 Add researchlike (innovational) tasks which are difficult for the outsider to evaluate and which increase your autonomy.

Advocacy

All these structural maneuvers require more than the idea; they require forceful advocacy on the part of the leader of the group, department, or function. Since ideas will be in competition for the attention of top management, they have to be sold by persuasive logic and persistence. Managers learn that they must be able to make forceful, convincing presentations. Top management is largely in the position of responding, not initiating; they give the nod to one or another proposal coming up the line. For this reason managers have to learn the skills of presentation: assembling convincing data, designing tables and graphs, articulating an appealing line of argument. Lacking a forceful leader, some departments will atrophy as they lose out to more energetic parts of the organization. Recognizing this, astute junior executives will seek to work in areas headed by ambitious advocates with proven track records for selling programs.

Illicit Power Ploys

We have been describing the strategies used to increase the power of particular departments and, of course, the managers of those departments. There are obviously a variety of Machiavellianlike activities which inflate, usually temporarily, the personal power of an executive.

These typically involve monopolistic practices of one kind or another. It can be a monopoly of information—gaining and holding on to critical knowledge which others must use and therefore depend upon you to provide. The monopoly may revolve around the ability to deliver favors, for example, by controlling access to certain kinds of permissions or resources.

Bill Allen was a hospital administrator who made sure no one else had access to the director. If you needed something that required the director's approval, you had to go through Bill. Bill was also careful that, if anything was requested and obtained, he would be the one to tell the "lucky" recipient. Thus, when the head of surgery asked that one of his staff be given office space and the request was granted, Bill made sure the good news was communicated by him, not by the department head.

Such people become bottlenecks because they are loath to delegate to subordinates or even to allow outsiders to communicate with their people. They also are typically afraid that subordinates will learn too much about their hard-won techniques and know-how, so they hold back on training, insist on doing part of the job themselves, and give only limited information. Often this becomes a self-confirming prophecy. When they are asked to delegate more because work is backing up, even when they wish to do so, their long-established habit of withholding information and know-how makes subordinate failures more likely. This encourages such managers to feel they have to do the job themselves to ensure success. Such monopolization tactics often have their roots in insecurities of one kind of another. These bosses cannot tolerate the possibility of subordinate failure, which might reflect on their own abilities in the eyes of upper management.

We have called these "illicit" ploys because they injure the organization: subordinates aren't developed, information gets withheld, and needless bottlenecks occur.

INTERGROUP STRUGGLES FOR POWER

Professionalizing the Department

Of course, all of these moves toward higher status, increased "professionalization," and power for your department don't come unopposed. Not only is such power usually garnered at other managers' expense, but others also seek to accomplish the same objective at the same time. Each time a new job is created, a new activity begun, or a reorganization effected, there will be a great quantity of maneuvering—to obtain more auditing, stabilization, and earlier work flow positions and to get rid of easily routinized functions.

Who wins depends on who has the most facility with the tactics of lateral relationships. The following case study highlights the types of tactics that are available and how they can best be employed.[7] It is a blow-by-blow how-to-do-it of power acquisition.

CASE: The Ambitious Purchasing Agent

The purchasing agent's original functions were (1) to negotiate and place orders for materials with outside suppliers at the best possible terms—but only in accordance with specifications set by others—and (2) to expedite orders, that is, to check with suppliers to make

---

[7] The research described here was completed by Professor George Strauss, School of Business Administration, University of California, Berkeley. Strauss's study and analysis are taken from Leonard Sayles and George Strauss, *Human Behavior in Organizations*, Prentice-Hall, Englewood Cliffs, N.J., 1966, pp. 429–443. Much of the description is Strauss's original wording.

sure that deliveries were made on time. This arrangement gave the PA broad power to deal with suppliers, but he was little more than an order clerk within the company.

An ambitious PA feels that placing orders and expediting deliveries are but the bare bones of his responsibilities. He sees his most important function as that of keeping management posted about developments: new materials, new sources of supplies, price trends, and so forth. And to make this information more useful, he seeks to be consulted while a product is still in the planning stage, before any requisitions are drawn up. He feels that his technical knowledge of the supply market should be accorded recognition equal to the technical knowledge of, for example, the engineer and accountant.

One way of looking at the PA's desire to expand his influence is in terms of work flow. Normally, orders flow in one direction only, from engineering through scheduling to purchasing. But the PA is dissatisfied with being at the end of the line and seeks to reverse the flow. Such behavior may, however, result in ill feeling in other departments, particularly engineering and production scheduling.

Conflicts with Engineering

Engineers write up the specifications for the products which the PA buys. If the specifications are too tight or, what is worse, if they call for one brand only, the PA has little or no freedom to choose among suppliers, thus reducing his social status internally and his economic bargaining power externally. Yet engineers find it much easier to write down a well-known brand name than to draw up a lengthy specification which lists all the characteristics of the desired item. Disagreements also arise because, by training and job function, engineers look first for quality and reliability and thus, the PA charges, engineers can be indifferent to low cost and quick delivery, qualities of primary interest to purchasing.

Purchasing finds that costs escalate because engineers are reluctant to standardize parts and components. Each engineer, in fact each project, might end up requiring a different size screw. Inventory costs are raised, paperwork increases, and the opportunity to lower bids by larger order sizes is lost. Purchasing feels this results from an absence of any constraints on ordering. "Obviously if nothing is lost by thinking through every design problem from scratch, the engineer has no incentive to use what is a stock item or can be a common part ordered by many departments." While the engineer's rebuttal will stress why his or her best judgment must prevail as to what is required, purchasing exerts pressures in the opposite direction. When successful, this results in requiring the engineer to justify departures from standard-parts lists for the most common components. In other words, rather than simply responding to a servicing order, purchasing assumes a stabilization role: being able to require permission *before* the order can be entered on the books.

Conflicts with Production Scheduling

The size of the order and the date on which it is to be delivered are typically determined by production scheduling. The PA's chief complaint against scheduling is that delivery is often requested on excessively short notice—that schedulers engage in sloppy planning or "cry wolf" by claiming they need orders earlier than they really do—thus forcing the PA to choose from a limited number of suppliers, to pay premium prices, and to ask favors of salespeople (thus creating obligations which the PA must later repay).

Techniques for Handling Lateral Relations

Understandably then, the successful PA develops a variety of techniques for dealing with other departments, particularly when he wishes to influence the form and content of the purchase requisitions he receives from other departments. As an example, let us look at some of the techniques which might be used if production scheduling submits a requisition with a very short lead time.

1 Rule-oriented tactics
   a Appeal to some common authority to direct that the requisition be revised or withdrawn.
   b Refer to some rule (assuming one exists) which provides for longer lead times.
   c Require the scheduling department to state in writing why quick delivery is required.
   d Require the requisitioning department to consent to having its budget charged with the extra cost (such as air freight) required to get quick delivery.

2 Rule-evading tactics
  a Go through the motions of complying with the request, but with no expectations of getting delivery on time.
  b Exceed formal authority and ignore the requisition altogether.
3 Personal-political tactics
  a Rely on friendships to induce the scheduling department to modify the requisition.
  b Rely on favors, past and future, to accomplish the same result.
  c Work through political allies in other departments.
4 Education tactics
  a Use direct persuasion, that is, try to persuade scheduling that its requisition is unreasonable.
  b Use what might be called indirect persuasion to help scheduling see the problem from the purchasing department's point of view. (In this case it might ask the scheduler to sit in and observe the PA's difficulty in trying to get the vendor to agree to quick delivery.)
5 Organizational tactics
  a Seek to change the work flow pattern—for example, have the scheduling department check with the purchasing department about the possibility of getting quick delivery *before* it makes a requisition. (This puts the PA into a *stabilization* role.)
  b Seek to take over other departments—for example, to subordinate scheduling to purchasing in a new integrated materials department.

Like it or not, the PA of necessity engages in power politics. In doing so, he develops allies and opponents. Each department presents a special problem.

1 *Engineering.* Unless the relationship with engineering is handled with great tact, engineering tends to become an opponent, since value analysis invades an area which engineers feel is exclusively their own. (In "value analysis" programs, purchasing agents evaluate parts ordered by the company to see if cheaper or simpler parts might be substituted.)

2 *Manufacturing.* There is often a tug-of-war between purchasing and manufacturing over who should have the greater influence with production scheduling. These struggles are particularly sharp where purchasing is trying to absorb into its own department either inventory control or all of production scheduling.

3 *Comptroller.* The comptroller is rarely involved in the day-to-day struggles over specifications or delivery dates. But when purchasing seeks to introduce an organizational change which will increase its power—for example, absorbing inventory control—then the comptroller can be a most effective ally. But the PA must present evidence that the proposed innovation will save money.

4 *Sales.* Sales normally has great political power, and purchasing is anxious to maintain good relations with it. Sales is interested above all in being able to make fast delivery and shows less concern with cost, quality, or manufacturing ease. In general, it supports or opposes purchasing in accordance with that criterion. But sales is also interested in reciprocity—in persuading purchasing "to buy from those firms which buy from us" (in order to increase sales, of course).

5 *Production scheduling.* Relations with production scheduling are often complex. Purchasing normally has closer relations with production scheduling than any other department, and conflicts are quite common. Yet these departments are jointly responsible for having parts available when needed and, in some companies, they present a common front to the outside world. Unfortunately, however, production scheduling has little political influence, particularly when it reports relatively low down in the management hierarchy.

The shrewd PA knows how to use departmental interests for his own ends:

> Engineering says we can't use these parts. But I've asked manufacturing to test a sample under actual operating conditions—they are easy to use. Even if engineering won't accept manufacturing's data, I can go to the boss with manufacturing backing me. On something like this, manufacturing is tremendously powerful. . . .

Modifying the Organization

Above we have described a variety of tactics by which a purchasing department may seek to introduce changes in the organization. For the most part, these are efforts to get others to adopt behavior and attitudes that will facilitate the objectives of the purchasing group itself. There is another method of introducing change in organizations which is often more powerful than these techniques of persuasion and pressure. When an employee's position in the organization changes, that person's behavior is likely to change. This tactic means changing the division of labor: who does what with whom, when, and where.

Below we shall look at only a few examples of this modification of the structure of the organization. In the first, job patterns are changed so that one department does not have to initiate as much to outside departments. The second example involves a change in departmental boundaries, or formal jurisdiction.

Inducing Others to Initiate Action   In most of the examples discussed here, a purchasing agent seeks to initiate change in the behavior of other departments. It is the PA who is trying to change the engineer's specifications, the production scheduler's delivery schedules, and so forth. The other departments are always at the receiving (or resisting) end of these initiations. As might be expected, hard feelings are likely to develop if the initiations move only one way, just as they do in one-sided, superior-subordinate relationships.

Recognizing this, many of the stronger managers seem to be trying to arrange their relations with other departments so that others might initiate changes more often for them. Specifically, they hope to induce the other departments to turn instinctively to them for help whenever they have a problem—and at the earliest possible stage. Thus one PA explained that his chief reason for attending production-planning meetings, where new products were laid out, was to develop an advisory relationship, to make it easier for others to ask him questions. He hoped to encourage engineers, for example, to inquire about available components before they drew up their blueprints. Another PA commented, "I try to get production scheduling to ask us what the lead times are for the various parts we order. That's a lot easier than our telling them that their lead times are unreasonable after they have made commitments based on these."

Some purchasing departments send out what are, in effect, ambassadors to other departments. They appoint "purchase engineers," people with engineering backgrounds (perhaps from the company's own engineering group) who report administratively to purchasing but spend most of their time in the engineering department. Their job, again an advisory one, is to be instantly available to provide information to engineers whenever they need help in choosing components. They assist in writing specifications (thus making them more realistic and readable) and help expedite delivery of laboratory supplies and material for prototype models. Through making themselves useful, purchase engineers acquire influence and are able to introduce the purchasing point of view before the "completion barrier" makes this difficult. Similar approaches may be used for quality control.

Work assignments within purchasing are normally arranged so that each buyer can become an expert on one group of commodities bought. Under this arrangement the buyer deals with a relatively small number of outside salespeople, but with a relatively large number of "client" departments within the organization. A few purchasing departments have experimented with assigning people on the basis of the departments with which they work rather than the products they buy. In one case, work assignments in both purchasing and scheduling were so rearranged that each production scheduler had an exact counterpart in purchasing and dealt only with that person. In this way closer personal relations developed than would have if the scheduler had no specific individual in purchasing to contact.

Even the physical location of the PA's office makes a difference. It is much easier for the PA to have informal daily contacts with other departments if his or her office is conveniently located. Some companies place their PAs away from the main office, to make it easier for salespeople to see them. Although this facilitates the agents' external communications, it makes their internal communications more difficult. Of course, those companies that have centralized purchasing offices and a widespread network of plants experience this problem in an exaggerated form. Centralized purchasing offers many economic advantages, but the PAs must tour the plants if they are not to lose all contact with client departments. Of course, the alternative is to decentralize purchasing, putting a purchasing group under each plant manager.

Value-analysis techniques sharply highlight the agent's organizational philosophy. Some agents feel that value analysis should be handled as part of the buyer's everyday activities. If the agent comes across a new product which might be profitably substituted for one currently used, he or she should initiate engineering-feasibility studies and promote the idea ("nag it" in one agent's words) until it is accepted. Presumably, purchasing then gets the credit for the savings, but resistance from other departments may be high. Other agents, particularly those with college training, reject this approach as unnecessarily divisive; they prefer to operate through committees, usually consisting of engineers, purchasing agents, and production personnel. Though committees are time-consuming, communications are facilitated, more people are involved, more ideas are forthcoming—and, in addition, the purchasing department no longer has the sole responsibility for value analysis.

Initiating Formal Organizational Change The final approach is for the manager to seek to expand the formal grant of authority given his or her department (which might mean a larger budget too), as, for example, to place other functions such as traffic, stores, or even inventory control and production scheduling in one combined materials department.

In the examples above we have seen how managers, and groups, enhance their position through professionalization. We've seen, for instance, that most purchasing departments start out as a relatively low-status "service" department, performing a highly useful function, to be sure, but at the "beck and call" of line departments and with little opportunity to exercise professional discretion. To professionalize their role in the organization, they seek to add work flow and advisory patterns to their jobs. Insofar as they also undertake value analysis, purchasing is evaluating or auditing previously made engineering and manufacturing decisions, seeking to find budget "fat" in materials and method specifications. Of course, the tactic of insisting that engineers justify departures from standard parts represents adding a stabilization function. Thus from one low-status administrative pattern purchasing can expand to the full panoply of management roles.

The same empire building can be observed in the case of a packaging design department.

Initially, the department's work consisted of recommending (advising) the type of package design and materials for the company's products. Over a period of time, the manager discovered that he was often not consulted, was consulted too late to be effective, or was not given enough leeway to make effective recommendations, and so he worked to secure changes that would allow his department to:

1 Participate in early discussions concerning new designs for company products, so that packaging needs could be considered with other requirements (change in work flow sequence)

2 Add designers to draw up preliminary specifications for packaging, taking this function from the industrial design department (change in boundaries)

3 Require all engineering managers to get approval from his department before changing the physical shape of the product (addition of stabilization role)

4 Establish a small group within his department to do research on better packaging materials and maintaining durability at lower cost (addition of critical innovation responsibilities)

5 Evaluate existing product designs, shipment sizes, and routing policies and changes in them for their impact on packaging costs (addition of auditing)

6 Serve as a transmission link to connect the engineering design department to purchasing for the ordering of packaging materials (addition of new work flow sequence)

7 Request that the shipping department be shifted from the jurisdiction of packaging to production, on the grounds that packaging does not handle routine business (change in boundaries)

8 Be available to assist cost reduction committees (addition of advisory role)

9 Eliminate the practice whereby the production department requested packaging studies and instead have such studies originate in the cost reduction committees (decrease in importance of service work)

10 Require that all contacts with outside testing laboratories that evaluated packaging materials be handled by packaging personnel (change in boundaries and shift of position in work flow)

Note how, in these examples of professionalization, what is added is always justified in terms of improving effectiveness, lowering costs, and aiding in the accomplishment of reasonable organizational goals. Unlike union-management struggles, which are usually in terms of who will pay more or give less, "professionalization" seeks to provide more work for the same pay, to do a better job, and to assume more responsibility. Of course, the problem is that when all managers are doing this, the task is complicated by the conscientious interference of their colleagues.

Below is a case describing the actions and skills of a manager who understood these bases for power and influence and the organizational changes they produced. In reading the case, consider the skills and "career strategies" discussed and decide whether, on balance, they contributed significantly to the overall organizational goals.

CASE: The Evolution of Power and Status

Information Access, Inc., specialized in the sale of econometric forecasts and consulting services to businesses around the United States. The firm prepared separate forecasts for a number of sectors of the nation's economy. Since IAI's primary output was specialized information, expertise was a central part of the overall product. Then shifting status and power structures within the firm began to cause major problems for management.

IAI's hierarchy, not surprisingly, was designed around the specialized forecasts. Each forecast had a product manager, who was typically an MBA and who was responsible for the depth and accuracy of the forecasts and of the insights the forecasts offered to customers. Expertise was the hallmark of these consultants, and their centrality to the primary product and close contact with customers made their position a very high status one. In fact, it was an open secret that some product managers had higher status than the president of the firm. On the other hand, the majority of positions within IAI were involved with computer operations, and the "databankers" who filled these positions had little or no customer contact.

IAI dealt with customers at two levels. Typically, managers from client firms negotiated for IAI's consulting services and signed a contract for both services and data to be supplied by IAI. The secretary or assistant to the client firm's manager then accessed the data directly from IAI's computer through a telephone link. For this reason, IAI had to deal with questions raised by the managers' subordinates about difficulties in accessing the information as well as with specialized questions raised by the managers themselves about how to interpret the data.

When IAI was first established, project managers, serving as consultants, dealt with *all* the questions—with technical problems in accessing the data, with administrative problems in billings, and with problems in interpretation of data. But as the firm grew and faced more substantive competition, it was felt that an 800 number would be more efficient in responding to customer questions about technical and administrative problems. The original plan was for the number to be used in a reactive manner only. In other words, the phone line would only handle incoming calls from customers. A number of college graduates (mostly BAs) were hired to handle these calls. Since they staffed the phone banks, they were soon nicknamed "bankies." For most, it was their first job out of college.

The real reason for establishing the 800 number was, of course, to free up the consultants, and the bankies were instructed to respond directly to any issue that did not warrant the attention of a consultant. Soon after the number was put into service, however, there were some unplanned changes in procedure.

Susan Faraday was the first manager of the 800 number. She had been with IAI for six years and had been promoted quickly through several positions. Then in the course of reorganization, her job was eliminated. She applied for the job as manager of the 800 number, but was turned down because it was felt that she had too much seniority for the position; the low status envisioned for the job fit neither her salary nor her grade level. However, when no other suitable candidates for the job were found, she was given the position.

The 800 number was an immediate success with customers. Activities went smoothly under Faraday's direction, and everyone at IAI was pleased with the outcome. As soon as the dust settled, however, Faraday moved to increase the status of her position. Her first action was to propose that her group undertake some informal market research. After all, she argued, her subordinates spoke to clients across the United States. Over a two- or three-month period, her group had contact with the majority of the firm's clients and was in an excellent position to "ensure that clients were happy with their consultants."

The consultants reacted with some annoyance. It bothered them to think that some lowly bankie who handled a customer's minor questions would be "checking up" on their performance. The bankies would not be speaking with the decision makers who were responsible for the purchases in the first place, the consultants argued, but with people who would be able to provide only indirect evidence of their performance. A poor relationship between a client manager and his or her staff could easily affect the subordinate's perception of the consultant's work. In addition, the bankies would have no way to assess the status of the relationship of consultant and client at any given point in time. If the client firm was negotiating a new contract or was temporarily dissatisfied, any comments elicited might not be indicative of the normal status of the client-consultant relationship.

The consultants felt that the best way to evaluate the effectiveness of their work was by the amount of money that they brought in from clients. Regardless of what information the bankies collected, if the clients continued to purchase services then they must be reasonably satisfied. Faraday responded that under that philosophy, the only way that IAI would become aware of problems would be for clients to stop paying or to allow their contracts to lapse. By that time, the client-consultant problem would be too serious to resolve easily.

Though the consultants did not like the state of affairs, the bankies began to solicit information regarding customer satisfaction. Along with the change, of course, came a large boost in the status and power of Faraday's job. For a time, things progressed without a major incident. Then Faraday decided that her group should be more "proactive" in their client contact. The market research effort was no longer to be limited just to clients who called into the 800 number, but would extend to all IAI clients. Faraday assigned her bankies lists of firms to contact and query in regard to their relationships with IAI consultants. In addition, she began tabulating "client satisfaction sheets." The sheets effectively assigned "grades" to consultants based on the clients' perceptions of their work. Needless to say, the consultants hit the roof. To make matters worse, Faraday began to set up meetings at client sites to "straighten out the problems" created by consultants. Over the consultants' strong objections, Faraday was able to consolidate her position and accrue increasing status to her department at the expense of the once-powerful product managers.

POWER BEGETS POWER

Thus the power seekers endeavor to institutionalize their base by accruing activities, job slots, and roles that will involve the opportunity to initiate and to control the work of others and to resist having to defer to those others (in service and routine tasks).

It is also useful to adjust the information system and communication linkages so that critical data concerning organizational problems flow to you rather than to your competitors. Those who have the information will be more likely to understand the important problems and even to propose solutions.

To maintain a dominant position, coalitions can be important, and astute managers seek to reward friends and supporters from other units by aiding them in getting funding, sharing scarce resources with them, and bestowing status. Of course, just being associated with a dominant group or department will be prestigious and a reward for staying as part of the coalition.

While these maneuvers never cease in most organizations, some stability emerges. Gradually, certain executives and departments are recognized as having substantial power. In turn, the deference they receive, the quickness with which their requests for aid or information are responded to—all serve to announce to other managers that they are a power to be reckoned with. Therefore, whenever a new activity or program is recommended, their support is sought, their concurrence requested. As everyone recognizes their status, such departments and executives get still greater status. It builds in a spiral.

Deference; -----→ Higher status -----→ Still more -----→ Still higher
battles won   and power   respect and   status
                                    deference

Future battles over jurisdiction and decisions become easier to win, and support grows from other managers who want to be close to, who want to be seen as supporting, these prestigious winners. Thus after a while their position becomes almost unassailable; they are surrounded by their supporters, empowered by their high-status activities, and have the ability to veto almost any new proposal.

That's how to win in organizational politics! But there is a danger here.

The problem for the organization is that this becomes a vicious circle. While at some period in its life the organization may have been "hurting most" in finance—finance was the big problem and deserving of the most attention—this may no longer be the case. Still, over time, the influence of finance continues to discourage other functions. Everyone sees marketing, for example, as a routinized function, with no challenge, no need for new breakthroughs or accomplishment, not much chance of getting major budget increases. Organizational perceptions then predetermine that marketing will be poorly handled. Management's impression that few good people in marketing are worthy of promotion will be confirmed by marketing's performance. And this, in turn, makes it even more difficult to get innovative work out of marketing.

After a while management wakes up and "tears the place apart." It replaces most of the people in marketing because "we have a lousy marketing department"—not realizing it became mundane and unimaginative because the management-controlled status system (where promotions and deference are given) decreed that its work should be of low quality.

Management needs to exercise care that it doesn't force key functions to become second-rate by a too-biased distribution of rewards and resources. Business organizations can become very political, and it behooves managers to understand the bases for power and the tactics and strategy which provide these.

Managers need to comprehend the logic of these basically unplanned kinds of organizational changes and be able to predict their occurrence. They center on the quest for status and its accompanying power and rewards. By understanding the dynamics of these processes, managers can protect their own leadership position and prevent its erosion in the daily give-and-take of lateral relationships. Just as important is the ability to identify which of their subordinate managers is doing the job as assigned and which is seeking to increase status and probably making the jobs of other managers more difficult by failing to be responsive and accommodative. Subordinates can easily substitute increasing the status of their functions for doing the more difficult job of fitting the division of labor prescribed by the design of the organization. However, these managerial initiatives can also enhance the functioning of the organization.

CHAPTER 7

WORKING THE HIERARCHY: THE SKILLS OF MANAGING UPWARD AND OF DELEGATING RESPONSIBILITY

Most experienced managers have learned that gaining commitment from subordinates and cooperation from peers requires both skill and patience. They are prepared to work on these relationships. But managers are often unprepared to "work the hierarchy," to work on relationships with their superiors and with the subordinates of their subordinates. Establishing and maintaining relationships with people on both ends of the scale represent quite different sets of problems, and we shall analyze the behavioral content of both sets. The first aspect of "working the hierarchy" is often referred to as "managing upward": how to influence the boss. The second aspect relates to the traditional management skill of delegation. (We shall see that the "traditional" view may have serious limitations here.) Handling both sets of relationships effectively is critical for successful leadership.

MANAGING UPWARD

As we have seen, managers gain the status of leaders when they are successful in representing and protecting their people

135

and their area of responsibility. Many, if not most, decisions about schedules, budgets, space, and time contain ambiguities. As we saw in Chapter 6, status and power help determine whose priorities get served in the face of such ambiguities. Given this, one can see how extremely important in protecting and aiding the interests of any group is the ability of its manager to gain and hold the confidence of his or her superior, the ability to persuade and motivate upper management, who are in the position to make decisions that may appear to disregard the legitimate interests and needs of the individual group. How does the group's manager cope with this? Successfully countering the normal top-down flow of initiations requires significant capabilities. What are they?

The ability to accept profound differences in perspective
The ability to deal with the contradictions resulting from being "in the middle"
The ability to persuade the boss

Accepting Differences in Perspective

Although certain "facts of life" may be frustrating and are rarely comfortable, astute managers learn to accept them. Their bosses are necessarily going to have different priorities and perspectives than they do.

> Moving that equipment outside my area was going to increase my coordination costs enormously and slow down my work. We used the equipment 100 percent of the time, but my manager put great pressure on me to allow it to be moved to the second floor. At first I thought this had to do with those old claims that our air conditioning was inadequate for the delicate electronics, and we did need more space for operators. But then I learned that he was looking three years down the road when other departments would learn how to use this new technology. He felt that its being located in our work area would inhibit their use of it and give everyone else the idea that we had sole control. I argued and argued that we needed it now and couldn't afford the efforts to coordinate between two floors if we were going to work off this backlog, but he insisted that "longer-run" issues had to take priority over my current work problems.

When managers are asked what is most difficult about their jobs, they consistently place near the top of their lists concerns like this:

"My boss just doesn't realize how much is required to meet his demands; he doesn't even know how inadequate my staff is."

"She keeps expecting more and more, even though my plate is already full; she doesn't seem to appreciate the workload I carry."

Predictably, these same managers reiterate in turn that their subordinates can't grasp the "larger picture," don't accept the need to balance short-run with long-run considerations, and aren't helpful enough to other units in the same division.

While frequent exchange and communication can minimize these differences, the manager seeking to influence the boss has to accept the fact that "what you see depends on where you stand." The boss is inevitably going to see the world differently.

Being in the Middle

Managers also have to learn that working in a hierarchy is going to involve them in "role conflict," in that they will always be in the middle of legitimately and persistently conflicting demands from those above and those below. And their job involves "taking the heat," that is, accepting this conflict as an ongoing fact of life. The conflict gets resolved only to the degree that the leader is able to keep the contradictions within reasonable bounds. An example may suffice:

Eells had four outstanding subordinates. Without their loyalty, he would never have been able to implement the new technology in record time. This enabled him to meet what he first considered an impossible deadline: to improve productivity in the unit by 30 percent by the end of the first quarter. Eells wanted all four to receive the maximum bonus of $2500. But Ray, his boss, told him that there was no way she could get that amount for him and still have anything to give the three other units she supervised. In Eells's eyes no one in the other units had done anything that even approximated the effort and creativity his people had shown. And the results they'd achieved had been so spectacular that his people now expected some kind of significant recognition. Eells felt strongly he would be letting his people down, but he also understood that Ray did not want to appear unfair to her other units.

Eells has to accept the reality that while his people unequivocally deserve the reward, his manager has additional *legitimate* concerns reflecting broader measures of equity. While he should vigorously argue the case, he should also retreat gracefully and good-naturedly when he is overruled. This communicates his understanding of the broader decision criterion of the boss and the reality that he lacks the power to implement all his recommendations.

But a retreat doesn't have to be a rout. Eells may well be able to obtain reasonable awards for his people and/or negotiate some assurance that they will receive maximum merit increases when salaries are reviewed.

The effectiveness of these upward initiations depends in part on the realization by upper-level management that the leadership status of their managerial subordinates depends upon their ability to win benefits for their staffs. Thus superiors have to be receptive to initiations from below, even conceding on some issues just to aid lower-level managers to maintain their status within their groups. Status, after all, depends upon their being able to show that they have both influence with upper management and the courage to represent their people, even when it challenges upper-management demands.

> My boss was urging me to get that order out—regardless—by Thursday: he needed it then and no excuses. My staff insisted that we had to live up to our own hard-won technical standards. Every unit and component had to be completely and fully tested even if it took all month. They were professionals who believed in what they were doing and they weren't going to be panicked. They said it was my job to get them the time to do high-quality work.

On the other hand, when upper-level executives see managers who are never willing to push unpopular orders, they should know these managers are not filling their jobs properly. Weak managers will always blame upper management for orders that subordinates resent: "If it were up to me, we wouldn't be doing this that way, but you know how stingy that front office is!" An unambiguous sign of weakness is the refusal to represent subordinates and the desire to always "yes" the boss.

Ideally, managers should be identified with those above and those below by showing the capacity to accept initiations from both, but not to the exclusion of the other. Poor bosses are "unbalanced." They either act like a sieve, passing down—even amplifying—everything that comes from above. Or, just as bad, they seek to immerse themselves in the work group, pretending to be "just one of the gang."

Persuading the Boss

Obviously managers are used to directing their subordinates; they are less accustomed to, and surely less comfortable with, being directed by their subordinates. While the latter is a less frequent occurrence, a subordinate at critical times will need to persuade the boss to do something he or she is reluctant to do, even to change a decision. It is worth looking in detail at how effective managers redirect the decisions of their superiors.

> I worked as a programming manager in the computational lab of the company. I began on the technical side, then shifted to management and became quite successful. But I knew promotion to top management came through sales, and I wanted a sales management job. My boss couldn't help me and sent me to the head of administrative services. At first she rejected my request, but when I persisted, she agreed to make an appointment for me with the VP of marketing. My record was good and I think I made a good impression, but he said that he was up to his budgetary limit, and further, it was most unusual to have technically successful programmers become "marketeers."

The problems here are easy to outline:

1 Initial rejection by immediate supervisor
2 Request violates norm (technical people don't do well in marketing)
3 Request violates rule (don't exceed budgeted personnel quota)

The first problem was solved by persistence, courage, and initiative on the part of the programmer: willingness to go against the grain and refusal to be discouraged by initial rejection. Problems 2 and 3 took more ingenuity and persuasiveness. Listen to how the programmer handled the VP:

> I know that this hasn't happened before but it would make a big difference if there were people in marketing who understood programming. Marketing could get much better service from the company's computer facilities if they knew what to ask for and how to evaluate the services they were getting. I can put your managers in personal touch with just the right person for their problems, and further I'll be a liaison person between the two departments. Just give me the chance to try out for six months, and then we can decide whether it's worth pursuing further. In the meantime I'll try to get programming to keep me on their budgeted personnel count—if you'll pick up the salary. This way there's no need to get anyone to approve an exception, and if I don't work out it's my loss.

Sometimes there is no need to go over the boss's head; there is adequate authority at the lower level, and what is needed are the proper persuasive skills. Many subordinates are tempted to assume that they must accept orders and decisions without questions or they'll incur retaliation. In fact, not all managers thrive on a constant chorus of "yeses"; they even actively seek dissent.

> I judge subordinates on their willingness to disagree with me and to stand up and say why I'm wrong. Of course I expect them to have sound reasons and to be able to mount a reasoned argument supported with good analysis and, where possible, facts.

Conformity, the constant "yesing" of superiors is favored primarily:

1   Where the boss is insecure and/or despotic
2   In highly political situations, where threats abound, and where loyalty, per se, is all-important
3   Where it is difficult to evaluate performance, where there are no obvious results, and therefore loyalty and absence of friction become more important than performance

Where these conditions are absent, subordinates can learn to challenge the hierarchy. Suppose a manager serving under an autocratic boss wishes to increase substantially his own freedom of action—and still remain within the organization. Can he do anything about it? The following case, by William F. Whyte, of how one manager coped with a highly autocratic boss is instructive.[1]

CASE: Dealing with an Autocrat

Wes Walsh was superintendent of a plant. He came in under a works manager widely known in the company for his type of autocratic control. Furthermore, the offices of the two men were within a hundred feet of each other, so that although the boss was also responsible for other plants in the area, he could keep a close watch over Walsh. Nevertheless, Walsh was able to manage his plant very much according to his own notions, with little interference from above. How did he do it?

The previous superintendent had been constantly at swords' points with the works manager. He advised Walsh to keep away from the manager's office. "The less you see of that son of a bitch, the better you'll get along." Though Walsh and his predecessor were good friends, Walsh decided to disregard the advice. If it hadn't worked for his predecessor, why should it work for him? Instead, Walsh saw to it that he had frequent contacts with the boss—and contacts that were initiated primarily by Walsh himself. He would drop in, with apparent casualness, to report progress or to seek the works manager's approval on some minor matter, carefully selected so that the boss could hardly veto it. Walsh was getting his boss used to saying yes to him!

Major matters required longer interaction between the men, carefully prepared and staged. Consider the problems of the materials-reprocessing unit.

With increasing volume of production going through the plant, it had become apparent to Walsh—as indeed it had to his predecessor—that this unit was inadequate for current requirements. It was too slow in operation and too limited in capacity. This condition seriously hampered production and created a storage problem in the plant. Materials awaiting reprocessing were strewn about at the end of the operating area.

---

[1] William F. Whyte, "Taking Initiative with the Boss," in Leonard Sayles (ed.), *Individualism and Big Business*, McGraw-Hill, New York, 1963, pp. 170–173.

Walsh's first step was to propose to the boss that he pick a time when he could spend a couple of hours with Walsh in the plant, so that they could look over some of the problems the plant was facing. The manager set the time, and the two men spent the hours together on an inspection tour. To some extent the physical conditions the works manager saw spoke for themselves, but Walsh also supplemented these visual clues with an account of the way in which the inadequacy of the materials-reprocessing unit hampered his operation. The boss had to agree that the condition was undesirable. Eventually he asked, "What do you propose?"

Walsh was ready with a carefully worked out proposal for the purchase of a new type of reprocessing unit at a cost of $150,000. After a brief discussion of the impact of a new machine on costs and production, the works manager authorized the purchase. It is noteworthy that essentially the same proposal had been made more than once to the works manager by Walsh's predecessor. Made no doubt in a different form and fitting into a different context of interpersonal relationships, the good idea had received simply a flat rejection.

So effectively did Wes Walsh handle his superior that he won a large measure of freedom from a man known throughout the works as an autocrat. And the works manager was more than happy with the relationship. In fact, several years later, after his own retirement, he was boasting to others about how he had discovered and developed Wes Walsh!

Walsh adds two qualifying comments to the story of his success. He points out that the works manager was approaching retirement, that he lacked firsthand experience with the plant managed by Walsh, and that he was preoccupied with pressing problems in another plant. "If he had been ten years younger, he would have found the time and the energy to get to know my plant inside out, and then he would have given me a much harder time." We should add, nevertheless, that the same conditions had prevailed for Walsh's immediate predecessor, and that he had been completely unable to gain any freedom of action.

Walsh suggests these rules for approaching a big decision with an autocratic boss:

1 Prepare the ground carefully; don't just spring it on the boss.

2 Don't present the problem and the proposed solution at the same time.

3 Present the problem in stages and in such a way that no solution will be immediately apparent to the boss. This will help assure you that he does not commit himself before you have had a chance to make your full case. Once an executive of this type has committed himself, it is almost impossible to get him to reverse his decision. If you can bring him through all phases of the problem with the solution still unclear in his mind, then your chances of getting your solution accepted are greatly improved.

Laying the Lateral Groundwork Before challenging the hierarchy, the subordinate should seek to learn the constraints to be expected from the various groups whose cooperation will be required in implementing his or her proposal. (See Chapter 5.) Part of any persuasive presentation to a boss is evidence that the subordinate has a realistic understanding of *who* will be involved, *where* they stand, and *what* it will take to gain their support for a new activity. Thus there is a great deal of interplay with peers required of the manager who is "working upward." The results of these contacts and negotiations with peers need to be cited in any verbal or written presentation. Consequential omissions are very damaging: "You mean you didn't get a commitment from data systems on what the connection costs were going to be?"

It may be as important for the subordinate to seek greater autonomy and acceptance of ideas as for the boss to encourage this. A skillful, determined subordinate can win reasonable autonomy even in an autocratic setting.

Keeping the Boss Uninformed Astute subordinates with self-confidence usually discover that there is an alternative to appealing the boss's rejection of their request or idea. Where they are reasonably sure that what they want to do will show benefits after the fact, they do it without asking permission and receiving a predictably negative response. Here is an example of what we mean:

> I knew my boss would never agree to having me ship the customer a unit different from the one ordered. It is against our procedures. But I knew that the customer needed the equipment and couldn't

afford to wait, and that the new model would do the job even better than the one with which they were familiar. No amount of phoning or letter writing would work; they had to see it. So I took the chance of shipping it with no order. I knew if I went to the boss he would have to go by the book. This way I didn't put him in the tough position of being caught between wanting to trust me and wanting to do the right thing. If I was wrong, I would get the blame and no one else's neck was on the line. But if I was right, as I was sure I was, I would have saved one of our best customers.

Proving Your Loyalty Almost every manager has more to do than time and resources support. A great deal of effort is spent on lateral relations, cajoling and persuading others to cooperate and share resources or provide authorizations. In that demanding world filled with people who can and do say "no," managers expect their subordinates to say "yes" at least most of the time.[2]

Thus the subordinate who seeks to persuade a boss to change a decision or who wants his or her criticism taken seriously has to have proved loyal *in the past*, have demonstrated loyalty *prior* to the negative response. Loyalty in organizations is not vague fealty but observable responsiveness. Simply put, the subordinate has to show that most of the time he or she consistently follows through on requests without a great deal of grumbling and "naysaying."

Given what we have already said about differences in perspective, many of the decisions and orders of the boss will be troublesome. From the vantage point of the subordinate, many will appear ill-informed or poorly timed; many will be difficult to implement. Still, to build up future credits, the subordinate has to follow through responsively and responsibly.[3]

But loyal subordinates can also be critics. In private meetings with superiors, they can candidly raise objections and press issues that may have been overlooked. And they don't automat-

---

[2] Chapter 3 treats of leadership techniques for increasing the likelihood that subordinates will give a positive response. See Chap. 5 for a description of "audit" and "stabilization" staff who are in a position to constrain line managers.

[3] Of course, if the order is unclear, a sensible subordinate seeks clarification and whatever information is necessary to assure that what gets done will be consistent with the expectations of the superior.

ically have to say "yes" or patronize their more powerful superior by obeisance during discussions. But, and this is an important "but," when the manager says, "This is important; I've considered your objections and I still want you to implement my order," the subordinate must give way. (The only exception would be when the order involves an illegal action or promises extraordinarily destructive results.) In the British system, it's the role of Her Majesty's "loyal opposition": after a decision has been made, regardless of earlier differences, you close ranks.

Ironically, the proven loyal subordinate is allowed the greatest amount of free speech and criticism in a hierarchy. It is the subordinate who can't stop objecting and/or who doesn't respond quickly and unstintingly when the boss has made a decision who loses influence upwards.

A subordinate also demonstrates loyalty by keeping the boss informed of any problems that may cause embarrassment or disappointment. For example, if costs are beginning to outrun the budget or a technical glitch is threatening to delay the completion of an important project, a loyal subordinate alerts the next level of management. Otherwise, that next-level manager is not going to be able to deal effectively with peers and other subordinates:

> I was in a meeting with a senior VP who was asking questions about how we were doing on the conversion of the IFD system. I assured her that things were going well. Then the bomb dropped. Did I know that the first full systems test had been a complete failure? Of course I didn't. My people must have been covering up and hoping that they would get things moving again before the word leaked out. But since tests involved our computer service area, it was inevitable that one of the "techies" would start talking. That manager let me down by not keeping me informed, and I'm going to keep him on a shorter leash in the future. I felt like a fool—worse, a boss who didn't know what was going on in his area.

Among the most delicate issues of loyalty are those involving outsiders. Bosses expect that subordinates will not embarrass them by revealing departmental flaws or major mistakes. On the other hand, in the course of lateral relations, there will be times when it is important, for example, to alert the next stage in the work flow that a delay is likely because of some internal problems (as discussed in Chapter 5). It takes intelligent sensibilities to distinguish between internal work flow problems that can be discussed externally (because they are not significantly embarrassing to the boss) from those that cannot.

> We exchange information all the time with the other departments. Recently, however, I have not told shipping how far behind we are. My boss had reassured senior management that we had this backlog under control. Then the equipment failed. Now nothing's under control, but I've still got to stick to the party line so as not to contradict her.

Below is another example from our research data. Was the manager right to consider her subordinate disloyal? Where does one draw the line between allowing a free flow of information for better decision making and controlling information in order to support the boss?

CASE: Being Upwardly Mobile or Being Disloyal?

A meeting had been called in which market research, headed by Lisa Evans, was to present their proposal for a marketing approach for the company's newest financial service. The meeting, which would be attended by several financial types and representatives of the product group that had developed the new service, was typical of those held in the next-to-last stage of the company's decision process. From this meeting the proposal would go to the VP who would decide whether to adopt or veto the idea.

Meetings on this level were generally quite informal, with everyone being encouraged to speak forthrightly, yet with the underlying assumption that this was not the place to betray any internal dissension within a department, especially in the presence of "outsiders," in this case, an important user of the department's services.

Prior to the meeting, Evans had some discussions about the proposal with Jay Lit, a member of her group, and she discovered that Lit was not enthusiastic about it; he made no secret of that. He felt that much more study was needed and that the proposal was marred by several flaws in analysis which could lead to failure in the marketplace. Evans, knowing that their time had run out and that the company was eager to get into the market before several competitors jumped in with look-alike products, felt that the plan the group was proposing was a reasonable one, given the time they'd had and the risks being taken. She explained that to Lit and considered the matter closed.

Evans was therefore shocked when Lit spoke against the proposal at the meeting, voicing the same objections he had raised earlier with her. On the basis of this performance—and because of some other things she had observed in Lit's behavior—Evans decided that he was probably not a good long-run bet. She felt that he would probably continue to try to gain visibility with "outsiders" and to show off his independent and unorthodox thinking, even at the expense of hurting the department and embarrassing her.

Other cases can be used to exemplify the choices that must be made between showing loyalty and establishing necessary and useful lateral relationships, between protecting internal interests and gaining external support:

We had been asking for permission to hire ten more people, and I think my boss had tried to get the budget. But the total company was becoming "lean and mean," and new positions were hard to come by. Fortunately I was at the meeting in which several staff people told the division head about the consequences of the delay in my project. It wasn't too hard to piggyback on their comments and describe our unanticipated technical difficulties and the problems of sharing staff with another operating group that needed our technical expertise. Without actually making a pitch for more people—after all, that was my boss's job—I think I got the message across that we were really going all out even though we were strapped for personnel.

I am in charge of a data processing group. Our workload has almost doubled recently, and we've been hiring people as fast as we can. We've not only outgrown our assigned space, we need at least 50 percent more. In our company, all space is controlled by a staff group—real estate. They've told me that we have to wait until another group vacates an area adjacent to our current space. But if I can't put my new people to work soon, I'll be handicapped in efforts to reduce a huge backlog of projects. We've had two big systems failures recently, and trying to debug these has held us up on routine maintenance. My immediate boss is embarrassed by the situation and spends a lot of time reassuring our internal customers that we'll soon be getting to their work; these customers have no idea of the extent of the backlog. I want real estate to know how much we need the space, but I need to protect our group's reputation too. That makes it tough to go all out in trying to persuade RE to give me the space.

Some subordinates will never get this sort of opportunity to negotiate with outsiders. Their bosses, excessively timid managers who have no leadership capabilities themselves, grant them no chance for visibility. To enhance their own status, such bosses insist that all contacts with outsiders be funneled through them. Thus they not only fail to develop the managerial abilities of their subordinates, they discourage the work of highly motivated subordinates and at the same time impede communication.

Upward Bypassing   A more risky tactic for changing a decision is to go over the boss's head. Almost all managers resent being bypassed like this, seeing it as a clear sign of disloyalty. It is not only a threat to their leadership but a danger to internal unity. Problems may well be revealed that will be interpreted to their detriment.

Nevertheless, most organizations believe in "appeals channels" as a method of getting around implacable superiors. It is assumed that the channels will be used exclusively for problems in which the "appellant" is seeking redress for a serious inequity or where the boss is hiding serious problems of dishonesty or inefficiency. In the latter situation, the appeal is often called "whistle blowing," and it takes great courage. That was demonstrated in a recent case where a chief scientist in a pharmaceutical company protested to top management and the FDA that middle management was allowing the distribution of unsatisfactorily processed ethical drugs.[4] Such bypassing can be encouraged when senior executives encourage dissatisfied employees to come through their "open doors." But realistically it is anticipated that such appeals will be few in number and will deal only with grievances of major proportion.

Regrettably, but realistically, the whistle blower faces a hard time surviving the anger of those bypassed.[5] Successful bypassing requires substantial diplomacy and tact. In providing infor-

---

[4] *New York Times*, March 1, 1988, p. 39.
[5] That is the classic argument for trade unions, which serve as an appeals channel and protect the aggrieved from unjust retribution.

mation to more senior managers in the hope of influencing their bosses' decisions, subordinates must take great care not to cause embarrassment to their bosses as they pave the way for beneficial change.

RESOLVING STALEMATES

Even without an appeal from some lower-level manager, an executive often must step in and resolve an intramanagement dispute that is threatening to disrupt the ongoing routines of the organization. Upper management has the role of arbitrating and resolving—quickly and expeditiously—disagreements which otherwise might fester and delay needed consensus:

> The Fado Company was designing a new piece of equipment for an important customer. Design and manufacturing were in dispute over whether a particular new feature was practical. Design engineers insisted it could be made to work reliably; manufacturing claimed the feature would always be troublesome and in need of repair. Their common boss delayed making a decision either because he hoped the department heads themselves would or because he was reluctant to antagonize either one of them. As a result, the disagreement simmered for weeks, delaying the project until the customer canceled the order.

To some managers this need for intervention is not only painful, it is evidence of poor performance on the part of their subordinates: "If those department heads were doing their jobs right and weren't prima donnas, I would never have to get involved." But the modern organization purposely builds in conflict by establishing units with unique and even incompatible goals and values. Manufacturing and design, in the case above, have legitimate differences, and there will be times when a higher-level "judge" will have to and should decide who is right or how the dispute should be compromised. Where there are many unknowns and ambiguities, one often hears remarks similar to those made by one program manager.

> I often don't know who is right; the technology is too new, and there are too many unknowns. But I know that it's important to get a settlement quickly to keep the work moving, so I make a decision. It may be wrong, but it's better than no decision.

Of course, a high frequency of such intervention is undesirable. At best, it suggests that lower-level managers are unable to cope with lateral relationships. (In fact, such need for intervention is a good control measure indicating poor performance and the need to reconsider current structural arrangements.) As many have pointed out, interventions take time from other tasks and often are less well tuned than would be a settlement by the parties to the dispute. After all, the parties know many more of the details, and it takes a long time for upper-level managers to gain the requisite information to make good judgments.

The case below poses some interesting problems in lateral disagreement. For the boss involved, it threatened stalemate. For the managers involved, it demanded some skillful upward management.

CASE: When Push Comes to Shove

Joe Trill runs a quality assurance laboratory for Asta, an electronics company. Every component produced by the firm must go through the lab. Joe's lab has been so successful at improving quality and handling ever-larger workloads that a satellite QA lab on the West Coast is being shut down and its work consolidated in Joe's area. Joe is pleased with the implicit recognition being given his ability to handle ever-increasing workloads and to improve productivity while doing it. His success, he realizes, stems from the high level of commitment of his work force and supervisors and the extraordinary performance of a new line of automated test equipment which the lab has recently installed.

But the impending consolidation has brought with it some horrendous problems. Perhaps the most difficult for Joe has been his battles with real estate, a staff group within Asta responsible for allocating space and conducting remodeling.

Joe has approached RE about a recently vacated area in his current building which would easily handle his expanded equipment and personnel requirements. But Asta is in the midst of a cost-cutting campaign and real estate feels that they could save the cost of moving all of Joe's existing equipment by remodeling his present area.

This seems like being "penny-wise and pound-foolish" to Joe. Given the productivity of the new equipment he has found, recommended, gotten budget for, and implemented so successfully, he is already saving the company more than 50 percent over its testing costs of just two years ago. Converting the present area to accommodate a larger work force and more equipment will not only reduce the amount of work space per person for his highly productive people, it will also put his new technology at risk. And remodeling will also mean constant interruptions in the power supply. Every time that occurs it will take several hours to restart the equipment. Even more serious is the threat that dust and other particle matter created by construction work will damage the equipment, putting it out of action for extended periods and hurting overall output.

Real estate won't budge from their position. They had come under substantial criticism for a major cost overrun the previous year, and they have now gone on record that remodeling is the most economical way of incorporating the West Coast lab into Joe's operation.

Joe's protests are easily written off because he is known as a "fighter" who always wants to get his own way. Joe's own view is that if he were not a "fighter" he would never in the first place have been able to convince a reluctant boss to buy this equipment which is now proving so effective that it will pay for itself in 2½ years. Yet this same boss is reluctant to take on real estate.

The boss, of course, has his own reasons. As he explained to Joe,

> I know you feel strongly about this, and you may well be right, but look at it from my position. I've got to deal with real estate on a number of other things, and they are riding the corporate "be-mean-and-lean" bandwagon. They've got numbers that say they are right. I know you feel that they've inflated the moving costs and have ignored all the risks to the equipment and to continuity of production, but my hands are tied. If you work with them, I think you can get them to do things in ways that will protect your equipment. And with overtime we can make up for those power outages.

Joe knows that his people are already exhausted from overtime. He also knows more than his boss about the sensitivity of the equipment and about the insensitivity of real estate's contractors, invariably the lowest bidder, the one who acts as if taking extra pains to keep operations going will eat up any profit on the contract.

As Joe thinks about the problem, he becomes more and more angry about the injustice and stupidity of it all. Here he is defending the company's welfare, while real estate is playing politics. He needs to "get the goods on them," to show that they are threatening corporate profitability while claiming some illusory savings. (By Joe's figures, the losses in output could equal as much as $200,000, over against a relocation cost of under $10,000.) But he knows too he has to control that urge to get even.

And he knows he has to walk a tightrope with respect to how hard to push the boss. No pressure means little movement will occur; too much pushing, and he'll be discredited as a troublemaker. Joe needs his boss to fight for him and with him. He can't cross over that narrow line between being a vigorous fighter for necessary improvements and being a troublemaker who pushes too hard for "pet projects."

For many students of management and for new managers it comes as a disturbing surprise that managers in the same organization should differ from one another. They fail to grasp the importance of differing perspectives in an organizational world that has more problems than can be solved, more issues than there is time to deal with, and legitimate conflicts over priorities and even over objectives.

DELEGATING RESPONSIBILITY

Most textbooks on management, and most managers, have a simple, straightforward chain-of-command view of "delegation," the assignment of tasks to subordinates:

1 Delegate as much authority as possible so the subordinate can make most decisions *without* referring back to the boss.
2 Hold subordinates responsible for results; let the results be dependent on the subordinates' decisions, not on the boss's.
3 This distancing of the "delegator" from the delegated assignment provides two significant benefits:
   a Since the task, in every sense, becomes the subordinate's, he or she will be motivated to produce good results, which are, after all, the ultimate proof of ability.
   b Such "complete" delegation not only motivates—and trains— subordinates to make tough decisions (given the responsibility and discretion), it frees the boss to do other things.

This is an appealing management technique, and it certainly contains more than a kernel of wisdom. But it is an incomplete description of reality. Bosses sometimes need to get involved and not wait for results. Further, at times they not only need to interact with subordinates concerning these delegated tasks but also to bypass the subordinates in order to be in touch with the actual operations.[6]

Dealing with Subordinates before the Results Are In

Managers are often in a better position to identify systems or external problems that make it difficult for their supervisors to meet their performance targets than are the supervisors themselves. Simply waiting for the end of the task period and playing the judge, awarding merits or demerits, is not conducive to being perceived as a "facilitating" leader.

Ellis noted that costs were beginning to creep upward and that her supervisors were always behind in their workload. She got involved and discovered that a newly adopted software system was creating a number of unforeseen problems. When the system was reprogrammed, the workload declined substantially and productivity rose.

Also, managers need to reassure themselves that subordinates are handling the more ambiguous elements of their jobs in ways that reflect the values of senior management.

In talking with his human resource supervisors, Leib discovered that they were placing a great deal of emphasis on monitoring merit increases in order to assure themselves that they were within the guidelines set by the division president. This led to many confrontations with line managers and arguments about the interpretations of policy. In the process, the supervisors were neglecting other aspects of their job that Leib considered more critical. In particular, they were doing little to build up goodwill with line managers by demonstrating the value of the newly installed quality-circle program. Leib moved quickly to reemphasize that HR staff, at least in his eyes, had as a primary task the

---

[6] Our discussion assumes that there are at least two levels of supervision.

strengthening of the capabilities of line managers to meet their goals—in this case, high-quality production. He insisted that his people prove that they could get the confidence of those managers, not threaten them.

There will also be times when a subordinate may make a commitment that would be difficult or costly to reverse if trouble should develop. Staying close to that subordinate and the situation may help avoid a major loss—for the subordinate *and* for the organization.

There is, however, a trade-off. By getting more involved and engaging in a "hands-on" management style, the manager runs the risk that subordinates will not make the tough decisions on their own.

> Jim has worked for me for several years; he's a fine engineer but he is reluctant to make tough decisions in his projects. When there is a risky decision, he comes to me and asks my advice. If I'm not careful, he simply takes my "advice" and that becomes the decision. If it doesn't work out well, he is quick to say, "But I was just following your instructions."

The manager has to exercise care that the subordinate understands he or she is still responsible. The manager is providing information and advice which has to be factored into the decision but is *not* the decision:

> I learned from my boss today that the vendor from whom I was hoping to get our new photocopier has a poor reputation for service. That was news to me. If I still go in that direction, given how much I can save on my equipment budget, I am going to insist that the first year's maintenance be "unbundled" from the price. These companies like to sell you both at the same time, but I see no reason why I can't get them to change, given the size of the order. Then I can contract with a good service company.

Order versus Inputs

Naive managers assume that when the boss speaks it is always to give an order. (Regrettably, the same managers are also likely to assume the contrary: there is no need to go into action without the boss's initiative. This reduces the likelihood that subordinates, who are closer to operations, will initiate needed improvements.) They have not learned that the boss wants to be in a position to voice an opinion, share information, and express frustration without presuming that everything will be taken as an order to do something.

Good leaders want to share as much information as possible with subordinates, including their own priorities, values, and problems. They recognize that all can't be solved, or even helped, by an immediate response from a subordinate. What they hope for is that subordinates factor into their own decision making and priorities this knowledge being shared by someone with a broader purview.

Thus the manager who has been delegated a responsibility needs to accept a variety of inputs from above, some of which will be based on information the boss may have gleaned from "bypassing downward." However, these suggestions, questions, and comments do not mean that the boss is assuming the delegated responsibility.

This is the same leadership issue dealt with in Chapters 5 and 6. Managers in most modern organizations don't have the luxury of having total authority equal to their responsibility. They must be responsible for results that depend on "outside" units—audit, stabilization, and service groups, for example. But their dependence on resources that they don't directly control does not mean that their managers, in turn, should not expect them to meet their goals. It means that the goals have to be met in the context of negotiation for needed resources and approvals.

> I told Stein that I thought it was a mistake to try to get systems to lend her a programmer to finish that work that had been going so slowly. I doubted that they would give her anyone but a "loser," and I told her so. At the same time I told her that I needed her capital budget by May 1, not June 1 as we had originally planned. Well, you could have knocked me over with the proverbial feather when she told me this week that the project I had assigned her in January wasn't going to be completed on time. Her reasons were that I had stopped her from getting a programmer whom she saw as absolutely essential, and then when I had moved the capital budget date up, she had just assumed that I was willing to see the project date slip. Nonsense! It was her job to get a programmer if she really needed one—I had only expressed some doubt about the way she was going about it. And every manager has to learn to juggle a lot

of balls. The fact that I'd given her a new deadline on the budget wasn't grounds for lessening effort on an earlier assignment. Her job was to figure out how to do a variety of things that competed for her resources and energy.

Understanding Operations

The more traditional views of delegation would have the manager responding solely to results. When results were poor, of course, that might signal the need to get involved. However, to play a facilitator's role—and because results often provide very limited or even distorted views of what is really taking place in the organization (to be discussed further in Chapter 8)— successful managers seek to "pierce the veil" of their subordinates' functions. In effect, they bypass downward.

Right up to general managers, executives need to be familiar with operations. Managers have to have a good sense of what is problematic about the work delegated. Several important objectives are served by getting firsthand experience. Lower levels of supervision may not have the perspective to spot consequential trends or underlying forces that are hurting results and need remedial action. The following is the experience of a third-level executive:

> When I got into the field I discovered that we were missing our deadlines as the result of an unannounced change in data processing's schedule. They had been using the slow overnight period to process the orders and requests that our people worked with. Gradually other departments had made demands on that time, and now some of our people were sitting on their hands until ten or eleven in the morning waiting for data to come in. My supervisors had missed reporting this change because it had worsened only gradually, and I guess they thought that somehow they could overcome the handicap. Of course, they couldn't; it was like working with one hand tied behind your back.

Only with the "feeling for operations" that comes with firsthand observation can an executive interpret the numbers that are supposed to reflect performance. Many of these reports will compress a variety of factors into a single "result":

> Our costs for doing engineering work for other divisions were considered very high, and I always assumed that this was because we were somewhat overstaffed while we awaited an upturn in external

business. It was only after I began talking with our engineers that I learned that one of our major hidden costs was a tendency by our technical staff to make almost automatic decisions to use the most costly methods, materials, and specifications. For years our biggest internal customer had said not to spare any expense—absolute perfection was the priority. Those work methods got embedded in both our written and unwritten rules on how to do engineering. Other customers who didn't need that kind of extraordinary quality were getting it regardless. I had my supervisors looking at every conceivable way of saving money, short of dropping personnel, but I had never thought of looking at the basic parameters of the engineers' decisions.

The responsibility of the more senior manager to recommend or endorse changes (in methods, equipment, or personnel) can best be fulfilled if he or she has a real sense of the problems that are frustrating people and inhibiting performance.

I had always assumed that our people spent most of their time doing analytical work. Until I got involved I didn't know that there were enormous delays involved in getting approvals, making copies of fiche-stored documents, and trying to interpret garbled work orders. Learning all of that, I was able to justify the purchase of an optical storage device in our most recent capital budget.

Even heads of large companies (like the dynamic founder and CEO of the supermarket chain Wal-Mart, S. M. Walton) attribute their success to an intimate familiarity with operations and customers, and they regularly appear at the work level to get a firsthand feel for what the company's business is really like.[7]

Many managers presume that employees resent or are unnerved by what they consider "snooping"—observation by managers who outrank their supervisors. Quite the contrary. Most employees are delighted that their work is considered sufficiently important for the "brass" to seek firsthand understanding. When senior managers demonstrate an interest in their work, it serves to reduce the status gap between employees and management and gives prestige to the real heart of any

---

[7] See Jan Carlzon, *Moment of Truth*, Ballinger, Cambridge, Mass., 1987, for a description of how SAS, the very successful Scandinavian airline, has forced middle managers to get intimately involved with operations. The author is the president of SAS.

business—operations, including even the more menial tasks. Rather than withholding information, most employees relish explaining what they do and how they do it and what can go wrong. There is almost no question that elicits a more enthusiastic response than "Tell me about your job." Not only does information move upward, but morale and motivation are increased. After all, under these circumstances, employees are educating and controlling the behavior of upper management rather than merely following orders that have moved down an impersonal chain of command.[8]

Managers who are involved to that extent get much higher levels of commitment than those who manage solely by numbers and impersonal reports. The latter never taste the real "flavor" of the work, sense the rhythms and frustrations that form the core of getting out the finished product or service. In turn, their subordinates know that they lack real empathy for what it is like "in the trenches." Managers who show that they do have this familiarity gain great credibility right down the line.

Some Dilemmas in Assigning Responsibility

In describing how a good leader handles delegation, it is easy to oversimplify. What first comes to mind is the classic situation in which a subordinate is given a well-bounded task and most of the resources necessary to accomplish it. The result is the product of the subordinate's energy, resourcefulness, and dedication.

Reàlity blurs those neat compartments. Subordinates are often interdependent, and it is not easy to say who earned credits or, in the case of failure, demerits. For example, who is responsible for the results in this well-reported tragedy?

A ship belonging to a British shipping company sank just offshore Zeebrugge, Belgium, on its way to Britain in March 1987. The ship was carrying a large number of passenger cars below decks, and the accident occurred when water entered the improperly closed bow hatch through which the cars had been

---

[8] This kind of bypassing downward was endorsed strongly in the successful firms described by Tom Peters and Robert Waterman in their noteworthy study, *In Search of Excellence*, Harper & Row, New York, 1986. They called it "walking-around management."

loaded. Quickly filling with water, the ship capsized, and 188 people lost their lives.

The ship's original design was unsatisfactory, in part because there were no bulkheads in the hold. Newer versions of the ship had warning lights on the bridge to alert ship's officers when the hatch was not secured, but older ships, such as the one that sank, were never retrofitted. Two years before the tragedy, a sister ship had sailed out of a harbor with its bow hatch unsecured, but a disaster had been averted because the seas were calm.

A union of naval officers sought to require management to hire an extra officer for the vulnerable ships on the grounds that, though the duty officer was supposed to double-check the hatch, other tasks often kept that officer from doing it. Management rejected the union's argument.

On the ill-fated voyage in 1987, the crew member who was supposed to close the hatch after the autos had been boarded had fallen asleep, and the officer who was supposed to double-check on him had been kept busy on the bridge. The hatch went unchecked and 188 people died.[9]

Who was to blame? The sleeping crew member, the deck officer who should have checked the hatch, the captain responsible for the safety of the ship and its passengers, or the shipping company's top management?

In identifying responsibility, it is important to recognize the leadership issue. Good leaders do seek to build a sense of responsibility. While there are often grounds to shift the burden of responsibility to others "above" or "below," the manager has to supervise in such a way that the subordinate has both a sense of responsibility and the ability to take initiative to deal with issues that may be beyond the scope of the immediate job.[10]

In the political world, this is often quite easy to see, particularly in the use of the prestige of the office of the presidency. Arthur Schlesinger described John F. Kennedy's tactics:

---

[9] *The Economist*, June 20–26, 1987, p. 14.

[10] Observers frequently cite the temptation for managers to blame subordinates for the failures and to take credit for the successes. See Robert Jackall, *Moral Mazes: The World of Corporate Management*, Oxford University Press, New York, 1988.

The President was in this respect very much like Roosevelt or Churchill. If he was interested in a problem like the Congo and wanted to control what was going on, he would not follow the chain of command as President Eisenhower, I gather, did. In other words, say, tell something to the Secretary of State, who would tell it to the Under Secretary of State for Political Affairs, who would tell it to the Assistant Secretary of State for Africa, who would tell it to the Congo Desk Office, and similarly the Congo Desk Officer would replay through the same chain of command. This would often dilute the message both ways, divesting it of any pungency of character. President Kennedy's instinct would be to call the man and ask him or tell him, and this had the effect of not only giving the President much fresher information and sharper opinion, but it also would imbue the machinery of government itself with the sense of his own purposes. It's a very exciting thing to get a call from the President and an exciting thing to have some direct sense of what he wanted, and this had I think a tonic effect throughout government.[11]

Higher levels, aware of the filtering and suppression of information, want to "see" for themselves what is occurring—the problems and the progress. This is also a natural hedge against the departure of a subordinate manager. Managers above always want some direct contact with those levels below who might otherwise have loyalty only to the manager who leaves (or is replaced). Such contact, it is hoped, will build loyalty "up the chain."

CONCLUSIONS

Managers with no sense of leadership look upon hierarchies as simple chains of command. They expect to be directed solely by orders they get "down" from their immediate superiors and to rely solely on information they get "up" from their immediate subordinates. In contrast, managers with leadership skills recognize that there will be inconsistencies in the demands of lateral peers and their line management and even in the directions of their bosses. Similarly, there is the need to initiate more frequently to subordinates and to go "below" their direct reports to learn and observe the actual operations of the organization.

---

[11] Quoted in Henry Brandon, "Schlesinger at the White House," *Harper's*, July 1964, p. 58.

This is in sharp contrast to the traditional, almost mechanical view of delegation.

These patterns that depart from a strict view of hierarchy require subtle skills. The manager must demonstrate loyalty and responsiveness before gaining the leeway to depart from automatic conformity. And in bypassing downward, the manager needs to protect the status of his or her direct subordinates. The manager must be wary that in aiding and shaping the work of a subordinate, such involvement does not detract from the subordinate's responsibility for the results of the assignment.

The confrontational aspect of bypassing upwards can be reduced. Astute managers learn how to get information to superiors about their needs and problems without directly challenging their boss. They accept the decision but clarify the implications and trade-offs.

The shift from being an austere judge who only looks at results, giving rewards or demerits commensurate with those results, to being a "facilitator" of a subordinate's performance should actually help the manager to improve motivation. Sitting impersonally "on high" is not a role conducive to easy relationships with those in a less elevated position, while facilitating leads to firsthand knowledge of the operations and brings a manager in touch with subordinates.

Thus a more hands-on management style has the multiple advantage of keeping superiors informed about the real problems confronting the organization, allowing them to influence the directions taken by their subordinates and to be perceived as a source of support, not just an appraiser of performance.

CHAPTER 8

DESIGNING WORKABLE, VALID CONTROLS

One of the oldest tenets of management, known by almost every manager, is to use feedback: learn how well you're doing so course corrections can be made. Regrettably, designing controls that both do this and accomplish the other purposes served by good controls turns out to be much more difficult than most managers recognize. Measuring performance and accomplishment is easier said than done. Further, it's often more destructive than constructive.

THE USES OF CONTROLS

Typical managers expect to be concerned with getting orders accepted, persuading reluctant or indifferent employees to do something. Few managers are aware that an even more difficult problem is knowing what orders to give. Another way of saying this is that managers must have methods of appraising ongoing operations to know where interventions (orders, explanations, etc.) are necessary and where operations are proceeding well enough so that managerial time and energy can be devoted elsewhere.

The manager's need to know what is required is usually matched by the subordinate's concern with what is expected. The typical job has multitudinous requirements. While the basic tasks may be obvious, most of the "how" and "when" are far from obvious. How many of the rules really have to be followed? What should be emphasized, what deemphasized? What does the boss favor, ignore, dislike? In a pinch, what are the priorities? How should effort be distributed? Like the student beginning work in a new course, the employee seeks to feel out the boss and the situation.

We shall see that both boss and employee find it far more difficult to assess how work is progressing or even what work is expected than most inexperienced managers anticipate. This chapter, then, will be concerned with the design of controls to provide feedback to both manager and subordinate to resolve these ambiguities.

Types of Controls

One of the most significant tests of good leadership is the ability to understand and make use of a diversity of controls. Most managers don't understand the differences, nor are they able to "tailor" the controls to the job. The results are disastrous because subordinates are encouraged to do the wrong things, and managers lose control over their scarcest resource: their own time.

It is just assumed that managers should have one set of books, so to speak—one set of controls. As we shall see, this is impossible, given the diversity of tasks that must be accomplished. Whatever the controls instituted, they must enable the leader to:

1 Train/constrain and motivate subordinates (low-level controls)

2 Allocate leadership resources to identified problems and appraise the "promotability," or worthiness of subordinates (middle-level controls)

3 Assess the overall performance of the organization to reassure sponsors, directors, and at times, outsiders (high-level controls).

These goals require three sets of books and controls which are very different from one another.

Typical Problems

Managers are likely to confuse the data and measures useful in convincing sponsors and higher management that their operations are progressing satisfactorily (high-level controls) with measures they need themselves to monitor their own operations and assess where intervention is required (middle-level controls).

Managers usually don't distinguish between the feedback that motivates employees to improve performance (low-level controls) and measures which assess how well overall operations—the organization as an organization—are holding together or the system is being maintained (high-level controls).

Managers are tempted to concentrate on controls representing the most easily quantified aspects of the job and thereby encourage a number of destructive reactions on the part of subordinates, reactions by which they meet standards but injure the larger system. For example, controls should encourage employees to handle the full breadth of their jobs, but many quantitative "targets" encourage concentration on those elements which show the quickest observable results.

LOW-LEVEL CONTROLS TO CONSTRAIN AND MOTIVATE SUBORDINATES

Not unlike their superiors, subordinates also have a number of uncertainties about their jobs. They are told many things (and not told a number of things) and, out of a welter of information, orders, observations, and rumor, they must fashion their jobs and, more specifically, how they allocate their time.

"I'm told that quantity and quality are important, but I see that people only get reprimanded when quantity drops below par."

"It isn't in the job description, but you get evaluated around here by how many bright answers you have to questions the division manager raises at those two-hour Wednesday meetings."

"The people I work with make it pretty clear that you had better share good customers, or else!"

Sensible managers, then, seek to be more than passive participants in this process by which subordinates "psych out" the situation to assess what's important, what's trivial, and what's forbidden.

Managers have three methods of shaping emphasis at what we shall call "low-level" controls. They are:

1 Using reinforcement/learning techniques and attention-focusing devices
2 Establishing rules
3 Setting motivational targets

Positive Reinforcement for Every Job Element

Subordinates almost inevitably seek to narrow their jobs. Just as managers want routinization and predictability, so do subordinates want to do those things where results are easiest and most assured. Sales representatives ignore missionary work; supervisors shortchange personnel development; bank tellers are accurate at the expense of good customer relations; teachers concentrate on publishable research, not better teaching.

Thus managers seek to evaluate the full range of activities that the job encompasses. In the early stage, learning theory is an important consideration here. Managers, in the context of encouragement (positive rewards), seek to reinforce the elements that have been performed well and to keep reminding the employees of those that are being neglected and done less well:

> Abe, you've made a good deal of progress since we last reviewed things. You're now keeping other departments informed about our schedules, and you check daily with incoming orders to be sure there's no additional work. I also like the way you cope with orders that need to be backlogged. Now, in terms of what we've been saying about the full scope of this assignment, that just leaves two activities that I think need some more attention. One is reviewing the previous week's record and highlighting for me and for accounting where there are significant variances. The second requires spending some time, at least several times a week, in the lab talking with the

technicians who may be having trouble but are too busy or timid to contact you.

The manager is using what's called "conditioning," "positive reinforcement," or "stroking," to do three things: encourage repetition of desired behavior by giving a positive reinforcement, call attention to omitted aspects of the job, and put the whole thing in the context of positive encouragement as distinct from negative punishment. This is sound training technique. The technique further requires that at the early stages there be a one-to-one correspondence between behavior and reinforcement, but this should become more intermittently random over time. Thus, after the learning period is over, the manager randomly samples job behavior to inhibit the development of narrower jobs.

Perceiving Trends   In addition to the tendency to ignore or underplay the less desirable aspects of their job, subordinates will be tempted to do other things which good low-level controls can correct.

They will fail to see problems which build up slowly. For psychologists, this is "adaptation," or "accommodation," the tendency to accept as normal or not significant that which continues over a long period.[1] This shows itself in the manager who ignores the gradual accretion of labor troubles, safety hazards, or poor work practices. Because the problems increase slowly and are present over a long period, they become like "noise" in a system, ignored as random disturbances as long as the real signal can still be heard. To counter this, the leaders must originate a series of measures to call attention to the problem, perhaps contrasting one unit with another and/or with some base period.

This is the purpose of ongoing measures of quality, downtime, turnover, customer complaints, stock-outs, and the like.

A more serious problem is subordinates' tendency to see

---

[1] I have heard that some instructors in elementary psychology demonstrate the accommodative powers of living organisms and how such traits can be self-destructive. A live frog is placed in a beaker of water, and the temperature is very gradually increased. By the time the water reaches the boiling point, the frog is dead. If the same frog had been placed in boiling water, it would have jumped out at once and saved its life.

only those things which their routines, group norms, and past practices define as relevant. Within any work situation many problems and opportunities will be ignored because conventional practice in the group doesn't allow these things to be seen.[2] Here again the leaders have the problem of broadening the definition of the job to include the full range of relevant subjects.

Not-So-Hidden Cues In seeking to shape the behavior of subordinates to fit and cover the true dimensions of the job, managers have to consider their unintended signals and cues. At the very time managers may be seeking to emphasize the importance of one element by explicit statement, their behavior can contradict this:

> In the March Advertising Agency, the head of creative services gave great emphasis to learning client tastes, even though these often had to be ignored. While she preached this to her associates, whenever the new copywriter sought to discuss a specific client, she was too busy or distracted to treat it as a particularly important topic.

At the very time managers are busy, distracted, or angry, subordinates may be raising an issue which will help shape the subordinates' view of the job. Most subordinates learn to assess by subtle cues what their bosses regard as trivial and important, what they find easily dispensable, and what "turns them on."

Rules and Standards

Ideally, rules establish the limits of permissible behavior and free subordinates to use discretion within those limits. It would be pointless to seek to work in the absence of rules unless there were no external interdependencies or dangers. Further, without explicit rules most subordinates would expend great effort to seek out the hidden standards or be loath to do anything

---

[2] The best study of this perceptual bias is Graham Allison's description of the various government agencies and departments which President Kennedy sought to mobilize in the Cuban missile crisis. See Allison's *Essence of Decision,* Little, Brown, Boston, 1971.

which might violate an implicit requirement. So managers should be quite willing to make these explicit in the checks or controls that are established.

"Only expenditures over $500 need approval from a financial officer."

"Every capital budget request must be checked by a knowledgeable financial analyst against a set of standards to be sure that the amounts are realistic."

"Every new product must be safe for even a young child to use; utilize only nonflammable components as prescribed by our testing department."

There are problems associated with such standards. Many are thought to be absolute technical or legal requirements, and managers want to assure themselves that all the proper steps have been taken:

"No checks can be issued without two signatures."

"Incoming supplies must be approved by the ordering department before being unloaded in receiving."

"No job openings can be filled without concurrence of the affirmative action officer."

Organizations gradually multiply the number of rules to the point where many are ignored, or individual initiative to cope with problems is inhibited or destroyed. A well-known technique to throttle an organization, much used by clever trade unionists, is the "work-to-rule" gambit. When employees live up to every rule on the books, nothing gets done because there will always be equipment in less than perfect condition or orders that require additional authorizations and the like. Recently business has criticized the federal Occupational Safety and Health Administration (OSHA) for endeavoring to design rules for every possible safety contingency, with the result that great costs and inefficiencies are incurred.

The other danger is that too many rules will be enforced by "stabilization" procedures, that is, obtaining permission from an authorized person before proceeding. This is much more costly in time and money than "auditing" procedures, which evaluate after the fact whether or not rules and standards have been lived up to.

There are all sorts of ways I could do my job more efficiently but there are so many rules and procedures that I'm not allowed to use any ingenuity. For example, even when the order has no combustible parts, I still have to go to product test and get their OK to proceed.

Current efforts to become more competitive by reducing red tape are associated with a variety of techniques to reduce stabilization-type low-level controls. For instance, in a certain company travel expenses no longer need to be signed off by three levels of management; employees now just sign their own. But "after the fact," a small number of expense sheets are sampled, and where an employee has overspent, he or she will receive a supervisory review.

Managers' desks are often crowded with requests they are supposed to review and approve—and to which they give only the most cursory attention. These requests should probably be converted from a "stabilization" task to one of sample "auditing."

As we saw in Chapter 6, groups whose work will be impacted by decisions made in other parts of the organization are reluctant to give up their stabilization authority. However, formal stabilization requirements are equitably reduced when interdepartmental task forces and committees meet to review and approve new activities at an early stage in the work flow.

Motivational Targets

Behavior that is positively reinforced tends to be repeated. That is the old psychological "law of effect," and it hasn't been repealed. Research confirms that employees work more diligently when they have clear targets.[3] (If those targets are developed by participatory techniques of supervision and accompanied by rewards, they are even more effective.)

In some organizations, employees who deal directly with customers and receive immediate plaudits from these people when they serve them well are likely to work harder at the ser-

---

[3] See Edwin Locke and Gary Latham, *Goal Setting: A Motivational Technique That Works*, Prentice-Hall, Englewood Cliffs, N.J., 1984.

vice task than their colleagues who might be engaged in important customer service activities behind the scenes and who never see or hear from a customer.

Almost every manager finds it useful to employ quantitative performance measures. In theory, these measures provide the critical feedback which will encourage subordinates to strive more vigorously, and they are seductively simple. Regrettably, they may not be as effective as they appear—or as simple.

The dilemma leaders face is this. Obviously, followers are motivated by clear, unambiguous feedback on performance; however, no incentive works as simply as its advocates would allow. Questions of equity, reward, intergroup comparisons, and pressures against "rate busters" for self-protection—all serve to vitiate their effectiveness. Nevertheless, the existence of targets and feedback on performance in relation to targets does motivate individuals and groups. Energy and enthusiasm are released by having what appear to be reasonable goals and by learning how one has performed in relation to these goals.

But experienced managers quickly learn to be wary of these potent tools because they also have many undesirable side effects. They can induce the opposite effect of the other "low-level" controls we have been describing; they encourage the subordinate to *narrow* the focus and even to *distort* the job to the point of injuring the organization in order to show good results.

> Some years ago a telephone company measured the performance of "back-panel wiremen," who handled changes in telephone numbers, by counting the number of new connections they made each day. To increase their output, the wiremen began neglecting to remove excess wire associated with disconnected numbers, with the result that the panels grew overweight with excessive waste wire and some collapsed.

> A computer company began measuring the work of their maintenance personnel by the speed with which they accomplished specified repairs on customer premises. To look good on more difficult repairs, the maintenance people ignored early reports from customers on difficult-to-diagnose problems and waited until the problems worsened or were repeated. Customers were incensed by the increased downtime.

Schoolteachers measured according to students' examination results began to "teach the test" and ignore other classroom activities.

Law enforcement officials who were measured in terms of numbers of crimes "solved" tended to ignore the difficult, complex cases—though those cases were the more important ones from the public's point of view.

Sanitation workers appraised by number of "truck dumpings" per day began dumping less than full loads. And when their work was measured in terms of weight of garbage collected, they began competing with each other for heavier, easier-to-collect garbage and ignored more dispersed and lighter garbage on the streets.

Managers measured on safety performance began hiding accidents by treating employees themselves rather than using the infirmary, and by keeping injured employees at work to avoid the stigma of "lost-time" accidents.

Executives who have achieved budgeted profits or sales seek to hide or hold over additional increments and save them for the next year. Similarly, marginally profitable activities are continued in order to avoid the penalty of "write-offs" associated with discontinuing a line of business. Profits are often overstated by overvaluing inventories, receivables, and even sales.

Quarterly sales results are inflated by shipping unordered, unwanted merchandise to customers who return it after the close of the inventory period.

Patients are kept in hospitals longer when hospital revenues depend on numbers of beds filled.

Distortions and Dissembling   The organization is the loser on several counts when these motivational targets are misused. Unmeasured aspects of the job are ignored, larger organizational interests are injured, and often cooperation with other groups is destroyed. Subordinates single-mindedly pursuing a goal of increased performance are in no mood to consider the needs of adjacent work groups for better quality, a change in schedule, or any accommodation, for that matter. Further, the information system of the organization becomes "polluted." Measures of performance become deceptive as subordinates ignore certain aspects of their job. The standards are further distorted by the tendency to inflate performance and deflate "bogeys" or the appropriate base against which to measure progress:

> It's common practice for supervisors and production workers alike to pressure to decrease their standards—whether the base for a piecework plan or the next year's budget for costs and sales. Efforts devoted to "proving" that the proposed base line is too high pay off as well as efforts devoted to improving real performance.

Thus managers who are told that all supervisors stayed under their cost budget for the year don't really know much—assuming the budgets had been bargained out—any more than do managers who are told that employees are producing, on average, 120 percent of base rates.

If result measures are to be used, they must be updated to reflect changed organizational values. Frequently, managers fail to detect how existing controls contradict or nullify *new* organizational goals.

> The president of a diversified company sought to get two divisions to collaborate. One had been highly profitable in terms used by the executive compensation scheme. Collaboration, to this division, meant developing products with lower profit margins and diluting current highly profitable activities. Although the president ordered cooperation, little was forthcoming.

> A training program began to shift from developing students solely for the private sector to training students for public employment. These graduates found it more difficult to get jobs and felt that the program's placement office was not effective. In fact, the placement office was evaluated in terms of the average salaries of students placed and, because of the lower salaries associated with entry-level jobs in the public sector, they really had little inducement to encourage those kinds of placements.

Seductive Goals As we shall see in the next section, employees can be seduced by the attractiveness of easily measured goals. Given the existence of an obvious performance standard and substantial rewards—or punishments—associated with the attainment of the standard, it is easy to lose sight of other aspects of the job.

> In an organization studied by one of my colleagues, great emphasis was placed on the sales volume attained by their new ventures. Managers eager to gain recognition for their fledgling product would be tempted to ignore every other aspect of their job—personnel retention, additional product development work, satisfying the demands of outside functional groups—to get the sales figures up. In the longer run these neglected aspects of their job would injure their reputations and even their operations.[4]

There is no simple answer to these problems. Quantitative standards, are motivating; they may even be inevitable. However, the wise leader doesn't overstress them and balances them with concern for the total job.

Some Fallacies in Managing by Results A widely held belief is that the good manager manages solely by results. This is presumed to foster maximum delegation, prevent excessive supervision, motivate subordinates to accept responsibility, and save the supervisor's time for really important matters. While much of the material here and in Chapter 9 explains why results are not an adequate basis for management control, the list below summarizes these reasons:

1 Looking only at results encourages subordinates to engage in behavior that may be destructive to organizational relationships. A subordinate may benefit, but the coordination necessary to meet overall organization goals suffers.

2 Such an emphasis encourages excessive competition for scarce resources—such as space, personnel, parts, maintenance facilities—and leads to neglect of the unmeasured aspects of a job.

3 It is difficult to pinpoint the cause or source of problems. Looking at results simply does not give one enough information. A man missed the schedule, the budget, or the specifica-

---

[4] Robert Burgelman and Leonard Sayles, *Inside Corporate Innovation*, Free Press, New York, 1986.

tions. But who is at fault, where did the problem occur, and what can be done to prevent its happening again? In most cases, the manager is at a loss to answer such questions because his feedback information tells him only that there is a problem. Typically, everyone and everything conspire to hide the blame or shift it to others. Measuring results encourages "buck-passing," "balloon squeezing," and "account poaching"—terms used by managers themselves to describe the illicit behavior in which they engage.

4   There is an increased number of instances where "crisis" measures must be taken because the supervising manager has waited too long; a potential loss has become an actual failure. By the time the results are in, it is too late to do much about it.

5   Many times good performance is not identified—only failures.

6   For many groups, such as staff, service, and administration, results are not easily assessed in dollars and cents. These groups find it difficult to justify their existence under this method of management without wasteful demonstrations of "programs" that they have initiated.

Effective Use of Targets

Targets, however, are important motivators; they are just more difficult to utilize than most managers assume. Subordinates who are motivated to succeed, who accept the legitimacy of their leadership, perform better when they have explicit goals and receive feedback on how well they are meeting these goals. For the process to work, the targets themselves must be designed with several goals in mind.[5]

Overcoming Accommodations   On a surprising number of jobs—particularly on technical, managerial, and professional—there are plenty of problems to solve but often no indication that any major change or improvement is called for. In fact, over the years, those working on these jobs become more accustomed to routinization, as we have already noted, and a

[5] An excellent summary of the experimental literature confirming the motivational value of goals and standards is provided by Arlyn Melcher, *Structure and Process of Organizations*, Prentice-Hall, Englewood Cliffs, N.J., 1975, Chaps. 9 and 10.

fixed level of effort. This regularity and resistance to change, or even the recognition of the need for change, is often called "trained incapacity."

Psychologists have also noted the extraordinary individual capacity to ignore cues, signals, and other evidence that change is necessary or would be useful, when such change is difficult or painful.[6] Individuals conveniently misperceive and rationalize away the need to do more or different things. The most extraordinary example of this involved the Navy command at Pearl Harbor who managed to interpret a large number of warnings from Washington in a way that didn't impose any need to accelerate the base's preparedness.

> On November 27, 1941, for example, Admiral Kimmel received an explicit "war warning" from the chief of naval operations in Washington, which stirred up his concern but did not impel him to take any new protective action. This message was intended as a strong follow-up to an earlier warning, which Kimmel had received only three days earlier, stating that war with Japan was imminent and that "a surprise aggressive movement in any direction including attack on Philippines or Guam is a possibility." The new warning asserted that "an aggressive move by Japan is expected within the next few days" and instructed Kimmel to "execute appropriate defensive deployment" preparatory to carrying out the naval war plan. The threat conveyed by this warning was evidently strong enough to induce Kimmel to engage in prolonged discussion with his staff about what should be done. But their vigilance seems to have been confined to paying careful attention to the way the warning was worded. During the meeting, members of the staff pointed out to Kimmel that *Hawaii was not specifically mentioned as a possible target in either of the two war warnings*, whereas other places—the Philippines, Malaya, and other remote areas—were explicitly named. . . . On December 3, 1941, Kimmel engaged in intensive discussion with two members of his staff upon receiving a fresh warning from naval headquarters in Washington stating that U.S. cryptographers had decoded a secret message from Tokyo to all diplomatic missions in the United States and other countries, ordering

---

[6] See Irving Janis and Leon Mann, *Decision Making: A Psychological Analysis of Conflict, Choice and Commitment*, Free Press, New York, 1977. The authors show how decision makers often manage to repress, misinterpret, or just ignore data that are uncomfortable, particularly data which will require the making of a decision with possibly unpleasant consequences. The authors call this "defensive avoidance."

them to destroy their secret codes. Kimmel realized that this type of order could mean that Japan was making last-minute preparations before launching an attack against the United States. Again, he and his advisers devoted considerable attention to the exact wording of this new, worrisome warning. They made much of the fact that *the dispatch said "most" of the codes but not "all."*[7]

Raising Consciousness Thus to be useful, the stimulus must overcome psychological inertia to hold fast, to be passive, to maintain continuity. For this reason, social psychologists since Kurt Lewin have stressed that individuals who are to be stimulated must be motivated to *perceive* the data correctly. This requires the managers to prepare subordinates to "see" or "hear" or "learn" the consequences of their behavior. How do managers sensitize, alert, and make ready subordinates?

This requires actively involving subordinates in setting the stage where a problem, discrepancy, or organizational need will be perceived accurately and can be confronted. How to do this?

1 Joint agreement or at least mutual discussion of goals, standards, objectives is needed—so there is some consensus on what are reasonable expectations. There is a good deal of evidence that goals which are "moderately" or "reasonably" higher than current performance are the most motivating.[8]

2 Subordinates should be involved in developing the methods and data by which goal attainment will be assessed. For example, managers being assessed on the basis of the profitability of their units often rationalize away unpleasant results when there are heavy and arbitrary allocations of corporate overhead and other uncontrollable costs. Survey data indicating that their employees have dangerously low morale can also be ignored, unless supervisors have confidence in the methods chosen to measure "morale." (The currently popular OD term for this is that managers being motivated have a sense of "owning the data." Thirty-five years ago this was called "action research" because the executive was presumed to be involved with those doing the measurement—or research—and would therefore feel

---

[7] Ibid., pp. 121–122. (Italics supplied.)

[8] Melcher, op. cit. Also, there cannot be too many goals or standards; perhaps no more than three to five is optimal.

bound to do something about whatever got disclosed, what the data showed.)

> In a large drug company, a divisional president was concerned that a key manager did not sense how badly a particular drug could be hurt if competitors were successful with some new formulations. The VP proposed that the manager undertake a study of competitor R&D—based on published papers, trade journals, industry rumors, and other informants—and summarize likely developments over the next five years. Nor surprisingly, when the study was completed, the executive in question felt compelled to undertake steps to improve his market position.

Of course, much of what used to be called "sensitivity training" does just this. The individuals learn first that the people around them are peers, have no special "ax to grind"—they're often strangers before the meeting—and hear them saying what appear to be candid things to others. They get involved in their deliberations. Then when the group is critical of them—say, for being too domineering or for being prejudiced toward women or minorities—the criticism comes across as credible and also shocking. Unprepared for harsh criticism, stunned by its frankness, the recipients may be motivated to try some change in their behavior. This is because they now perceive a *discrepancy* between the image they thought they projected (of decency or impartiality) and what they hear with their own ears, what people are saying about them. Obviously, this should have more of an impact than hearing lectures about good or ideal deportment or even hearing their boss criticize them. ("He's always criticizing me and this must just be another campaign of that silly personnel department.")

Instilling Confidence   As we pointed out earlier in our discussion of so-called path-goal theory, individuals can only be motivated when they believe that their efforts can make some difference and won't be destroyed, countered, or diluted by other people or events. Thus there may be adequate and accepted stimuli to do something, but if there are no apparent solutions, no slack resources with which to do anything, and a feeling of hopelessness, this "discrepancy" will be frustrating. It will be like being pulled in two opposing directions simultaneously.

As we noted in Chapter 3, subordinates must feel there is some semblance of equity and feasibility, that is, that the "game is worth the candle." In situations where change is punished—by peer displeasure, lack of recognition—or where failure brings major disgrace, individuals may see the need to take action but be inhibited by the possible costs (compared to potential benefits) of taking initiative.

Giving Feedback Obviously the likelihood of continued efforts to be responsive to crises and the need to change substantially depend on the availability of feedback. As the proponents of conditioning and the behaviorists have insisted, repetition of effort is dependence on positive reinforcement. Quite aside from the encouragement and learning provided (e.g., that initiative is appreciated, pays off, is worthwhile), feedback is necessary to know where you are in relation to your goal.

> Some years ago an industrial-psychologist friend noted that many managerial jobs are like a shooting gallery with no lights: you never know how close you are getting to the target, only whether or not you hit it.

Many psychologists believe this feedback is best provided by "noncontrived" methods—that is, where individuals see the results for themselves or some impersonal method is used to measure them. This contrasts with the boss's keeping score and potentially biasing the results. Even getting subordinates to maintain their own tally of how much has been accomplished each day, week, or accounting period or using unambiguous physical indicators (e.g., piling up counters to show how many cases were shipped) is preferable to supervisory evaluations.

The more individuals sense progress, the more they are motivated to continue the good work.

Targets as Simple, Single Aggregates

Perhaps the "bottom line" with respect to targets is that managers should use simple, single aggregates with care. It is always tempting to have a single measure that represents the "target" for the subordinate and the "control" for the manager. But on jobs with any degree of work diversity and complexity, it is rare for a single measure to encompass very much of the job, and it is common for both the job and the information received by the boss to be distorted to fit the measure.

It is the height of folly to encourage distortion and dissembling by associating high rewards with hitting the target, while at the same time, a great deal of time and energy is spent on rooting out the deviant and destructive behavior motivated by these very same targets.

Many ethical problems of business—for example, cases where employees violate laws and deceive managements—arise because the temptations have been made so great by the target-and-reward system.

MIDDLE-LEVEL CONTROLS TO ALLOCATE RESOURCES AND IDENTIFY PROBLEMS

Managers also need controls to signal where and when intervention is necessary. These are very different types of controls from the ones we have been describing and are much more likely to be ignored or misunderstood. Too many managers, in fact, utilize low-level controls for this purpose; for example, they assume that the quantitative targets will tell them how well the organization is functioning. Of course the targets won't do that for the reasons already discussed; they're useful as benchmarks and motivators only. What managers are seeking is a measure of *systems* performance: how jobs and job elements are coordinating and how the system is functioning as a system.

Assessment in Terms of the System

In appraising systems performance, managers need to know basically three things:

1 Are jobs being performed in such a way as to maximize organizational effectiveness? Our studies of effectiveness show that this requires the development of smooth routines tying jobs together and the absence of bickering, buck-passing, and conflicts over who should do what and how and when. Experienced managers spend time, in other words, monitoring job interfaces in order to assess how those boundaries are being handled.

2 Are the internal elements of a job being properly weighted so that employees demonstrate what is often loosely called "good judgment" in trading off time and emphasis among the various considerations they control?

3 Are subordinates responsive to unanticipated problems? Do they demonstrate the ability to change routines?

Thus at the core of the managers' "middle-level" control system are measures of:

Interface behavior
Trade-off decisions
Initiative and change

These are the three aspects of any job by which one can distinguish superior from inferior performance of subordinates and which determine the manager's allocation of personal time. As we shall see, these measures, while much more difficult to develop than the simpler low-level controls, do not self-destruct; that is, they do not tend to be destructive to organizational values over time.

Appraising Effectiveness The starting point for monitoring interfaces is obviously their specification. Using industrial buyers as an example, we can illustrate the technique and show how these measures provide a better method of appraising effectiveness than do the more traditional measures.

To simplify, these are some of the major interfaces of the industrial buyer's job:

1 *Response to requests from internal users for purchases.* Here the buyers must combine a service and a stabilization pattern. At least some of the requests will specify materials or delivery dates that are needlessly costly because they either ignore more modestly priced substitutes and existing inventories of parts purchased in quantity or they specify too tight a delivery date. Alert buyers seek to explore the needs of internal customers; where appropriate, they are responsive to service requests and, where necessary, they seek to modify the requests to obtain lower costs. Too much pressure (stabilization) on the customers makes the purchasing function a burdensome hurdle for responsible managers; too little effort to explore the real needs raises the cost of goods purchased. (For example, allowing too little time for delivery always raises costs by making bidding difficult.)

2 *Negotiation of terms with vendors and update of delivery.* A somewhat similar "mix" is required for dealing with vendors. Here negotiating skills are required, but too much pressure will often cause the vendors to give unrealistic delivery dates or prices (which at some point are likely to be violated). Too little pressure gives the organization needlessly high costs or unrealistic delivery dates. But, in addition, the buyers must keep checking back (that is, auditing) to be sure that nothing has intervened that will handicap the vendors in making their delivery. If this contingency arises, buyers contact the customers and alert them to the problem (that is, they act in a liaison capacity).

3 *Continual exploration of new supply sources.* Effective buyers are also alert to possible shortages, vendor deficiencies, and new sources of supply. For example, the possibility of labor strife or other contingency should initiate a broad search for more protected sources or substitutes.

Thus buyers are described in terms of organizational interfaces and assessed in terms of the ability to "work" these interfaces (demonstrating negotiating skill, responsiveness, initiative):

Buyer–customer
Buyer–vendor
Buyer–vendor–customer
Buyer–marketplace

More specifically, buyers are expected to handle the job in terms of its system characteristics. For example, they should be surveying certain published statistics, responding to requests for service, checking periodic reports, and the like. These may call for a certain response, given a specific criterion for action, if the data or information is above a certain predetermined threshold of action.

Work Flow Conception of Job

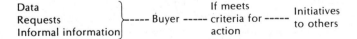

Services provided another example of developing middle-level controls on the basis of the work system. The president of Scandinavian Airlines described in a recent book how he broadened the scope of measures being used to "control" his air cargo staff and directed their attention toward the company's strategy of satisfying their customers.

Air cargo management in the past had assumed all was well if two measures looked good: (1) the volume of cargo carried and (2) the frequency with which paperwork accompanied the cargo.

These were replaced with measures that were more systems-oriented and that emphasized customer service:

1 How quickly customer calls were answered
2 How frequently dates specified to the customer were actually met
3 How frequently the cargo actually arrived on the flight on which it had been booked
4 How long it took to move the cargo from the plane, after landing, to where the customer could have access

Not mentioned but probably also important was the ability of the manager to improvise routing when difficulties emerged and to keep the customer informed when delays were incurred.[9]

Measuring Trade-offs A critical element of most jobs is the ability to trade off conflicting objectives or constraints. In the SAS example cited above, cargo supervisors face a trade-off: the increased risk of paperwork being separated from cargo if flights are shifted, against the customer disappointment associated with an unexpected delay in the original plane schedule.

Making trade-off decisions is often vaguely called "exercising good judgment," but we can give it explicitness and behavioral meaning. Most jobs contain conflicting requirements; too much concentration on one will injure the other.

[9] Jan Carlzon, *Moment of Truth*, Ballinger, Cambridge, Mass., 1987, pp. 109–112.

A utility employs telephone answering clerks to answer emergency complaints and route repair services. The clerks often have more calls than they can handle. They must learn to balance the value of more time with a given customer—which will often provide them with the ability to solve the problem by phone—with the need to handle a specified volume of calls. Too brief a conversation sends out more repairpeople than necessary; too extended a conversation overtaxes the lines, causes other customers to wait, and also runs the danger that a gas leak, for example, may cause an explosion while the problem is being explored.

Gate personnel for commercial airlines must balance the value of delaying a flight to assure all baggage is aboard and to pick up additional passengers from delayed connecting flights against the desirability and passenger demand for on-time departure.

Often these trade-offs also require interpersonal negotiation. The purchasing agents who do a good job seek to reconcile the legitimate needs of the vendors (for additional time, or money, or looser specifications) with the needs of the internal customers.

Thus what managers call "judgment" is simply the ability to handle individual problems with the proper trade-offs. This means using rules flexibly and dealing with each situation in terms of its own characteristics.

In fact, many subordinates are unwilling to do this; instead they evolve rules of thumb to provide either automatic answers or answers that will safeguard their personal interests, not the organization's. The latter usually manifests itself in what academics have called the "minimax solution."[10]

The minimax solution assures minimal risk for subordinates. Take this example in which an executive is evaluating the advice of a staff person that seems to contradict what the executive believes to be the right course of action. Rather than assess

---

[10] The term itself is the product of the mathematical analyses of Morgenstern and Von Neumann that became the basis for "game theory"—decision making where you have one or more opponents who are likely to take steps to nullify your decisions.

ing the possibilities in terms of their intrinsic merit, the executive makes the decision in such a way as to minimize personal political losses. In doing so, the executive uses a type of decision matrix that evaluates the personal risk:

		Manager Expects Advice to Be	
		Good	Bad
Executive decides	To accept	No risk; will even get some credit	Little risk; can blame staff
	To reject	Great risk; staff will blame executive as will superiors	No risk; staff happy to forget

Such a minimax matrix induces many executives to accept staff proposals uncritically because the greatest loss (to their status) can come from a rejection, and, after all, it's difficult to know what will prove to be right.

The same kind of "selfish" trade-off endangers the design of new aircraft. One of the obvious problems facing designers and development engineers is weight—the new plane tends to get heavier as design proceeds. The reason can be identified in the engineers' use of a minimax-type solution to the problems facing them. Thus the engineers designing a part ask themselves where the greatest risk of personal failure is. The answer is, always, a part or component that shows structural failure in testing. If there is a choice between sticking to the weight limits of the preliminary design or adding weight to ensure that the part meets its performance requirements, the engineers consistently add weight. The greatest risk is thus avoided. But since everyone is doing this, just about every new plane grows substantially in weight as a result of risk avoidance:

If part doesn't add weight to design and fails test—GREAT BLAME

If part doesn't add weight to design and passes test—Some credit

If part adds weight to design and passes test—Modest credit

If part adds weight to design and fails test—Some blame, but at least tried[11]

Managers who consider this an important element to monitor ought to find it relatively easy to separate flexible, adaptive subordinates from those whò have excessively routinized the decision-making aspects for maximum risk protection.

Encouraging Initiatives Many observers have sought to quantify the performance of what they call the "discretionary" component of a job. They argue, with substantial validity, that management is basically not interested in the individual performing the required portion of a job. If that portion is not performed, the individual should be discharged. (The required portion then becomes a low-level control.) What is worthy of commendation or censure is how the individual copes with the discretionary part:

A machine begins malfunctioning but is still producing within tolerance levels. Does the operator detect the early stages of a problem and notify the supervisor?

A "miscellaneous file" begins to get unduly large and not very useful. Does the clerk maintaining the file take the initiative in seeking to open new category files?

A schedule slips because of an unforeseen parts shortage. Does the employee doing the job take the initiative in suggesting some shortcuts to make up for the temporary delay, including perhaps changing the sequence of duties?

Another way of saying this is that every employee ought to know where existing routines are inadequate and when there is the need to introduce change. (This will be treated as the prime test of the leadership capabilities of the manager in Chapter 9.)

Guiding Delegation and Promotion Decisions Effective supervisors use delegation as a means of expanding (or contracting) the discretionary component of the job. Thus managers may have a number of analysts working for them with the same job title, but those who have demonstrated this trade-off or

---

[11] This example was suggested by Professor R. R. Ritti of Pennsylvania State University.

judgment skill are given more delegated autonomy. Their jobs may be broadened to include new responsibilities, and/or are subject to less frequent review, or are "checked out" less by the boss. The ability to demonstrate good control over the discretionary component of one's job encourages sensible management to offer still more discretion.

For managers, this kind of control assesses whether they have developed adequate internal measures to estimate where their own operations are effective. Upper-level executives should be able to observe managers "going into action"— increasing the number and breadth of their initiatives, for example—when these measures signal a problem.

> Some years ago we observed the near demise of a company highly dependent on a new product that calculated and printed prices for an important service industry. When government taxes changed, it was necessary to change the internal configuration of the printers located on customer premises. Because of unforeseen strikes and material shortages, the new parts were delayed in fabrication. The vice president in charge continued to exhort everyone to work harder, worried a great deal, but basically did nothing to change the procurement process. When the president was alerted to what was occurring and realized what anyone should have known—that customer failure to receive updated printing machines at the time the new tax took effect might endanger continued sale of the company product—he went into action. Additional suppliers were contacted, airplanes rented, extra shifts scheduled, and an entire emergency procedure instituted. The vice president was demoted for failing to take the obvious steps to remedy a problem. He had failed on the discretionary part of his job.

Why "Systems" Controls?

As we've seen, most measures have some motivational value, but these controls tend to injure the organization's functioning as an organization. Most managers are aware of this but tend to write it off as a necessary cost:

> We know that any control we use will be good for several years. Then it just wears out as people find ways of beating the system. So we just turn to a new one, and so on.

But this self-destruct characteristic is not inevitable. It is derived from the unrealistic presumption that one can assess a job in a vacuum. Traditional controls seek to look at job outputs as though the individual were solely responsible for some final product of a good or service. In reality, the organization depends on coordination and integration, and job performance needs to be measured in the same "systems" terms. That is the basis for recommending monitoring interfaces, trade-offs, and discretionary response (usually to unanticipated problems). Basically this focuses attention on the process of management, not simply on the end result.

Further, there is good evidence that one can predict—an important requirement of any control system—future technical breakdowns by observing organizational malfunctioning. Internal polarization (in relations among subgroups) and breakdowns in work flow exchanges consistently *precede* technical breakdowns, missed schedules, performance failures, and dollar losses.

HIGH-LEVEL CONTROLS
TO REASSURE OUTSIDERS

In all fields, not just the corporation, there is a growing concern with accountability: Is the organization accomplishing what it was established to do? Leaders of these organizations have to prove to their constituencies—higher management, government funding sources, community groups—that they are worth their cost and meeting their goals.

These measures of accomplishment are not controls in the sense that we have been using the term. They really are defenses against the outsider, buffers to protect the organization from being invaded by investigators or threatened by cuts in support.

They are often quantitative results, not unlike the motivational targets we described as low-level controls:

The number of patients treated during the fiscal year
The number and weight of rockets launched successfully
The profitability of the operation in relation to shares outstanding, revenue received, assets employed

With the increasing emphasis on what is called "evaluation research" in the public sector, there has been effort to get measures of *outcome*, not simply inputs and outputs. Thus it may not be adequate to say that in a public agency managers trained x number of people for new jobs; rather the managers must show how this training related to longer-run job tenure for these trainees and to increased family income and self-support. Such data are much more difficult and costly to obtain, perhaps more controversial. In this sense, they are far different from low-level targets because these evaluation studies seek to explore *real* results, above and beyond the measure of units processed or dollars turned over. These are results that can only be seen in the community, outside the walls of the organization.[12]

In pleasing sponsors of large-scale, diffuse programs, it becomes especially important to define goals that will allow for measurement. Thus goals must not be defined too broadly or too narrowly. An astute observer noted that the Office of Economic Opportunity (OEO), by defining its goals in global terms—attacking poverty—found it difficult to justify its existence, to prove its effectiveness.[13] At the other extreme, some would argue that NASA erred by overemphasizing a too-well-defined, finite goal: the moon landing. It had difficulty maintaining support after its magnificent achievement. When Ruckelshaus took over the Environmental Protection Agency (EPA), he sought to avoid these extremes by defining his goal for the agency as measurable pollution abatement, demonstrably cleaner air and water.[14] This would make it possible for him to demonstrate progress to EPA's constituencies.

Our earlier research on large, multinational government-funded projects disclosed related findings. If the projects were defined too broadly, each country had both the means and incentive to bend the purposes of the project to suit its own special, national interests. If the project's goals were too narrow—for example, a nuclear reactor with very fixed properties—the

---

[12] See Carol Weiss, *Evaluation Research*, Prentice-Hall, Englewood Cliffs, N.J., 1972.

[13] P. Wiehl, "William D. Ruckelshaus and the Environmental Protection Agency," unpublished working paper, Harvard University, Kennedy School, 1974.

[14] Ibid.

project had no room for new discoveries or for unanticipated barriers. Thus successful international projects had goals that were neither too broad nor too narrow.[15]

CONCLUSIONS

The most obvious thing to do is not always the correct thing. From the earliest days of scientific management, it seemed obvious to managers to measure and motivate subordinates in terms of how much they accomplished. Simply put, it is straightforward and attractive to hold people accountable for tasks as though their jobs or departments were neatly compartmentalized. This provides the greatest motivation and the greatest ease of quantification. Regrettably, however, such controls contradict the organization's requirements.

Managers must learn to use three very different kinds of controls. Each serves its own useful purpose; together they compose a control system and deal with the real business of management.

Low-level controls provide reassurance to the manager that subordinates are not violating critical standards. They serve as checks and checkpoints to assure the boss that harmful shortcuts have not been taken and that relevant procedures have been followed. They also provide "targets" for subordinates when they are used to establish goals and measure certain results—sales volume or units produced. Subordinates like being assessed in terms of targets they feel competent to meet, and such goals can provide both motivation and, when attained, a sense of job satisfaction.

However, clear quantitative targets have shortcomings in that they usually exclude important qualitative aspects of the job. They encourage a variety of actions which can subvert the real goals of the organization. They are most pernicious when they get reduced to *simple, single aggregates,* and everything depends, from the subordinate's view, on hitting or exceeding that one important number.

Middle-level controls aid the manager in knowing how the organization below is functioning as an organization. These

---

[15] Leonard Sayles and Margaret Chandler, *Managing Large Systems,* Harper & Row, New York, 1971, pp. 122–123.

controls are based on the organizational dimensions of subordinate jobs, and they assess how well that total system is being "worked": relationships maintained, decisions made on the basis of sensible trade-offs, and initiatives taken to deal with problems. Effective managers will utilize evidence of recurring systems breakdown as their signal that personal intervention is required to improve the job performance of subordinates and/or to introduce change.

Managers must make use of high-level controls to reassure upper management that their intervention is not required because good progress is being made.

9

THE CHALLENGE OF INTRODUCING CHANGE

Management effectiveness and introduction of change are almost synonymous. While traditional managers may have spent most of their time giving orders and overseeing the work, modern managers, with skillful delegation, are concerned more with intervention and change, with fine-tuning their operations.[1]

In many ways the ability to introduce change effectively into an established work setting is one of the real tests of managerial leadership. Without this capability, new technologies and improved methods of doing work will not be employed. Over time that creates an ossified organization. Further, when managed well, change can be a magnet that attracts the loyalties of motivated employees. Ambitious objectives, like introducing innovative improvements, can mobilize group esprit around the common goal. The manager who initiates this effort while maintaining a sense of momentum gains further legitimacy as a dynamic leader who "gets things done."

[1] For a reasoned assessment of the role, and some of the methods, of innovation in business, see Peter Drucker, *Innovation and Entrepreneurship: Practice and Principles*, Harper & Row, New York, 1985. A highly influential book that criticizes the nation's managers for not being adept at change is Robert Reich, *The New American Frontier*, Times Books, New York, 1983.

There are many similarities in the challenges presented by technological change and organizational change. This chapter seeks to deal with both by concentrating on work system improvements designed to eliminate the kind of work flow impediments identified by what we have called the manager's "middle-level controls." (See Chapter 8.)

As we have observed repeatedly, astute managers concentrate their leadership skills on *work systems*, not on isolated jobs. Managers must both oversee internal coordination—that is, the interrelationship of jobs within their own jurisdiction—and external coordination, especially the interchanges with groups just preceding and succeeding theirs in the work flow and with centralized service and support groups. The efficiency of the operations for which they are responsible is almost solely the product of work regularization and routinization in jobs interrelating at their boundaries—so that A facilitates B's work, who in turn fits into the activities of C. Given this systems view of work, we can identify the contribution of change. Managers engage in three distinct levels of change behavior:[2]

1 *Intervention.* To return the system to equilibrium
2 *Restructuring work.* To improve system performance
3 *Major reorganizations.* In response to serious internal work flow defects or new external problems or opportunities

INTERVENTIONS

Most of the leadership techniques described in Chapter 3 are responses to observed system imperfections. Subordinates must be persuaded to increase their tempo; conflict between two employees as to who is the source of a problem must be resolved; a shortage requires modifying a work procedure. All of these are designed to recapture the normal tempo of operations, to return the work flow system to a stable state.

Employees can distinguish good managers from bad in these interventions. The appreciated managers aren't looking to see

---

[2] A new study suggests that managers cluster their changes in relation to the length of time it takes to learn a new position and to gain some feedback on the effects of previous changes. See John Gabarro, *The Dynamics of Taking Charge,* Harvard Business School Press, Boston, 1987.

who is at fault, what rule or order is being violated, but rather what needs to be done to get the system going and in the process help subordinates reach their goals. In other words, managers are fixers, identifying holdups, making substitutions and improvisations.

Most organizations evolve special "emergency" routines for expediting lagging work flows that involve calling into play special problem solvers, up-the-line appeals for "relief" or temporary suspension of certain standards.

RESTRUCTURING WORK

Many times the work flow can be improved—that is, interruptions made less frequent, complaints from other departments reduced, breakdowns minimized—if some change can be introduced. Effective mangers identify misfits between job and personality and shift part of task A, formerly done by employee X, to employee Y, and, in turn, shift some of task B over to X from Y.

Even more important in most organizations are managerial skills in renegotiating external relations to facilitate internal regularity.

> My department was always in a state of panic on Thursday. We never knew what receivables would be asking us to do but we knew it was going to be rush and an emergency. I spent several weeks with accounts payable, our other big "customer," to see whether there wasn't some way we could rearrange our work commitments to get Thursday freed up. And then I developed a small group within our own department that would specialize in handling the work related to receivables. I even encouraged them to spend time over there to learn their procedures and needs and see if they could pick up early signals on what was going to be hitting us.

What's happening here? The manager is doing what all good managers do—spending time on the interface of the department, where it intersects the work of other departments. Where the "flows" are not regular, the manager is negotiating changes in both the division of labor and procedures to smooth out the instabilities. What most managers ignore is that they *do* have the authority to control, and can modify some of the structural variables that affect the functioning of their departments. Changing specialization, modifying procedures and schedules, calling for advance notice—all can serve to minimize work flow disturbances.

Using Participation

The typical method of instituting change in a hierarchy is an announcement tumbling down the line. It doesn't work, not because it's undemocratic, but because it's inefficient. The meaning gets distorted by the time it gets down to where it has to be implemented. Existing stereotypes and hostilities get focused on the change and a self-confirming prophecy develops: "Here is another management folly; let's be sure it fails." Of course, in the end, it does.

Managers often realize that employee participation in the change process makes the employee feel better, but there is much more involved than good morale. When subordinates are consulted about and contribute to the change process, many other benefits accrue:

1 Being intimately familiar with operations, employees can contribute suggestions and insights that make any proposal for change more realistic. And in the ensuing give-and-take between employees and management, the manager can learn important elements about the technology that were previously unknown or misunderstood.

> Our boss was going to eliminate the forms we generated for inventory control when we shifted to the new computer because they duplicated work done in production. What he didn't know was that some of our data had more up-to-date information and accounting often used the discrepancies between the two reports to check on customer returns.

2 Active participation releases energy. Debating, questioning, and making suggestions shift employees from a dull passivity to a more alert state and to greater productivity.

3 Participation reduces the status gap between superior and subordinate and contributes to legitimating the role of the leader as one who is responsive to subordinates. Employees also gain the security of knowing that management is likely to rectify harmful errors in planning or design.

4 Those who are involved in shaping a change will be more committed to its implementation.

With participation, trite as it may sound, the change becomes "our" change, tailored in part to our needs and problems and not a resented foreign imposition on an already problematic workday.

Managers as Their Own Change Agents

In recent years it has become popular to speak in psychological jargon about the role of change agents. In fact, there is now a management specialty, organization development, whose major focus is on how *outsiders*—"consultants," "facilitators," and "change agents"—can aid company management in accomplishing organization improvements it couldn't do itself. A real mystique has grown up surrounding these apparently charismatic (and expensive) consultants who can transform a rigid, conflict-laden, troubled business into an "open," flexible, and mutually cooperative enterprise.

In fact, these OD techniques can be practiced by the managers themselves without the interventions of an outsider. Let's try to understand the underlying theory of "change agents," stripped of the usual obscure jargon.

Back in the 1940s, a distinguished social psychologist, Kurt Lewin, developed what he called "action research," although the name is not important. What was important was the prescription he developed for change.[3]

Managers usually introduce change by recognizing a problem, developing a plan for solving it, and then implementing the plan. If they believe in employee participation, they ask employees for their ideas and even allow criticism of management's solutions. In any case, the change process involves moving from the managers' goals → to a strategic analysis → to specific tactics.

Lewin stressed a more motivational approach and a more evolutionary one. For people to be interested in changing their behavior, they must first be dissatisfied. Only when the people who have to change feel that they have a problem is there likely to be any movement. Since most efforts at change flounder because carefully executed plans are ignored or sabotaged, this first step is critical:

[3] Kurt Lewin, *Resolving Social Conflicts*, Harper, New York, 1948.

1 *Seek change when the people who are going to have to do the changing are distressed and feel they have a problem.* Now their problem may not be the same as the boss's problem—at least at this point—and their perceptions may be wrong, but at least they are in a state where they're looking for help. For example, management may be seeking to improve coordination between two departments so that work flow problems can be reduced. But each department feels that the only problem is the other person's; they're doing just fine, but the other department is causing holdups. When one, or perhaps both, have just missed an important schedule, breached their budget or come under pressure from above for improved results—i.e., when they're hurting—that's the time to move.

The next step involves getting them to accept some procedure for exploring how the problem can be solved. Department A is unhappy with the quality or timing of materials coming from department B. The manager (as "change agent"), or whoever else is going to act as the catalyst, gets the department to establish a study or miniresearch project on the problem:

- What kind of information is needed?
- Who can collect it?
- Who should analyze it and how? What is secret and what can be openly discussed?

2 *Get consensus on what kinds of data and what method of collection and assessment the group will accept as valid for evolving a solution to its problem.* The manager may have to help to get the project under way. It may require some outside technical aid, a survey, a review of old records, interviews with people in both departments. But whatever and however, agreement on possible solutions is reached. Then the study is made and, because the group has contributed to its design, the group is presumably ready to accept the findings. In most circumstances the study will produce some surprises. For example, the other department has difficulty in knowing what is desired when or if there have been conflicting signals or contradictory instructions. Perhaps the materials prepared in the criticized department also have to meet the needs of still other departments. Nonetheless, the exposure to this prevalidated data, which often highlights the discrepancy between the groups' presumptions and reality, serves to *unfreeze* their attitudes. In other words, they are prepared to change because they have learned at some "gut" level for themselves that they are, in small part or large measure, responsible for the problem.

3 *Make feedback the critical element; it becomes a catalyst to the people who will have to change, emphasizing the discrepancy between what they believed and the reality of the situation.* This is very much like what happens in most management consulting. Good ideas and diagnoses that already exist at lower levels of the organization are being flushed out and up; but here the "flushing-out" process is designed to make people accept what they see and hear because it isn't being imposed on them by a higher level of the hierarchy. As Lewin argued years ago, the discrepancy between what was believed and what is now discovered to be truth will motivate people to change.

4 *Aid people in coping, skill transfer, experimenting with new methods.* However, to accomplish the change, subordinates may well need help. They may need some new technology, new interpersonal skills, or just plain encouragement to try out some new behavior without fear of failure or criticism. So the manager's/change agent's next step is to provide both the psychological support in exploring new job behavior and the technical aid. For example, conceivably the group may want some personnel colocated between the two departments or want improved communication linkages, more phones. Or perhaps one group is composed of engineers and the other accountants; the separate groups may need help in understanding each other's different languages and viewpoints.

5 *Then the cycle is repeated.* Usually the first efforts won't be roaring successes; there will still be unresolved problems, and some innovations won't work as planned or hoped. So the group which is the focus of change is encouraged to continue to:

- Research/study the work flow problems by collecting more data
- Evaluate and feed back
- Consider further innovations
- Get help in implementing these
- Check as to how these are working

The emphasis is on the fact that the individual and the group must feel they are getting help with *their* problems to accomplish *their* goals. And they are changing in response to evidence they have helped collect, or at least authorized, and in response to discrepancies between presumption and reality that they can see and feel for themselves.

The manager's role is one of facilitator—stage-managing the process so that the individuals themselves will be motivated to change, in contrast to being told to change. Further, the process is, or ought to be, a continuing one. Over time the group learns to make this method almost automatic. For example, if there is internal dissension, rather than blaming one another, someone will suggest: "Let's have someone observe our departmental meetings so we can get some feedback on what seems to be happening, how we can end up with so much shouting and so little accomplished." In a week or two the "observer" reports back, and the group, on the basis of that, seeks to improve its functioning as a team.

Using Group Dynamics

Of course, this is the heart of what is called "sensitivity training"—or even "consciousness raising" or "assertiveness training." They are all similar techniques and employ a very simple method, though it's usually couched in jargon. In the group, individuals learn for themselves when their behavior is inadequate because their peers are critical, and one tends to accept peer group evaluation. Usually there is a substantial discrepancy between the person you thought you were and what others tell you they see in you: "Jim, you come across as a frightened rabbit; you're afraid to speak up, and you usually begin with an apology even before you've said anything." This hits Jim hard; he is shocked and wants help. If he didn't before, now he knows he has a problem.

Then the group is supposed to help the individual explore improved methods of accommodating others, try them out, and gain confidence in their use—all the time with direct, gut-level feedback.

Most of us don't change because we're told to change; we don't learn much by simply being lectured to or by reading reports. *We change by learning for ourselves the answers to the questions we have ourselves raised in response to pressures and problems we're experiencing.*

There will be times when bosses will want to use this *evolutionary* approach to introducing change. Rather than starting with the problem of "selling" their solution to the problem, they will seek to find common goals and common means. In doing so, they will adopt specific motivational techniques. That is, they will:

1 Respond to subordinates' problems, waiting until the subordinates feel compelled to find some improvement or change because they are blocked in reaching their goals (e.g., a sales representative can't meet the acceptable quota or an engineer discovers the schedule slipping)

2 Utilize impersonal confrontations that will create motivation to improve—"unfreeze"—behavior (e.g., send customer-complaint letters directly to production departments or let employees see reliability test results)

3 Take the role of facilitating the subordinates' efforts to reach their goals (e.g., ask, "What can I do to help you reach quota?")

MAJOR REORGANIZATIONS

The third type of change is both the most basic and the broadest form of change. Sensible managers introduce major reorganization as a *result of,* or in *response to,* the frequency with which minor day-to-day changes have to be employed and in light of their relative effectiveness.[4]

As we have sought to demonstrate elsewhere, both internal and external structural "faults" show themselves in *excessive* requirements for managerial intervention and initiation, and in polarization. Further, of course, the frequency of disturbance to the work flow system is costly in terms of both managerial time (the greater the number of interventions required, the smaller the span of control) and efficiency, since output is correlated with continuity in most work systems. Thus the need for major reorganization is signaled by one or all of several work flow symptoms.

---

[4] Insofar as "major reorganization" necessarily results from new methods of work and new technologies, effective managers think first of this type of change when they learn that a new technique or new equipment can improve productivity or quality or both.

Symptoms of Need for Structural Reform

Recurring Problems Problem situations repeat in a highly predictable fashion. "Every week I get involved in at least one hassle with the . . . department over schedules." Similarly, problems of unbalanced workload for subordinates, persistently scarce resources, or constant seniority grievances—all may drain the managers' time and energy resources. Each time they invoke emergency measures to change the behavior of an individual or of a number of people associated in a work flow, they commit themselves to a difficult task, and potentially neglect other parts of their job.

"High-Amplitude" Problems Disturbances that involve major deviations from planned patterns of interaction and work flow are very costly. Taking everyone from the regular work to tackle last-minute rush jobs, crash problems, and task force investigations devours managerial time and disturbs the regular work habits of subordinates. Even though irregular in occurrence, such problems are worth identifying because of their seriousness.

"Long-Chain" and "Spiraling" Problems Figuratively, an initial infection (disturbance) in the organizational system "spreads" to other flows, and these new upsets cause further reaction. Thus the original difficulty is magnified as many groups become involved. As managers make compensating adjustments to deal with their own problems, these accumulate and begin to create their own backlash of disturbances. Similarly, failure on the part of key managers to take decisive action on critical problems shows up as "long chains." These problems may not be recurring; they just are never solved.

"Spiraling" appears when the absence of continuous work flows creates the necessity for the use of remedial channels. Their use, in turn, creates additional upset and more breakdowns. These then act as pressure on line management to increase further their use of short-term remedial measures, until the organization literally falls apart from the internal stresses that have been set up.

The managers' monitoring system should include a summarization of their own use of short-term remedial actions. They should know where and for what they spend their scarce time resources. The incidence of such disturbances identifies problems that may require long-term, as distinct from "fire-fighting" or short-term, managerial actions. In the same fashion, repeated requests for aid can identify internal problems in the work flows of employees. Thus managers at any level in the hierarchy can monitor the intersection points of the flows over which they have jurisdiction, as well as some of the internal dynamics of the jobs of managers below them. All, however, represent second derivatives—the rate at which deviations show up.

Polarization Organizations where internecine conflicts are rampant require some major managerial interventions. The evidence is usually unambiguous: departments are predictably opposed on any and every issue; continual backbiting and buck-passing destroy most cooperative patterns; there is no mutual accommodation, so that any new requirement or departure from routine cannot be absorbed without substantial hassling and mutual recriminations.

Approaching Major Organizational Change

This type of analysis suggests a management paradox—easy to express, but difficult to accept:

```
Change ----→ required to maintain routine and efficiency
Routine ----→ required to provide the managerial time and
              energy to devote to the problems of change
Change ----→ creates profound management problems because
              it destroys routines
```

Expressed even more simply: managers must accept the fact that there are substantial costs in undertaking change. Organizations with few or no established routines are unlikely to have the management "surplus" to invest in the very substantial effort required to introduce change—because change interrupts, yes, destroys, routine. But without periodic change, organizations grow increasingly internally divisive (as problems accumulate) and externally irrelevant. That's the paradox.

The Myths of Change

Many, if not most, managers are unprepared for the rigors of the change process—even assuming they know when and where the efforts should be made. In part, this lack of preparation is cultural; Americans particularly are brought up to believe both in change and in its simplicity. Our culture values:

1 Risk taking, because we are forward-looking and confident about the future; we assume tomorrow will be better than today (and what was good enough for our forebears is certainly not good enough for us).

2 Optimism combined with pragmatism; we are less concerned with immutable laws than with what will work and with improvisation. In fact, we are neither awed nor intimidated by authority, protestations of "it won't work," and the resistance of our senior and more prestigious superiors.

3 Encouraging initiative at lower organizational levels; specialists as well as managers believe in challenging the status quo.

While change and progress are generally laudable, some of the other values and beliefs we hold fast to are sheer myth.

Americans, given this cultural impetus for change, are overconfident about their abilities to change. They cite with pride vast new programs to implement new technologies: the Manhattan Project, NASA, and the like. In these government programs, as in private industry, real innovations are often associated with new organizations or, at least, organizations for which the specific innovation is new. Electric typewriters became successful in a computer company; automatic washers were perfected in an auto parts company; and the camera that develops its own pictures was not perfected by a film or camera company.

Almost every major change program requires, in both time and money, double the original estimates, and part of this can be attributed to such illusions about change as these:

1 Managers welcome change; it's only workers who resist.

2 The problems are largely centered around job security.

3 Good managers plan change down to the last detail—in advance.

4 Effective change progresses in a one-way sequence from conception through to implementation.

5 A really good idea is the best guarantee of success.

The reality is that change threatens managers more than workers and the problems are questions of power, of breakdown of accustomed and efficiency-related routines. Even the most carefully contrived plans will be found faulty, and to overcome these problems it will be necessary to go backward as well as forward: to return to early design problems during later development stages and to consider final uses at the very beginning. The idea itself is the smallest part of the problem; implementation is the key problem.

Putting Implementation in Perspective

Schools and organizational experiences often cause managers to put a great deal of emphasis on the big, profitable idea. Both in government and business, it has become obvious that ideas are relatively easy to come by; the problem is making them work. Even brilliant breakthroughs in the war on poverty and in new technologies turn out to be frustratingly difficult to get to work. Enormous amounts of money are expended in programs to retain workers, yet few get permanent jobs. For decades we've known about thermoelectricity and techniques for making oil from coal, yet converting these breakthroughs into cost-efficient industrial processes eludes those organizations that keep trying. What are the managerial challenges in undertaking necessary change?

Euphoria and Exaggeration The early stages of the change process often generate undue optimism; in fact, the bias gets built in. Managers whose ideas are likely to be accepted are those who feel strongly that the results are going to be great, if not miraculous. Further, the organization often favors the self-confident, strong-willed, highly persuasive sponsor over the more cautious executive. For the most part, budgets get allocated on the basis of the possibility of major gains, not marginal improvements. Further, the managers are likely to be working with and "working up" a small number of like-minded associates who generate internal enthusiasm, even euphoria, as they repeat to each other the likely "miracles to come."

Thus both government bidding practices and internal company competition for budget items encourage what have come to be called "buying-in" practices. Managers are induced to understate problems, costs, and impediments and overstate anticipated benefits, performance levels, and reasonable schedules, in order to gain the nod from sponsors weighing alternative bids. Program managers tacitly assume they can bail themselves out of these commitments by future breakthroughs, hard work, and later changes of the contractual terms or their verbal commitment. They reason that once the institution is committed to going ahead and they can "taste" the future returns, they will be able to wheedle additional concessions—revised specifications, higher costs, etc.

The institutional realities that help convert technical managers into salespeople are matched by the small-group factors that develop "true believers." There is a large body of research on how a small group induces in its members common and often exaggerated beliefs about reality. Thus the colleagues surrounding an articulate and often charismatic entrepreneur–program manager become convinced and convince each other of the practicality of the new approach or idea.

Unanticipated Costs   What these predictions almost universally neglect are the administrative challenges of introducing change. Managers must learn to cope with a string of compelling, usually unanticipated, challenges to their skill and perseverance. Among the most vexing will be these:

1   Plans and prognoses, however carefully worked through, will consistently omit or neglect some critical factor that will reveal itself later and threaten the viability of the total project.

2   More groups and elements of the organization will be impacted than anticipated, and their concerns and cooperation will be more difficult to resolve than the fears of the managers' own subordinates!

3   The change process not only destroys routines that are the source of efficiency but encourages "plundering"— purposeful disturbances of the status quo, designed to benefit some groups at the expense of others. This occurs in part because of the differential impact of the change.

4   As unanticipated problems occur, anxieties about slipped schedules and faltering budgets will encourage those management pressures most likely to discourage the very flexibility among employees and managers that is required.

5   Unforeseen eruptions of complaint and protest occur.

Incomplete Plans   Managers are frequently urged to plan meticulously: conceive of every contingency, systematically work through procedures and responsibilities, and compare costs and benefits.

The reality every manager discovers is that all plans are incomplete. There are always unforeseen and unforeseeable defects. Recent studies suggest that actual returns on new corporate capital investments compared to predicted returns vary by a factor of 10.[5]

Even projects planned by the World Bank with an army of engineers and economists turn out to be faulty because some major factor was forgotten or suddenly turned adverse, such as climate and water supply.[6] Some years ago we watched a major American metals company meticulously plan the adoption of a new automatic smelting process licensed from the European innovator. The technology transfer, worker training, and cost and output schedules had been worked out to three decimal places. But the whole project was first threatened and then destroyed because the plans neglected roofing material! (In Europe, tile factory roofs provided convection currents that turned out to be indispensable to the new smelting process, but the United States version had been built with galvanized material.) By the time the omission was discovered, so much money had been spent seeking scapegoats in union and worker recalcitrance and lower-level management ineptness that the project had to be given up.

In a similar incident, a new gauze-making machine failed to perform to predicted output levels. Output just could not be improved, even after long, arduous negotiations with engineers, workers, and union over where the fault lay. Departmental efficiency continued to suffer until, by chance, it was discovered that a new elevator shaft produced air currents that tended to tear the gauze.

---

[5] See Joseph Bower, *Managing the Resource Allocation Process*, Harvard Business School, Division of Research, Boston, 1970.

[6] See Albert Hirschman, *Development Projects Observed*, Brookings, Washington, D.C., 1967. Hirschman surveys the management of a number of World Bank–funded major redevelopment programs with an emphasis on what went wrong. For a contemporary horror story describing all the things that can go wrong with a major effort at innovation inside a large corporation, see Christopher Byron, *The Fanciest Dive*, Norton, New York, 1986.

The Contagion of Change Most managers are short-sighted concerning who will be impacted by a change. They must learn to anticipate how widespread the effects will be.

NASA engineers were anxious to develop practical spin-offs for space age innovations. They conceived of improving fire fighters' life-support systems on the basis of those developed for astronauts. The problem was originally conceived as technological, but over time it became apparent that a diverse number of groups had to be "sold" on the efficacy of this new technology and the technology had to be modified to meet their diverse interests and standards. The groups included:

1 Manufacturers who would have to find this a practical product to fabricate in volume and for a profit
2 City managers and other political officials who would have to find the costs and benefits sufficiently attractive to increase fire department budgets
3 Various safety groups and associations who would have to approve and "warrant" the usefulness of the new system and who had performance standards
4 Fire chief organizations who would have to recommend its use and initiate requests that it be ordered
5 Active fire fighters and their unions, who would be concerned with its weight, bulkiness, and how it affected their mobility and agility during a threatening fire, and who would have to find it comfortable and preferable to existing equipment

Also in the public arena, efforts to improve sanitation department productivity by developing a new, larger truck floundered when a whole bevy of union officials; motor vehicle, safety, and finance officers; and purchasing agents had to evolve a consensus.[7]

Even in more modest changes in industrial setting, it is difficult to "contain" the change:

An engineer conceives of a better piece of equipment. To work out the bugs, time must be secured from one or more production

---

[7] See Erwin Hargrove, *The Missing Link: The Study of Implementation of Social Policy*, Urban Institute, Washington, D.C., 1975, p. 28.

departments. Any interferences with their schedules will affect a variety of other departments before and after them in the flow of work. Conceivably, quality control and safety standards will have to be renegotiated to be compatible with the new equipment and its tolerances, as well as production scheduling. Personnel departments may have to develop new training programs and reevaluate jobs. The existence of these "new" jobs will affect existing formal promotion ladders and informal status systems: "Hey, those are cushy new jobs being created over there and, given our seniority, we ought to be able to bid on to them rather than having them go to those junior workers now in that department."

And the problems spread as various routines are interrupted. Each new "infection" will require renegotiations of the manager because past working arrangements have now been interrupted or destroyed.

In this regard it may be useful to review our (Chapter 5) discussion of unstable equilibrium. With any change comes an avalanche of ricocheting requests for aid, modification, delay, speedup, increase, reduction, and so on. Each one sets off a new chain of interdependent renegotiations. All require time and energy, patience and flexibility—all of which are in short supply in a frenetic effort to meet budgets, schedules, and specifications.

In sum, the social organization and habitual work routines support—that is, facilitate, maintain, and serve—existing technology. In contrast, they are likely to be in conflict with or at least inconsistent with new technology and innovations.

Everything we know about employees as individuals and as groups tells us the importance of routine and regularity. Over a period of time, employees stretch and shrink their jobs to fit their personalities, doing a little more of task A because they like it and a little less of B because it's more difficult. Learning how to get extra supplies by conditioning the person in the stockroom to respond to your joking ways and how to avoid the needling of the inspector are just a part of the job.

Impact on Work Groups The same accommodation occurs within the work group when it becomes a tight web interrelating people, tasks, status, informal leadership, work locations, procedures, and everything else. Management always understates how much has to be worked out by the group in order to obtain smooth reciprocities, nonconflicting give-and-take that both encourages productivity and eliminates the interpersonal conflict. It is only when there is change—which destroys these carefully evolved routines (i.e., the teamwork)—that managers appreciate how complex and useful were these informal arrangements which filled in all the cracks left by the incomplete formal requirements.

Just one example may suffice:

A group of analysts shared a common database incorporated in a set of files. When the analysts needed some information they would go to the file, extract it, and then return it when the task was completed. For various reasons, the analyst group was then broken up into separate departments. They became competitive and, no longer trusting one another to take only one file and return it promptly, each was tempted to take extras, particularly ones that were likely to be critical for the day's activities. The analysts also made use of the "special problems" section which was supposed to handle a certain category of problem beyond the capabilities of the regular analysts. Increasingly, as a result of the restructuring and the new competitiveness, more problems were classified as "special problems" and shunted to the other section.

The resulting allocation problems of the files and the crush of work in "special problems" created the need for new staff who would filter, approve, and monitor the use of both files and "special problems" designations. In turn, the analysts questioned the ability of these new people to properly evaluate their work habits and considered the new arrangement both an interference and a blow to their status.

The point of all of this is simply that these work flow problems didn't exist before a change that was designed to solve another difficulty. But work group routines, once cracked, often crumble completely. Then, with an attempt to replace the equanimity comes competition for status and recriminations.

Similar disruptions occur within and between very simple jobs. For example, a major furniture store sought to increase output by breaking up the truckers' jobs—they brought in a dock loader to pack each van, leaving the delivery to the trucker. The results were the opposite of what was anticipated. It was discovered that the truckers had worked out a highly personal and functional method of packing their own trucks so that the furniture was easy to unload along their preferred sequence of stops, given the way they could handle furniture and liked to drive. There were now endless battles between trucker and loader over how to "sandwich in" the furniture.

Change usually violates formal controls, status relations, and informal understandings. An effort to develop a new line of electronic water purification instruments failed to bear fruit because a high-status electronics group would be penalized under the company's profit sharing plan by cooperating with a low-status water treatment division with its notoriously lower margin on sales and its reputation for being inept. Most organizations also have social contracts or informal understandings which are threatened by change. In a large mental hospital, the too-busy psychiatrist had given increased autonomy to the nurses, in exchange for the nurses' assuming the burden of a "custodial," nonrehabilitative culture. Efforts to improve the effectiveness of the hospital ran smack into this unwritten agreement which both doctors and nurses had every incentive to maintain.

Symbolic Issues As routines, status, and reward-punishment systems are violated or threatened, it is likely that a small number of symbolic issues will emerge. These pose profound challenges to managers because symbolic issues are notoriously difficult to resolve. Since they represent so many hidden and otherwise unspoken fears and vested interests and are deceptively simplistic, management finds it difficult to attack them realistically:

> In a major airline undergoing rapid change, a new management sought to get gate personnel to wear red jackets to enable customers to spot them more easily. Resistance was extraordinary. It was asserted that the old jackets were in the traditional color of the airline and the new color was demeaning—"what a bellhop would wear." Management couldn't understand the intensity of the resistance because it failed to recognize that the jackets were simply the symbol of all the anxieties relating to the major changes sweeping through the organization.

A not-too-different problem occurred when a mining company sought to introduce a safer type of explosive. Much to their surprise, the employees complained about it and sought to get the company to continue the use of the traditional explosive. They justified their reluctance to use the material on the grounds that it was difficult to discharge and unreliable. Management was convinced this was simply blind opposition to change.

In actuality, the employees were resentful of the way they had been treated on a number of issues, and the explosives question was just the most convenient to protest. However, mine management had been oversold by the vendor of the new explosive; there were some real problems involving blasting caps. Because of the vehemence of employee resistance, management failed to consider what real technical problems there might be. Only after a number of months were a series of tests undertaken which showed that the employees were partially correct.

This was the same problem we saw with the tile-roofed smelter. Managers detecting employee resistance and inadequate work performance under the new technology are likely to seek *attitudinal* solutions when part of the problem is technical. Because workers are protesting and recalcitrant, managers are likely to assume these are purely emotional difficulties. In fact, the upset created by employee relations problems makes it difficult to work through the technical-level problems systematically.

Dissension and Plundering In the mêlée created by the change process, the upset of routine and the search for new routines, it is always possible for individuals or groups to seek to improve their position at the expense of others. In turn, this effort to exploit the situation further threatens the established status and power system created by work group actions.

Most new ideas have a differential impact on various groups and interests in the organization. Take a simple case of a new product proposed by an executive. Each functional unit will have different requirements for the new product which may well be contradictory:

Sales wants to be sure that the innovation is completed quickly enough to get the product to market and head off competition—and, usually, the lower the price, the better.

Engineering wants a product with exciting, challenging new features that will prove their technical mettle and justify a fairly high price to cover foreseen and unforeseen development costs and contingencies.

Marketing wants simplicity, lots of lead time for tooling up— and the fewer models, the better.

Finance is concerned with building in a profit level that will provide a short enough payback period to justify the initial investment.

These vast differences in starting point assure conflict. When, for example, the marketing group is too specific in what it needs for the marketplace, engineering resents the reduction in its autonomy and creativity; when guidelines are too loose, engineering complains about marketing's "vagueness." On price, engineering is sure to complain that marketing wants "everything for nothing," and engineering is convinced the target price is too low and the time schedule too short.

Here is another example. A large hospital sought to substitute the so-called unit dose system for having inventories of drugs at every nursing station. Under the new procedure each patient would be sent proper medication several times a day via a "cart" prepared by centralized pharmacists. The nurses resented the implications that they were incapable of preparing the right dose and that there had been some stealing of drugs under the old decentralized system. They sought to discredit the new system, which wasn't difficult since during the start-up phase, drug carts failed to arrive in a timely fashion and occasionally individual prescriptions were missing. Even more problematic, the pharmacists used this turmoil to seek greater status and recognition. Here is how the pharmacists viewed the new situation:

> Both doctors and nurses consistently make mistakes in giving patients drugs. In the past, we were in a poor position to monitor prescriptions for a single patient that might be mutually contradictory or incompatible. Also, we were in no position to undertake studies of the efficacy of certain new drugs for specific illnesses. Now we

have much better records on what patients are getting and can seek to stop an inappropriate prescription when we compare it with what the patient is already receiving. We also have both the excuse and the information to justify floor visits to check patient records and improve our studies and service.

Of course, what this head of pharmacy meant was that he wanted to change his status in relation to nurses and doctors. In the past, pharmacists had just been servicing the medical staff; now they wanted to initiate and control. They were using the change as a lever to pry open fixed status relations and then to improve their relative organizational position. The risk they took in turn was that they would become the scapegoats for any inevitable start-up problems.

Management Pressure   Everything we have said about the unanticipated problems in any change—the spread of the impact to many areas of the business not considered, the distress of employees whose routines, values, and status (as well as ease of doing the job) are threatened—all produce pressures on management. The individual managers seeking to implement change are usually the focus. Upper management detects the discrepancy or gap between the overoptimistic expectations and the reality. The larger the shaded area in the graph below, the greater the likelihood of pressure emanating from top management for quicker and better results.

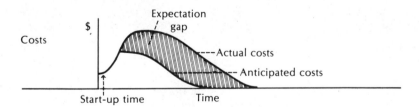

And the reaction to this pressure will illustrate the distinction between leaders and inadequate managers. The typical managers react by transmitting the pressure downward; threatened themselves, nervous about results, they center their efforts on forcing improvements.

Unfortunately, the result is often the opposite of what is intended, not simply because many subordinates resent or resist excessive and threatening coercions, but because of what the change process requires. It requires the evolution of new work methods and routines, often involving individuals and departments who have heretofore been foes or, at the least, strangers. And these new routines can only develop through a process of trial and error requiring permeable group boundaries and job "properties."

These difficult new patterns, establishing reciprocal relationships with former strangers and shifting from an accepted role to a new role—all must often be accomplished at the worst time. Development upsets all of the basic rhythms of an organization, and the inevitable delays, overruns, and unanticipated problems increase management anxieties. As we noted earlier, projected costs and schedule benchmarks are always unduly optimistic. Anticipated savings are less, and learning curves are more stubborn than the sponsors promised.

During this period, many levels of management and their staffs are likely to descend on hapless technicians and operatives while their professional managers are being called "on the carpet" to explain the overruns. Under such pressure, most managers and work groups react with a variety of defenses, almost all of which serve to make communications and trade-offs more difficult and complex. Further, they become less cooperative and less willing to compromise for the sake of another group's technical needs. Thus at a time when quick, mutually helpful interchange is most called for, the organization induces participants to become tighter and less responsive. Secrecy, blaming others, and insisting on "no changes" convert what might have been a reasonably open system to a set of closed subsystems.

It is not unusual to observe that sound innovations get killed off during this period when they are most vulnerable.

Employee Pressure In addition to pressures coming down from upper management, managers seeking to implement change are buffeted by their own subordinates. A predictable reaction to stress, anxiety, and uncertainty is complaint. As management seeks to initiate more to subordinates (with the added quantity of direction and persuasion required by the new

jobs, the absence of automatic routines, and the constant unforeseen problems), the employees seek to maintain some equilibrium by initiating more themselves. To be sure, some of this
increased interaction takes the form of in-group grousing and
rumor mongering, but there is also likely to be a large measure
of complaining up the line:

"There is no room for our personal belongings in the new
work area."
"My new office is too hot [or noisy or cold]."
"I need more time for make-ready on the changed job."
"The rates have to be higher."
"I can't work with that other department."

All this times time and energy and is additional pressure on
managers.

Thus, as we said at the outset, many managers, having experienced this endless grief, forswear a leadership role, ignore
the need for change, and opt for the status quo. Of course, in
doing so they doom their organizations to increasing irrele-
vancy and maladaptation.

But knowing the problems provides leaders with the means
of introducing change. We now turn to that more positive side.

LEADERSHIP IN CHANGE

In part, the best advice to be given managers who anticipate undertaking major change is to anticipate—that is, be realistic
about the euphoria often associated with new ideas, the bias toward overoptimism. Recognize the costliness associated with
disrupting the fine network of social relations that produces efficiency. But more is needed than this big, cold gulp of realism.
Leadership skills are also critical.

Every Manager a Project Manager

To implement change, managers must be able to tie together elements of the organization often not closely interrelated:

1 Handling subordinate reactions and suggestions
2 Moving back and forth from early plans and designs
through the final use stages

3 Facilitating trade-offs between and among groups when their coordination patterns have been changed or when cooperation is required.

In other words, the change process upsets existing routines, and the solutions require a reworking of nearly all the interfaces and interdependencies. Someone in a position to see the whole and comprehend the implications must "manage" these exchanges. While, obviously, top management or the president has titular responsibility for major changes, there will be many organizational innovations which appear to be of more modest dimension, even to be limited to a single department, which will still spread via the "epidemics" we've described. Here lower-level managers must learn to be project managers.

We use the term "project managers" to describe a role in which managers make rather few decisions but seek to get others to make both timely and relevant decisions—forcing choices and discouraging stalemates. The full dimensions of the project managers' roles will be described in Chapter 10; here we shall just identify these exchanges.

Taking Time and Being Open Managers who want to be change agents must expect to receive many more initiations and to accept many more during the change process. As we noted in the mining example above, some may well incorporate new and useful information—a consideration omitted in the plan, an unforeseen defect—as well as anxieties and anger.

> Many observers of the Japanese success with rapid technological change attribute this to the meticulous, slow working-through of problems. Even assembly line employees are encouraged to look at mock-ups of a new line and work stations and evaluate how well they are likely to work out. Criticisms and suggestions are taken seriously by engineers who seek to incorporate them into final designs. At Sony the first-line production supervisor is also an engineer who can incorporate employee complaints and suggestions into changed procedures.

During the process of change managers need to devote a great deal of time to problem solving and to responding to an admixture of distress, difficulty, and despair. Managers can't expect to distinguish easily between legitimate complaints ("The new process really isn't working"), distress ("I don't expect it to work"), and despair ("It's working, but it's hurting me in some way"). What's needed is time to hear out the protest, to communicate interest in the other person's problems and observations, and then to sort out what is a new factor worthy of investigation and what is simply a human relations problem worthy of supervisory skill.

Thus "participation" needs to be viewed not as a technique for improved feelings, but as a legitimate means of uncovering new information and problems. Subordinates are the closest to the work situation; they can see, firsthand and close up, elements that even experienced managers may ignore or not be aware of. In our earlier cases of the new gauze machine and the metal smelting process, employees complained there were *technical* defects. Management was so convinced this was either malingering or unfamiliarity with new technology that they refused to listen.

While it is indeed psychologically wholesome to be listened to, managers also have good technical reasons for favoring participation.

A city sanitation department sought to improve employee productivity by changing work schedules. The previous schedule had the men working six-day weeks (through Saturday) but, in compensation, receiving periodic three-day weekends (Saturday through Monday). The problem was insufficient personnel on Monday—when garbage accumulation was the greatest. The present system put the smallest crews out on that day. After a consultation with the men and the use of some statistical techniques, it was possible to devise alternative schedules that would be appealing, yet more efficient. (The solution entailed mid-week two-day-off periods—when many recreational events would be less crowded—plus continued Sundays off.)[8]

Integrating Developmental Stages   Left to their own devices, the various groups who contribute to the evolution of change from inception to application will insist on their auton-

[8] Erwin Hargrove, op. cit., p. 30.

omy. They perceive the development process as consisting of a linear progression of stages. Each of these four stages is assumed to be compartmentalized:

I		II		III		IV
Problem definition		Specification		Development		Use
&	$\longrightarrow$	&	$\longrightarrow$	&	$\longrightarrow$	
idea stage		design		trial		

Experienced project managers know that these typical four stages in a development program cannot stay independent of one another. Further, there is no neat, sequential progression from stage I through to stage IV.

The involvement of employees in later development stages is essential to realistic planning; there must be a "user in the loop." And these exchanges cannot be one-time or one-directional, either. It is not enough to have the user or the development group tell the designer or conceiver what it needs. There must be frequent exchange: "What will happen if we try to do it this way," "How will that affect your operations," and "If you can't live with this kind of operation, what do you need to permit you to fulfill that requirement?" The project managers then act as mediator/liaison persons, encouraging trade-offs and acting as honest brokers:

> Jane, if you'll modify that requirement for one week, just long enough to let them run through the new program from beginning to end, I can get the reliability group to both defer their tests and send you some extra personnel. Then, if it just won't work, Bill will be willing to specify a lower input.

Thus managers expect a good deal of back-and-forth trading off; of iteration, as the engineers call it; of trial and error.[9] This is in sharp contrast to the naive belief in meticulously constructed, detailed plans in which all contingencies are thought of in advance by far- and foresighted planner/technicians. Plans evolve

[9] An excellent description of what is sometimes called an "incremental approach" to major change is provided by the case studies of James Quinn, *Strategies for Change*, Irwin, Homewood, Ill., 1980.

and are shaped by real-life experiences and problems. There is just no way that hundreds, if not thousands, of permutations and combinations involved in putting together new systems can be either tested or even anticipated. This is one of the more obvious reasons why new automobiles have "bugs." It's not simply because of inadequate or shoddy test procedures. Just a few new parts that must interact with hundreds of older parts in a vehicle to be driven with countless driving styles—under highly variable road, climate, and maintenance conditions—make for an unpredictable new vehicle.

The change agents work the entire system by keeping in contact with the entire flow, knowing that a problem at one stage has repercussions and requirements at every other stage of the development cycle.

Facilitating Intergroup Relations   Within work flow stages there is a similar need for a liaison role. As we have seen, the various work groups that must utilize the new methods or technology, whose prestige and economic security may be threatened, and who are anxious about being able to master the new techniques are also likely to come under additional management pressures to make the new system work quickly and efficiently. Pressure plus fear induces fixation.

Alert managers seek to buffer their own groups, to restrain their temptation to pass along pressures from upper management for quicker results. The objective is to encourage more openness, not fixation. Under pressure, groups will seek to protect their jurisdictions and habitual routines and will devote their energies to proving the outsider is wrong. Note our previous case of the analysts using common files and a "special problems section." Under pressure, they overtaxed the files and the special section and were unable to develop "workarounds"—compromises or adaptations that would facilitate the operations of the new system.

A project manager's major concern is stalemates that can be costly in time and money and lead to symbolic confrontations, e.g., where group A insists its very existence is threatened by a group B requirement. To avoid this, managers seek quick resolution of intergroup work conflicts; their interest is more in resolution than in whether the solution is technically the very best that might have been developed. For many issues, settlement is better than perfection. Once the issue has become a symbolic confrontation, an inordinate amount of negotiating time will be required to resolve the superficial and underlying issues.

Sensitive to the trigger reactions of upper management regarding the "expectation gap," change-oriented managers thus seek to keep the system moving, to be the metronome, as will be described in Chapter 10.

Project Management Techniques of Change

Change agent managers have a variety of special techniques at their disposal. They can take the following approaches.

1 Seek out quick successes, demonstration projects, and other sources of easy reward for participants. This may entail doing easy parts first, "masterminding" some early successes, and otherwise assuring early and encouraging reinforcement.

2 Take advantage of "natural" occurrences to modify plans. For example, the early departure of a potential dissenter might be a good reason for doing necessary work in that department and delaying work in other departments still led by the "opposition."

3 Where possible, go "with the grain," that is, utilize as much of the status system and social organization as possible. If existing and respected symbols and higher-status people can both continue to occupy critical positions, that's helpful. For example, if an insurance company begins writing a new type of policy that is considered inappropriate, lower-status, and unworthy of this fine old-line company, that new line of insurance should be handled by very prestigious personnel in a high-status location who make use of some of the elements associated with the old-line policies.

This is called "syncretism" by anthropologists: incorporating elements of previously accepted institutions into the new.

4 Emphasize structural modification over "conversion." Managers are tempted to "sell" change on the basis of expected improvements, provision against security, and the real "need" for the change. A better approach is to induce acceptance by changing structural elements: location, controls, division of labor, and the like. For example:

It was very common during the early days of automation to find supervisors resisting the new equipment. Part of the problem stemmed from their inability to cope with the extra time and the absence of employee contacts when the automatic machinery reduced the need for order giving and questions. When supervisory jobs were restructured with other elements to give the supervisors the opportunity to assert themselves and keep busy, much of the resistance to the change disappeared.

In other words, managers learn that behavioral change precedes—not follows—attitudinal change. If subordinates can be induced to adapt their behavior to be consistent with some change, attitudes supportive of that behavior and the change itself will be forthcoming. It is much more difficult to persuade them that they *should* change their behavior.

5   Use ceremony to gain recognition for the profundity and legitimacy of various elements of change. When well handled, these little rituals can arouse supportive emotions and instill an understanding of and respect for new facilities, people, and practices. Ceremonies involve boldly illustrating new relationships by formally introducing, installing, and highlighting that which is new, and dramatizing its relationship to the old:

A new facility was opened by having a formal dedication in which the most respected senior employee "officially" cut the ribbon that opened the door. Speeches stressed the significance of the occasion in relation to the agency's history.

6   Lay the groundwork for change by unfreezing old attitudes as well as encouraging new ones. "Unfreezing" often takes the form of helping people see the inadequacy of current methods. This can be done through:

Data presentations that emphasize the problem—comparative statistics illustrating performance in various units and organizations over time.

The airing, by trusted sources of information, of problems and discrepancies. For example, a well-known public relations firm gained its reputation by tape-recording candid employee comments about the company, which were then played for key officials.

Small-group exposures which encourage individuals to consider what others think of them, and thereby "raise their consciousness."

7 Of course, provide reasonable security, guarantees, and assurances that those involved won't be hurt by the change.

8 Be realistic about length of time required for adaptation. The longer that jobs have gone unchanged, the less experience with new learning, the longer it may take for employees to both unlearn old skills and learn new ones. Remarkably enough, change involving some manual skills may require up to six months of retraining for employees to regain their prior efficiency and ease. What appear to be simple new patterns of coordination may require lengthy learning periods before they become automatic, nontiring routines.

9 Remember how insecure and anxious employees become when they lose their comfortable, assured skills and routines. During the period when they are trying out and learning new skills, they will need substantial security, supervisory reassurance, and a "moratorium" on critical evaluation.

10 Expect to deal with three organizations during change instead of one. Many times, parts of the old organization have to be maintained to assure continuity of output. Managers will be seeking to construct the permanent new organization that will be consistent with the new technology. And, at the same time, there will be an interim organization, often the "pilot plant" or "breadboard" organization, which is necessary to work through the defects and omissions of the original designs.

11 Practice—literally—new patterns of interworker and intergroup coordination just because they are strange and unfamiliar. Project managers must literally rehearse the new production by a variety of techniques which allow employees to self-consciously consider what they should be doing in relation to what others are doing. In other words, each job and activity interface is highlighted, discussed, and tried out—first verbally and then behaviorally, as in a simulated countdown.

Everyone involved cross-questions and challenges the work and plans of their peers in order to smoke out hidden incompatibilities, omissions, or potential troubles. Such conferences become a vigorous forum that provides a rethinking and justification of nearly all prior decisions and procedures. Note that upper-level management cannot conceivably provide this detailed reanalysis—only those who know the details of the system are in a position to question or respond.[10]

Unanticipated Problems It should be instructive to view in close detail the unanticipated implementation problems and the solutions associated with new technologies. As we've seen, innovators overstate the immediacy of the benefits and the degree of "perfection" of the new processes, and understate the costs of moving from development to operations. These understatements can be the product of small-group self-hypnosis (euphoria!), the organization's preference for optimism, and, most importantly, unfamiliarity with something new. It is just impossible to know all of the nuances and all of the operating and maintenance problems of something which has never worked before. (In fact, this is what we mean by "know-how," and why it's so valuable—it's all the unwritten, uncodified practical wisdom which converts good theory into something which works.)

The case that exemplifies all this involved a new antipollution scrubber, designed to remove sulphur from coal smoke and attached to an electric utility's power generation plant.[11] The operating company discovered that it took nearly four years to develop the knack of using what was supposed to be a relatively simple and well-understood process. After installation and start-up, all sorts of problems emerged: leaking, freezing, part failure, buildup of scale. Nineteen of the twenty-seven operators assigned to the new equipment requested a transfer on the grounds that it wasn't workable. Because of the enormous costs involved, the company determined to make it work. This is what it did:

> A newly trained crew of fifty-one was given to a manager with a reputation for handling difficult jobs. New protective devices were installed to protect the operating units from snow and

[10] See Quinn, op. cit.

[11] The data were reported in the *Wall Street Journal*, June 14, 1977, p. 1, and grew out of the experience of Kansas City Power and Light with a wet limestone scrubber.

sleet. Many of the fans and pumps were clad with stainless steel to resist corrosion. In other places acid-resistant paint was applied. New procedures were developed to control the acidity of the "slurry" so that the scrubber wouldn't get fouled with scale. (Management notes that it took three years just to develop this knowledge about the effect of acidity on scale and the technique for coping with it.) Finally an additional maintenance step was instituted: each night one of the eight scrubber units was closed down and flushed out with high-powered hoses.

As a result of all of these new procedures, plus newly designed equipment, the scrubbers now operate at high efficiency, rarely break down, and actually exceed the system's expected performance (removing 99 percent versus the expected 80 percent of sulphur dioxide particulates).

A 36-million-dollar investment many assumed was wasted was converted into a technological success by patient trial and error. Management worked through the implementation "bugs" in the face of massive discouragement with the apparent white elephant that had failed to live up to expected benefits. Rather than handwringing, recriminations, and lawsuits, the company did what any organization must do when it seeks to make a technological change actually work. It systematically worked through all the "bugs" and developed innovative operating procedures:

1 Many parts of the original equipment were inadequate and had to be modified.

2 The anticipated operating procedures and personnel were inadequate; very different procedures were required and a more highly trained, motivated crew.

3 Special maintenance techniques had to be improvised.

In the case of the failed "ordertron" below, it is possible to see, by their absence alone, the many facilitations that a manager should effect during change. The problems and the leadership issues associated with change that we have described previously are illustrated here in this one case. Consider the need for a "champion" who could have guided the ordertron through the dangerous shoals, providing the leadership that would have forestalled the failure.

CASE: A "Simple, Quick" Improvement in Technology

Kriss manufactured a variety of ethical and proprietary drugs sold through drug stores. The sales process was straightforward: orders were mailed to a central sales office, which in turn sent copies of the orders to the appropriate decentralized warehouse for shipment to the customer. But it was an inefficient system. For years sales had complained that relationships were injured and customers and commissions lost because of late deliveries.

To satisfy the legitimate complaints and facilitate a shorter response time, the company purchased an electronic device (an "ordertron") that allowed sales personnel to access distribution's warehouses directly. The new system seemed simplicity itself—and was greeted with enthusiasm by everyone in sales as a long-overdue improvement. At the retail outlet the salesperson would enter into the device the item code number, the quantity requested, and the customer code number. At some point during the day the salesperson would then call a special number at the nearest warehouse and place the ordertron over the phone's mouthpiece. The ordertron would then "down-load" the accumulated data into the phone line, and the order would appear on a printout in the warehouse. This printout would be used to fill orders and prepare invoices.

The first problems to appear were trivial. Some of the very same salespeople who had clamored for the device found difficulty in using it. Sometimes it had to do with using the wrong sequence of instructions or miscoding the product or customer name. (Though internal checks had been built into the software, confusion arose because some products and customers had basically the same number as other customers and products, with only one digit transposed.) Also, the device was fragile and broke easily if mishandled. To make matters worse, a busy signal often greeted the salesperson, whose impatience would build with repeated dialing. (It was discovered only after several months that because of a technical error in installation, the new phone system, which had been specially purchased to receive these orders, did not disconnect when an order throughput was completed. In effect, the phone did not "know" when more data were forthcoming from any given sales call.)

Gradually more serious problems emerged. Under the previous system, the written order arrived in a sales office, not in distribution. Sales had a weekly updated inventory list and could choose the appropriate warehouse, one not in an "out-of-stock" position, for relevant parts of the order. Although it was not according to the rules, experienced order editors had taken to breaking up orders among warehouses so as to get the total order filled as quickly as possible. These same order editors also caught mistakes in product codes since the name *and* number appeared juxtaposed on the written order. Through all of this, informal relations had developed between some of the order editors and the more experienced sales staff. When an important customer demanded quick delivery of a critical drug, the order editor knew how to override the system to expedite an order that might mean the difference between keeping and losing a big customer.

But with the new system there was no longer anyone in sales with contacts in distribution, and there was no way of getting special treatment for special customers. As the sales staff began to experience these phone-line problems, misdeliveries caused by inaccurate code numbers, equipment failures, and the new system's inflexibility, they grew more and more discouraged with the new devices. Many flatly refused to use them, telephoned the appropriate distribution center directly, and sought to get a staff member there to take a verbal order. (Interestingly, it was the longer-service and more prestigious sales personnel who first began to revert to verbal contacts instead of using the electronic device.) The distribution staff quickly felt overwhelmed by this influx of voice orders and sought to discourage the practice except for "emergencies." This led to a series of confrontations between sales and distribution. Sales staff complained to their sales supervisors of rudeness, of even being cut off by distribution. Distribution personnel complained to their supervisors as well, and a series of higher-level meetings was held to try to sort out who was causing what and what could be done about it.

At these meetings another issue arose. Sales didn't want its field staff in contact with nonsales personnel. Many of the field staff were experienced, highly valuable representatives of the company, with contacts and skills that were much sought after by competition. They expected to be treated courteously and even catered to. They also felt that there was information from the field that was being lost with this new sales distribution link. Salespeople were less likely now to pass on questions and observations to their order editor, where in the past, district sales managers had periodically interviewed order editors to pick up fast-breaking trends in the field.

Order editors, of course, were especially aggrieved. While the job sounded mundane—and in many ways it was—frequent contact with field staff gave these people a great deal of informal training in broader areas of the business. Over the years, many order editors had gone on to higher-level positions in sales, particularly staff positions. This career line was now threatened.

Several of the sales staff quit in that first tumultuous six months. It wasn't clear whether the turnover was due to frustration with the new technology or to an unanticipated number of tense confrontations between field sales staff and their managers. Essentially, what was happening was that field salespeople were calling their managers to complain about the ordertron. The managers had less time to talk with them and to express empathy with their problems because the total volume of such calls was increasing exponentially even as the managers gave more and more time to dealing with the new frictions with distribution.

The controller's office even got involved. Under the old system, order editors had a list of bad credit risks, stores that were more than ninety days behind in their payments, and orders from these customers could be intercepted. When it was proposed that similar lists be sent to the distribution centers, sales balked. Experienced order editors knew that such lists were often outdated even when they first appeared and that occasionally a truly good customer would get behind. After checking with one or another sales manager, order editors would sometimes allow orders from such customers to go through even when, in theory, they should have been blocked, and credit losses had not been significant under this practice.

About this time, top management got involved. They had made the decision to convert to the ordertron because they had been told by their systems group that, for an expenditure of about $100,000 on this modest new technology that promised faster deliveries and greater customer satisfaction, they could expect a 10 percent sales gain *almost immediately*. Not only had the increase failed to appear, they were now burdened with a new conflict between sales and distribution.

Then sales began to demand that all orders under the ordertron system come into a sales office first. This would have a number of advantages. Mistakes could be caught and/or the salesperson called back to verify information. There would be an opportunity to break up the order so as to use the inventory of multiple distribution centers. And they could continue their use of special treatment for important customers.

Distribution was adamant that this shouldn't occur. Using multiple warehouses for shipments to a single customer raised distribution costs and came out of distribution budgets. The so-called overrides for special customers caused still more additional expenses. Now that they had experienced full control of customer orders, they had no intention of relinquishing this source of improved efficiency and going back to having low-status sales order editors initiate to them.

Given the conflict and poor results, the head of the operating division wrote a strong memo saying that he wanted the ordertron system working within thirty days or thrown out. This ramified through the entire organization, with supervisors becoming more demanding and subordinates more frustrated. Morale plummeted as everyone sought to find someone else to blame for the unanticipated difficulties.

About seven months after the "roll out" of the much heralded ordertron, the VP for sales at Kriss announced that its use was being discontinued, "given a variety of technical problems with its operation." Senior management in distribution immediately complained that they had not been consulted about the discontinuance and that the ordertron was both useful and necessary, given "a number of organizational changes we have made to take advantage of the potential for new efficiencies created by its development." The VP for sales then wrote a memo for broad distribution, indicating that after further study, hoped-for hardware improvements, and reevaluation, it was possible that ordertron would be used by his personnel sometime in the future. Most people in sales familiar with the experience doubted that ordertron would ever be reborn.

Unanticipated Opportunities During implementation it is easy to emphasize catastrophes—all the things that can go wrong. But nature is not always unkind, nor is fate always ill-tempered. Just as "hanging loose" provides the ability to cope with unanticipated problems, such an approach also provides the ability to take advantage of unforeseen opportunities.

In the United States space program, satellites sometimes perform better than anticipated. Rapid reprogramming allows NASA to add new tasks, to extend missions, and to take advantage of chance natural phenomena—ripe for exploration—encountered by orbiting spacecraft.

A public utility, to save costs, merged a number of managerial districts. The original plan specified that the change would not be fully implemented for two years to allow existing district managers to be placed in other positions. Much to management's surprise, many district managers, when they learned their units were to be eliminated, retired, quit, or asked to be replaced. By taking advantage of this, the cost savings anticipated by the reorganization could be realized much sooner than expected.

CONCLUSIONS

Change is an integral requirement of every manager's job at every level. Most managers are inhibited in exercising leadership in this area by, on the one hand, misinformation (or myths) about change and, on the other hand, sad experience. The myths concern the degree to which our organizations in fact encourage and are comfortable with change and the eagerness of managers in contrast to the reluctance of workers. In reality, most organizations and their managers inhibit change as much as do fearful workers.

Managers who are unsuccessful at change look for someone to blame: the faulty plan, the lazy workers, the treachery of another department. They are angry, litigious, and highly unrealistic in their expectations. Rather than expecting to persevere in working through problems with all of the relevant parts of the system, they seek to "bull it through" or find the culprit. "If I bought it, it must be right" is clearly wrong!

Perhaps most importantly, managers have to come to accept the fact that change is difficult; the problems are not primarily of communication, personality, and irrationality, but of substance. The most important of these is the destruction of vital routines that are, simultaneously, the source of personal effectiveness and organizational efficiency.

Naive managers expect that most of their investment in change will come in the planning stage and in convincing others to accept the change. (The "others" are usually "users" and subordinates.) In reality, most of their time and dollars will be devoted to *implementation*, not planning and selling. The early stages of the development cycle take the smaller proportion of time. Working through the implications, working the lateral interfaces, coping with unanticipated "bugs"—all these consume the major proportion of time and resources that the project will cost.

Change requires both extensive and intensive participation by managers who must learn the role of project managers: depending on others for technical assessments and holding a diffuse organizational system together long enough to allow for vital reciprocal accommodations.

10

THE SKILLS OF THE PROJECT MANAGER

Organizations have increasingly made use of a special kind of managerial role in the change process: project management. *Fortune* reported that General Motors credits the effectiveness with which it downsized its major car lines to the use of "this important managerial tool."

> [This] was probably GM's single most important managerial tool in carrying out that bold decision. . . . Its success, however, rests on the same delicate balance between the powers of persuasion and coercion that underlies GM's basic system of coordinated decentralization. "We become masters of diplomacy," says Edward Mertz, assistant chief engineer at Pontiac, who was manager of the now-disbanded A-body project center.[1]

---

[1] *Fortune*, January 16, 1978, p. 96. One of the most famous descriptions of successful project management is Tracy Kidder's *The Soul of a New Machine* (Little, Brown, Boston, 1981), which describes a remarkable effort to create a new computer. A wide-ranging description of line managers who assumed responsibility for pushing organizational innovations and new products is found in Rosabeth Kanter, *The Change Masters*, Simon and Schuster, New York, 1983.

Research and development organizations, of course, have made use of project managers for years. Increasingly, however, this kind of special managerial position is being created in other kinds of organizations—wherever top management wants someone to shepherd through a new fixed-life program, a project manager is a good candidate. This role poses some special leadership challenges. The two most critical are: (1) many of the resources necessary to fulfill the assignment are controlled by other managers, and (2) to make matters worse, in most cases the project manager will have but a small proportion of the technical knowledge necessary to make important decisions when the inevitable unanticipated technical problems of implementation arise.

WHY USE PROJECT MANAGEMENT?

Some of the reasons for using the project form of organization include:

1   Through the representatives of various departments who work within it, the project helps to disseminate support and understanding of some new venture or process.

2   Because the new activity will impact all of the represented groups, through their new participation on the project they can help make its specifications and functioning consistent with the existing constraints and needs of their parts of the organization. This speeds adaptation.

3   In turn, the project will benefit from the diversity of specialization, background, and experience—an important advantage over developments that grow out of a single group dominated by common values.

4   The routines of the represented groups can continue because the innovation is conducted "outside" by this new, temporary component of the organization.

The project can be the design of a new information system, a new common chassis (as in the previously cited case of GM), the solution of a persisting organization problem, or the creation of a new product. It is a temporary organization that draws on personnel and technical resources from the permanent sectors of the organization, each of which has distinctive routines and interests.

Peter Drucker presents a convincing case that future organizations will be information-based and have fewer hierarchical levels and fewer staff specialists to advise top management. Instead the "real" work of the organization will be done by highly trained specialists working at operating levels in temporary teams and task forces seeking to design and implement new products, services, and methods.[2] Clearly the skills of project leadership will be increasingly important.

Facilitating Change

Of course, these are the intrinsic problems of introducing change that we discussed in the previous chapter. Change inevitably impacts a broad segment of an organization and creates many unanticipated technical problems that threaten ongoing operations as well as the success of the new activity. No single manager comprehends all the ramifications of existing processes and the consequences of modifying the original plans and specifications. The sensible organization utilizes project managers to cope with the vagaries and challenges of the change process. How such leaders operate in a world filled with unknowns and outsiders is the subject of this chapter.

Whenever an organization, community, or agency seeks to get a new job done *without* changing its basic structure or division of labor (that is, without creating new jobs and lines of authority), it typically establishes a project, task force, or working group to complete this time-bounded activity. This is in sharp contrast to traditional managerial thought. In scientific management, a job assignment implies the creation of specific organizational slots under the direct control of bosses who have authority and resources commensurate with the responsibility given to them. Projects and the project managers run in a very different direction: clear responsibilities are assigned to get some critical task accomplished, but most of the resources are left where they are—in other people's departments.

The major impediment to implementing change is the shock and disruption to the ongoing routines necessary to achieve reasonable efficiency. Each impacted department finds count-

[2] Peter Drucker, "The Coming of the New Organization," *Harvard Business Review*, vol. 66, no. 1, January–February 1988, pp. 45–53.

less unanticipated costs of adaptation. A sponsor-facilitator exerting encouragement and pressure is essential if the innovation is not to flounder because one department or another finds it easier to slip back to its more comfortable and successful past routines. Further, the facilitator often acts as a broker to resolve stalemates—where one department can't cope with the innovation because another department isn't adjusting and refuses to make concessions until still a third department modifies its procedures. And the third group, in turn, is likely to be dependent on some concession from the first group. Such circularity and interdependence require the energetic intervention of an independent "honest broker" who wants the innovation to succeed and who can identify and help resolve the inevitable stalemates.

Both in government and in business we see an increasing need for people who can influence the decisions of widely diversified groups with disparate objectives—influence them toward consistency with some otherwise elusive and easily ignored goals. But influencing groups to work toward this new goal can be a difficult task for several reasons:

1   The goal involved might appear to be less immediate, relevant, or powerful than other goals and internal constraints.

2   Groups may believe that other units in the system have more to gain than they have.

3   Groups may be wary of making costly concessions when these might well be nullified by a more intractable unit.

4   Groups may not believe or trust the information suggesting that their present behavior is injuring the larger goal or that a change will facilitate its accomplishment.

The Role of the Project Manager

Project managers thus have a very different supervisory challenge: getting work done through outsiders. As we shall see, this requires rather unique skills and a theory of management that differs from traditional supervision. The emphasis is on monitoring and influencing decisions, not order giving and decision making in the usual meaning of those terms. The project managers have overwhelmingly more responsibility than they have authority. The groups and employees they will be dealing with not only work for other departments and functions which have their primary loyalties, but they have performance standards, built up over many years, that are consistent with these affiliations (although perhaps inconsistent with the special needs of the limited-life project). Project managers have the job of finding ways of correlating the outsider's standards of performance and the needs of the project in terms of cost, schedule, and performance standards.

Project Inception

Most projects begin when upper management creates project offices, assigns project managers, and gives them a budget which allows them to purchase "contributions" from outside departments. Even with this budget, project managers may still have to woo and win reluctant line managers—line managers who will question whether they should assign their better people and resources to the project, particularly if there are other project managers shopping for these human and technical resources. Line managers can be skeptical about the feasibility and prestige of a specific project. One such manager explained:

> I tried to keep most of our people off the X project even though it was reasonably well funded. I knew it was the kind of project that headquarters could cut off tomorrow, and then we would have all those disappointed engineers to reassign, people who have just gotten all excited about the work and then have to do something else. This creates serious morale problems, and I try to get my people projects that have a real chance of going down to the wire.

The critical skills for project inception can best be viewed when upper management is either undecided or ambiguous about a project or is allowing lower levels of management to initiate some new projects. Under these circumstances, the development and success of projects that will be funded, that will "fly," depend upon the selling ability of the would-be project managers. Those who are successful in this entrepreneurial function—really in starting a new business, albeit with a short life expectancy—can generate enthusiasm and confidence in other managers who can give the new project political and economic support. Here is how one successful project manager described the start-up function:

> I had gotten the green light from my boss to try to get support for a special computer project, which would develop a technique for let-

ting our large computer handle a great deal of the test work we now do manually. First I got every department head or a deputy to come to a meeting. There my function was to get everyone to agree, first, that we had a problem with our current test procedures and, second, on what kind of procedure would cope with these problems. I then tried to generate enthusiasm for the solution: this computerization project. This meant showing people that they would be in heaven if we could pull it off and that everyone would benefit. Of course, I wasn't above a little logrolling either, indicating I would back them on some things they needed. I also tried to play up the losses for those who stayed out. You find after a while, when you keep talking something like this up, the enthusiasm can become contagious, and they'll convince one another.

Often the charismatic entrepreneurs who get new projects off the ground resemble evangelists. They have so much faith in their special project, its workability, and its long-run value that they can convince doubting Thomases with all the vigor of the good pitchmen of old. It is not unusual to find that such zealots are hard on subordinates. They are loath to delegate and keep making all the technical decisions themselves, perhaps partially because, in the early stages, they are the only ones who see the big picture, the grand design or conception.

But such single-minded convictions—such strong desires to clutch everything tightly to themselves—are inconsistent with the needs of running an established and funded project. It is the special managerial skill—the ability to push a project through outside technical support and line departments—that is our primary interest in this chapter. This skill and related ones come into play after the promoters or major organizational supporters have won the battle of getting the project accepted. (At that point the originators may have trouble adjusting as they see their baby growing larger and being reared by strangers.)

KEEPING TIME

Although it is rarely stated this way, program or project managers are dealing primarily with time and organizational process. They cannot easily second-guess the technical prowess of their line-support groups. Obviously, they and their staffs often do or try to, but in the long run they are dependent upon both the goodwill and the technical judgment of the outside groups.

This means that they must respect the professional expertise of these groups even when seeking to negotiate change.

Balancing Time and Process

What project managers can and must do is control the organizational participation—as distinct from the technical contribution—of the line or functional people. This means making sure that they cooperate in two very important ways:

1   The project manager must induce the line manager to make the right decisions at the right time. For example, the line manager may want to study some problem extensively to arrive at an optimal solution, but the delay in making the decision may be much more costly than any increase in return generated by the improved decision. Of course, the opposite may be true. The program manager may want to encourage longer study of some issue that has profound "downstream" significance beyond the particular line manager's field of vision.

2   The project manager must encourage the line manager to tackle problems in the right sequence and the right time. Line managers may be willing to tolerate a certain problem buildup, e.g., in schedule delay or labor relations, that might be disastrous to the program. Program managers will pressure them to respond adequately to these "out-of-limit" situations and give them a priority based on program needs—even though such a step may be inconsistent with the management style or the managerial appraisal of the line managers.

It is this balancing act, resulting in technical decisions which reflect organizational considerations, that require most of the program manager's time and influence. A nice example is furnished by one small aspect of a large area project.

On a construction job, fire prevention equipment was being installed, and the safety and equipment people were intending to use their usual criterion in design and installation. Traditionally, this was that every effort must be made to design a system which was *sure* to function in an emergency. From the project management point of view, in this particular location it was more important that the prime criterion for design and installation be that the system *not* function unless there was an emergency. This would have a major influence on such technical considerations as redundancy in circuits.

Project managers act in the role of *marginalists*. They widen or narrow limits, speed up or slow down actions, increase the emphasis on some activities and decrease it on others. They can't make very many of the decisions themselves—both because of time and because they are not empowered to do so. That power resides in the line and functional groups, in most cases. Further, they wouldn't want to make the major decisions, since they usually can't know as much about the problem as someone closer to the work level. They chiefly want to be sure that the decision is made at the proper time, within the proper framework of knowledge and concern, and by the proper people.

But project managers must often seek to counter inherent conservatism, particularly when some managers, by "playing it safe," increase the risk for the total effort. Managers may wish to build only familiar hardware, use only well-known components or traditional standards, or "gold-plate" their contribution—approaches which, in terms of time, dollars, and performance, may be destructive to the specific project at hand.

Project managers function as bandleaders who pull together their players, each a specialist with individual scores and internal rhythm. Under the leaders' direction, they all respond to the same beat. To get people to adhere to their operational rhythm, managers make them see the consequences of their actions. In bringing the work of the various groups to their centralized beat, they may also seek to change their interplay. The project may require, for example, that group A now report to boss B instead of boss A; that group A be consulted earlier or more frequently; or that group A give its consent before x, y, and z are done. Such shifts in organizational relationships change the character of the response that any group will give to emerging problems and directions.

Project Management versus Traditional Management

Professional employees and their managers are supposed to be left alone to sink or swim—as long as they appear to be motivated to meet their self-determined (in part) objectives. But project managers must constantly try to penetrate the functional and technical groups upon whom they are dependent.

Alice Fine got concerned that costs were mounting and exceeding estimates. She sought explanations and justifications for the hardware specifications of the major design groups. She noted one item that represented a large sum for "special cabling." When she pushed the engineer who was responsible for that, he said that his group "always specified cabling with extra-thick insulation," though such cabling required both a special order and a premium price. Further discussion revealed that the extra thickness was an engineering norm that had developed some years before when much of the engineers' work had involved designing equipment for highly adverse environmental circumstances. Those conditions did *not* relate to this project at all. The engineer had made an automatic decision to use what his group usually used, not what was required by Fine's project. She pressured to get the specification reviewed.

Project managers must often get into the minutiae of decision processes to judge whether the desired system is being maintained (for example, whether adequate weight is being given to *x* factor, adequate consultation is taken with A group, the sign-offs are procured promptly from B group, or the appropriate appeals channels and conflict-resolution procedures are being used when stalemates appear). Time is of the essence and constant monitoring is the rule. Project managers must know *whom to contact*, *when*, and *how*.

BEHAVIORAL SKILLS OF THE PROJECT MANAGER

If you watch these managers, you see them engaged in a ceaseless round of give-and-take. They appear to be trying, by the weight of various influence techniques, to counter the frictional forces and fatal drift in the human systems—forces that lead workers and groups to go back to comfortable routines.

Bargaining

Project managers prefer to spend a great deal of time negotiating. In part, this is due to the continual appearance of unanticipated problems or opportunities. "What will it cost us to avoid this or take advantage of that?" the manager may ask when dealing with a technical department. And part is due to inevitable differences in judgment. "I don't care what the tests show; I am sure we can get by with the extra five pounds, or at least that's what I am going to try to get approved." There are the individual differences in objectives. A subcontractor wants to use a manufacturing method in which he has an interest, but the prime contractor is fearful that this variation may upset an already tight schedule.

In addition, there are the foibles of organizational life. Estimates, specifications, and requests tend to have "fat" in them, because everyone believes they are going to get less than they ask for.

What we learn by watching project managers is that words don't mean what they seem to mean, that agreements can easily be misunderstood or ambiguous, that no agreement ever covers all the unanticipated contingencies, that temptations arise to lure committed people to take chances which they would not risk under less pressure or with less provocation— and many other factors that, if ignored, can sabotage the best-laid plans.

Managers know there often are no precise, rational answers to most questions, whatever their source, but that the answers are a product of flexible give-and-take.

Coaching

In many ways, project managers are more like coaches than supervisors: they exhort, urge, cajole, browbeat, and pressure. By their very presence—their personal intervention and force of personality, their talking, pleading, and demanding—they try to counteract the various frictions that would slow down or misdirect the activities of other groups.

As in life itself, complex projects produce a variety of oppressive frustrations as well as destructive temptations. When parts shortages appear, facilities are not available, or parallel activities (under others' control) are slowed down, everyone tends to relax, to wait, to take a somewhat easier way out. Like an ever-present conscience, effective project managers urge key people to keep fighting, to keep pushing against time, to pretend that everyone else will be on time, to seek equally satisfactory alternatives when the original plans are no longer feasible.

The pressuring includes keeping people from falling back on old, familiar routines and ways of doing business. The project often requires nonstandardized approaches that may be inconsistent with habitual patterns and methods for any particular organization or group. "We never do it this way" has to be a call to arms for project managers. Sometimes their problem is that the functional group wants to "gold-plate" something, to overprotect or overtest. Or the opposite may be the case: the group is taking shortcuts, conducting inadequate tests.

Confronting and Challenging

One of the techniques most often used in deterring backsliding is deceptively simple and direct. Project managers confront and challenge, raising questions like these:

"What makes you think that those bearings are comparable to the ones we discussed last week?"

"What is your evidence that this redesign is likely to solve the problem? Prove it to me."

"What have you done to correct the malfunctioning that showed up on the special test we agreed upon?"

"Can you expect to catch up on the lost time when you haven't authorized overtime and there is no additional staffing?"

The project staff is in the position of trying to get those people with whom it works to justify their present course of actions, their decisions, and their choices. It is one thing to do something which seems reasonable to you under the circumstances—it is another to try to prove or rationalize your act to an inquiring, reasonably well-informed, and potentially critical observer.

The challenge is a process used by project managers to force people to face up to unpleasant realities. It is a technique of supplying the constant stimulus of a friendly critic who will demand answers to a somewhat unpredictable set of potentially embarrassing questions. Telephone calls, visits, and regular meetings are used for the purpose.

The confrontation process also visibly demonstrates and reminds people that the project managers are vitally interested, alert, and aware that everything is open to question. This is consistent with the unusual potential for problems inherent in complex endeavors, where hundreds, if not thousands, of variables interact and where problems are inevitable, although you can never be sure where and how they will appear.

Intervention and Participation

Many of the behavior problems we have been describing have both before-the-fact and after-the-fact qualities. Project managers are seeking to avoid problems or to solve problems. And they also play a more immediate, real-time role.

In working to maintain a forward momentum, managers attempt to avoid stalemates, polarization of issues, and entrenchment of vested interests. Fluidity and movement, accommodation, solving problems rather than assessing blame—all these are part of the distinctive point of view of program management.

To demonstrate concern, as well as to get a feel for what is happening and for the many facets that cannot be documented or transmitted in either verbal or written reports, project managers appear on the scene. During crucial tests, for example, many managers want to be present to observe as much as possible themselves.

Project managers also have the job of keeping things moving by maintaining a consensus, jelling decisions, and resolving holdups when those immediately involved are unwilling or unable to do so. In this regard, they will often be faced with conflicting technical judgments. It is difficult to decide who among a group of conscientious experts is correct. While managers may feel obliged to suffer through this kind of choice, it is not realistic under most circumstances to try to prove who is right.

It's more important that a decision be reached so that forward momentum can be resumed. Insecure, risk-fearing managers fret and fume so long over such decisions that, regardless of who is right, it is too late to avoid schedule delays. First and foremost, then, project managers want to force a choice when indecision may delay their work. Their own dispassionate position, somewhat removed from the battlefront, may aid this resolution—as do their prestige and force of personality. Furthermore, their intervention is also a means of gaining familiarity and a feel for the real situation, and of keeping in touch with technical realities.

Indirection versus Orders

Thus, in contrast to direct supervision, there is comparatively little ordering in the relationship between project managers and the outside groups and individuals they seek to influence. There are many reasons for this, aside from the fact that the groups and individuals are not immediate subordinates.

For one thing, orders may raise legalistic questions like "Is this a change in our original commitment? Who is to pay for the change?" They also encourage a similar rigidity based on an opposite reaction: "No, we can't do it; this is our only choice under the present circumstances."

Further, project managers often lack the information needed to give a specific order. They are never as close to the situation as the individual immediately responsible, and must therefore trust the specialist. On the other hand, they may have broader knowledge than the technical expert has (for example, concerning other parts of the system or external pressures). By sharing this knowledge, managers can often help the specialist do a better job.

The heart of both intervention and decision making is quickness of response—the focusing of collective energies on the solution of a very critical problem. Given the many unanticipated barriers to working through original plans, the interdependencies (which multiply the impact of any holdup) and the ever-present schedule problems of fighting time, managers must be capable of rapid adaptation to changed circumstances. Sometimes rules must be violated and established procedures ignored.

In fact, many effective managers insist that they can't wait for a problem to make itself known officially. Anticipating trouble requires very close contact—keeping in touch with the thinking and the planning of the key participants. Daily or twice-daily calls, weekly visits, and bimonthly meetings are therefore par for the course.

Because a good many situations allow for corrective action

only during a brief "window," quick action is the essence of the problem. Slow response can lead to costly mistakes, a lost customer, a missed opportunity.

In these circumstances, project managers and their associates talk to people face to face and on the telephone almost constantly, checking out the new requirements and exploring the feasibility of possible changes. Decisions require enormous quantities of interaction!

Distancing

Perhaps the hardest thing managers must often do is *nothing*. Seeing a potentially upsetting problem and not attempting to rearrange its components so that it is attacked differently or more massively takes great restraint. Project managers must learn when to slow things down as well as when to force faster action.

Experienced, astute managers know when to let the other person have the time to work through the difficulty and when it is necessary to intervene, urge reinforcements, insist on a different approach, and the like. Not only is moving in too early costly and disrupting, it also wastes the distinctive capacities of the support group handling the problem.

Staying aloof for an appropriate time also provides perspective which may be lost when one becomes personally involved in the emotional effort of struggling to solve recalcitrant problems. Surely many of the truly costly mistakes in any large program are the result of overlooking rather obvious trends.

In a sense, project managers want to play both sides of the street, to be outsiders as well as insiders, dispassionate observers as well as accepted members of the team.

Providing Assistance

Project managers need to balance pressure with aid. They often have priority access to scarce external resources (in effect, acting as expediters), or at least to resources beyond the organizational reach of line or functional managers. They can serve as "honest brokers," bringing together conflicting groups of factions.

Using Meetings

Some meetings are useful for the same reason that managers prefer to confront subordinates directly rather than by mail or telephone. Where groups are interdependent and risks are substantial, management hopes that face-to-face questioning will dispel doubts and answer nagging worries, such as the question of whether the other person is working in a way that will wreak havoc on one's own budget, schedule, or performance.

Clearly, even among like-minded professionals who share a common language and respect for technical approaches, the data are not always self-evident. There will always be innumerable ambiguities and questions that cannot be answered definitively except in face-to-face meetings.

Meetings also impart a sense of personal participation, of seeing and comprehending with one's own senses without having to use intermediary people, paper, or data. Moreover, meetings help to dispel the doubts that arise in any system where artificial barriers separate people, doubts about whether information or unpleasant facts are being hidden.

Thus various techniques involving direct confrontation are useful in imparting reassurance and dispelling fears that a disagreeable surprise may come tomorrow, although everything looks rosy today. Being personally involved and allowed to hear firsthand progress reports, status reviews, and debates concerning alternative approaches demonstrates that one is an accepted member of the team. On the opposite side, exclusion from these get-togethers communicates second-class membership: "They only call on us when there are troubles, when we've done something wrong, or when they're looking for a scapegoat."

Handling Different Groups

Project managers have to learn how to structure and handle different kinds of groups, depending on the nature of the problem being confronted. One text makes these recommendations.[3]

---

[3] Harold Leavitt et al., *The Organizational World*, Harcourt, New York, 1973.

1 If the problem is complex, poorly specified, the manager should encourage free communications, open challenges, and criticisms among the members.

2 However, if the problem calls for imaginative and unusual solutions, criticism should be discouraged.

3 If the problem involves sensitive issues that divide the group, leave lots of time to work through the difficulties, and, if possible, get people away from their usual work site.

4 Where time is critical, keep the group small and tightly structure the meeting; force rapid movement and decision on agenda items.

5 Where coordination is critical, make sure that all decisions reached by the group are spelled out in great detail; have all affected individuals restate their interpretation of all agreements that have been reached; and seek to identify any inconsistencies or ambiguities.

Ensuring Coordination

Of course, the most important and most frequent use of meetings is to provide technical coordination, to interrelate the work of interdependent groups and individuals. Such meetings review progress and plans and try to evolve solutions to actual or foreseeable problems. Plans for future activities and problem solution, when handled successfully, take the following operational form:

What is needed, wrong, or foreseen. ("We are going to require additional backup teleprinting equipment.")

Who is responsible for taking what actions, utilizing what decision-making criteria with *whom, when,* and *where.* (Through group discussion, an implementing procedure is worked out, and the persons responsible for specific actions are explicitly named.)

How to track the project. Arrangements are made for the organizational process by which the completion and effectiveness of the program can be validated and for the time and method for reporting this validation back to those who need to know. ("We'll put this down as an action item, to be reported back at our next meeting by Smith and Brown, who have agreed to meet within seventy-two hours to check out the new equipment.")

At these meetings, individuals find ways of expressing both their concern and their anxiety, and such open expressions fill a very important function. Thus one hears comments like "I want to reemphasize our very real concern that the existing reinforcing may be inadequate," or "While I know you are doing all you can to speed things up, we want to underline how important an earlier delivery date would be to solving our schedule problems." Many times, the same underlying problem is dealt with by multiple questions that endeavor to ensure that things really are going well.

PRODUCT AND BRAND MANAGERS

Very similar to their shorter-lived counterparts are product or brand managers who seek to influence other departments to foster their particular soap or cereal. They too cut across the "grain" of the organization, not to introduce a one-time change, but to further their product's interests in competition with other products.

All the company's products may be competing for the same marketing and manufacturing facilities. For example, a product manager will endeavor to persuade manufacturing—and packaging and advertising as well—to tailor its normal activities to meet the special overall needs of his particular product. To permit such managers to do this, top management usually gives them certain stabilization powers: they may have the power to approve functional budgets or plans for new facilities, work schedules, or final specifications. Let's look at an example.

CASE: Getting It All Together

Ellen Fisher is a product manager responsible for the introduction of new soap products. She works through several functional departments, including market research, the development laboratory, production, and sales. In designing the new product, market research usually conducts a test of consumer reactions. In this case, the market research head, Frank Fellers, wants to run the standard field test on the new brand in two preselected cities. Ellen is opposed to this because it would delay the product introduction date of September 1; if that date can be met, sales has promised to obtain a major chain-store customer (using a house-brand label) whose existing contract for this type of soap is about to expire.

At the same time, manufacturing is resisting a commitment to fill this large order by the date sales established because "new-product introductions have to be carefully meshed in our schedule with other products our facilities are producing. We aren't set up to produce overnight one huge order like that after development has okayed the new specifications. It's a three-month, not a three-week, job you're asking us to do."

Ellen's job is to negotiate with market research and manufacturing, assessing how important their technical criteria are, which ones are modifiable, and, overall, what is best for the new product's introduction. A huge, first-time order from an important customer has to be weighed against possible manufacturing delays that could injure other parts of the new product's introduction. Increased validity of more extensive field testing has to be weighed against time and cost factors and the delays already incurred because of development problems. Another factor is that this soap is very similar to one for which complete test results are available.

Of course, these alternatives are not merely weighed in Ellen's head, they are debated in meetings involving her and representatives of all four functional groups. Her goal is to balance the legitimate objections of manufacturing and sales, as she perceives them, against her own need to get the new product off to a flying start. If manufacturing is pressed too far to meet the big order, subsequent delays could hold up the general introduction of the new product. On the other hand, Ellen wants to avoid indecision or a stalemate. If sales or manufacturing proves too obstinate, Ellen can always invoke her stabilization power—but such power must be used sparingly to avoid impairing her future relations with sales and/or manufacturing. And there's always the chance that, pressed too far, sales and manufacturing will go over Ellen's head and appeal up their functional lines.

Product management pits the total work flow concerns of one manager against the technical standards set by functional managers. When all are good managers, the result is constructive compromises and a wholesome exploration of when it is desirable to be unorthodox and bend rules to make exceptions to existing standards.

MATRIX MANAGEMENT

Many product and project managers work within what are called "matrix organizations."[4] In the matrix style, some employees have two bosses, one for their functional specialty and one "systems" manager who is responsible for getting a project completed or maintaining a product's profitability.

Most organizations seek to equate authority with responsibility. Every manager, from first-line supervisor to company president, wants to control the resources needed to achieve his or her predetermined goals. To be sure, modern organizations equivocate on this traditional principle of good management. They have "dotted-line" staff who can wield power equal to that of line managers; outside service groups and vendors who have to be negotiated with rather than ordered about; and a welter of clients, regulators, and community pressure groups who constrain the manager's decision-making autonomy. But the ideal, both for the manager and for the student of good management, is still clear lines of authority backed by resources proportionate to responsibilities. The ideal is compromised, but not forsaken.

Many companies, in fact, tie themselves in semantic knots trying to figure out which of their key groups are "line" and which "staff." Since some versions of traditional management theory permit only one real line operation, the other departments by definition must be staff. This terminology contradicts the obvious power of the so-called staff to control critical resources and to be responsible for important corporate objectives.

By contrast, project and matrix management assumes that plans will have to change because of the inevitably unstable equilibrium in these highly interdependent systems. Given such uncertainty, minor unanticipated problems will lead to major dislocations as their impact is felt throughout the system. These impacts, in turn, require adaptive plans and a constant remaking of the consensus.

In contrast to decentralization that requires new organizations whenever new tasks or goals are conceived, project and matrix management stresses a fixed dynamic balance between

---

[4] For an excellent description of matrix organizations, see Stanley Davis and Paul Lawrence, *Matrix*, Addison-Wesley, Reading, Mass., 1978.

the parts of the organization. It *reuses* old units instead of creating new ones for new goals and problems. It forces organizations to keep changing themselves because of legitimately conflicting goals, values, and priorities and builds instability into the very structure of the organization.

These new organizational forms recognize the necessary and desirable role of both specialization and coordination. Decisions, they assume, cannot be made by a well-programmed computer or small, expert planning groups—not because such approaches are undemocratic or unparticipative, but rather because sensible systems decisions, whenever there is a reasonable amount of technological uncertainty, require the active and continuous involvement of technically qualified, key functional managers.

The trade-offs between unit success through suboptimization of goals versus larger system interests can thus be made in the context of the countervailing forces of project and matrix management. These encourage relevant confrontations over issues whose solutions can't be preplanned or solved by decision models.

The challenging task of coordinating managers is to act as a catalyst—to force accommodation and flexibility, to compel attention to unanticipated and boundary problems, and to achieve a consensus by means of an organized give-and-take between the constituent elements and individuals.

CONCLUSIONS

The modern organization creates a number of specialists whose activities and resources impinge on the managers. Sometimes these groups control scarce services (like repairs, communications, or computational facilities). Sometimes they control scarce "permissions" (like authorization for capital spending or a raise for a key employee). But the result is the same: managers don't control everything they need to get their work done. They must depend upon outsiders; their authority is a good deal less than their responsibilities.

Project management is a more exaggerated form of this reality. Here authority isn't even close to responsibility since most of the resources are located in other people's departments. The managers depend upon employees of other managers to do nearly all their work. To make matters worse, many of these employees are simultaneously working for other managers, and of course they are being supervised by another boss.

Project managers must therefore be skilled in techniques of influencing and persuading others and effective use of meetings. They must be aware that, because of their professional training and identifications, these other employees have different standards as to what constitutes good work. They have different conceptions of cost and schedules, too.

Thus the project manager's function is not to impose his or her own knowledge on others but rather to establish clear-cut limits on their discretion. The project manager seeks to define the constraints which will influence the other's decision making in the desirable direction.

> I keep telling them that we can't afford the best in this project because time is of the essence. We just need a fan that will work for a short period of time where there is extreme heat. It only has to last forty-eight hours, not a lifetime. They would love to design a really great new fan, but they know now they can't.

After constraints are established, the project manager works to keep the project from stagnating or getting hung up on problems. Every project, because by definition it represents a job that's never been done before, is going to meet unanticipated problems. Some can readily be solved. Others may take much more time or money than anyone anticipated. It's up to the project manager to find ways of spotting these holdups, to help work out procedures which will quicken the development of a solution, and to keep people from becoming demoralized or slowing down because they think the schedule will never be met anyway.

These are surely the most difficult and challenging kinds of managerial assignments because project managers can't fall back on power and authority. They use a variety of fast-paced techniques to confront, persuade, cajole, and pressure people to keep their eyes on the critical element and to ignore the noncritical elements. Thus they are catalysts, goads, coxswains—or conductors—who keep the system moving.

As we saw in Chapter 9, the introduction of change in an organization of any complexity unleashes an extraordinary quantity of contradictions and conflicts that had previously been submerged by the evolution of work routines fostered by informal collaborations. Once the "spell is broken" by the need to renegotiate the "who does what with whom, when, where, and how often," the organization shows its inherent instability. There are usually just too many interdependencies for simple planning and management alertness to resolve. Thus the project manager's role, which provides central direction and decentralized problem solving, is essential to avoid destructive stalemates and battles over who should dominate and who is right.

We have spoken before of working interfaces, making trade-offs, and introducing change as the most critical elements in a manager's job. This being so, the project manager has the most challenging type of managerial role.

11

IS THERE
A MANAGERIAL
PERSONALITY?

Acting the role of a manager requires very substantial personality strengths. Since so much of management involves relationships—with subordinates, peers, superiors—the manager's inner self is invariably exposed. Personality, interpersonal skills, and leadership are all tightly intertwined. While there is good evidence that managers have to be intelligent and must acquire substantial technical knowledge about their areas of specialization, it is their personal and personality attributes that appear to weigh heavily in success.

Stress resistance is an important component of the managerial personality. So much of management (as we have described it in preceding chapters) can be stressful. For many people the barriers, inconsistencies, and inevitable frustrations implicit in organizational behavior lead quickly to impatience, anger, and resentment. Such emotional reactions almost always injure performance. Those with whom the manager deals sense the pent-up or openly expressed hostility. They, in turn, become less responsive or helpful, either because they resent the emotional display or they can't control their own inner stress. Managers whose personality skills are inadequate for the inevitable and persistent pressures of the leadership role are thus "contagious." Unlike good managers, who absorb or deflect pressure, they amplify it, reflecting it in a destructive fashion to all those around them.[1]

By rethinking the descriptions of managerial dilemmas given in previous chapters, we can easily list the most stressful aspects of managerial work, many of which are not even factors in the more traditional professions, or in so-called staff—in contrast to line—positions.

Managers are caught in the middle and must be responsive to the frequently contradictory expectations of superiors and subordinates. Only if they stay in the middle, avoiding the temptation of being consistently upward-oriented or consistently downward-oriented, will they be successful. In other words, they have to be willing to "take the heat."

• Because data and services are often widely dispersed in the organization, managers may have to make, and take, a dozen phone calls to get a simple piece of information or to get someone to undertake some minor action.

• There is usually no "straight line" connecting a plan and its implementation; there will inevitably be "fits and starts," two steps forward and one back, unanticipated obstacles, the need to take longcuts and shortcuts.

• Almost every new activity that is not part of an already well-established work flow routine will take longer to accomplish than anticipated.

• Managers are always fighting time. Each day will consist of unexpected interruptions, disappointments, minor and major crises, and a host of activities that will destroy neat, well-planned work schedules. The result will be many unfulfilled objectives that will make the next day even more harried.

• The sense of completion is rarely achieved; many agenda items are always "open," with closure nowhere in sight.

• The "system" can be unjust as well as unpredictable. There is no sure relationship between input and output; sometimes

---

[1] It is likely that reasonable self-assurance and self-esteem are important in resisting the temptation to interpret obstacles and other people's frustration and hostility in terms that are personally threatening. For a good review of the correlates of self-esteem, see Joel Brockner, *Self Esteem at Work*, Lexington, Boston, 1988.

success comes easily, even unexpectedly, and many times there will be failure in spite of vigorous and sensible effort.

• Fulfilling responsibilities—for which there can be substantial rewards or punishments—is usually dependent upon external groups, preceding or succeeding the manager's own position in the work flow. Critical "outsiders" who control necessary service and support resources may not fulfill commitments, yet the manager will still be held responsible.

• Being human, subordinates can be unpredictable. Inevitably managers will be disappointed when subordinates for whom they have won benefits and/or whom they have defended forget or ignore these favors, and fail to "come through" when asked to put themselves out in return.

To summarize, the manager works in an ambiguous world in which there are no sure formulas for moving from problem to solution. Uncertainties abound, and only rarely is there the sense of closure, of neatly and surely moving through sequential steps to the logical outcome portrayed in textbooks on scientific management and decision making. Work is fragmented; few tasks move smoothly from start to completion. The manager begins to solve an important problem only to be interrupted by an aggrieved employee or another department head with a priority request. Most tasks are diffuse; they require inputs and cooperation from widely dispersed parts of the organization. To make matters worse, the required contribution of peers can be ambiguous; ambiguous too is the precise boundary which separates the manager's jurisdiction from the jurisdiction of adjacent work flow units. As a result, consensus on what needs to be done, or even on what the problem is, may be elusive. Different groups whose cooperation is necessary can see things quite differently. And, as we have seen, it is rarely clear whether these differences represent legitimate technical issues or power seeking and status striving.

No wonder the manager whose personality does not equal the challenge feels anxious and abused and shows marked stress. In contrast, the manager who can cope effectively with the contradictions and ambiguities of the fast-paced organizational world should be eagerly sought for critical leadership positions.

In this chapter we try to portray the explicit behavioral skills demanded by the many facets of managerial work, both to aid learning and to emphasize the broad range of personality strengths needed in the manager who successfully responds to fast-changing situational demands. We seek to answer the perennial question, "What predictions can one make concerning who is likely to be successful in a challenging managerial position?"[2]

CULTURAL VALUES OR INDIVIDUAL DIFFERENCES?

Superficially, of course, the personality of the successful manager is simply a mirror of what anthropologists have emphasized as the attitudes (or values) that epitomize the industrialized modern world and distinguish it from earlier agricultural/traditional societies. In other words, managers need to, and frequently do, incorporate in their attitudes the hallmarks of modern society:

Optimism about the future. There is no room here for fear of the future consequences of "evil forces" such as government restrictions and worldwide monopolies. This means confidence that there will be a sensible payoff for hard work, that most people are reasonably responsible and trustworthy, that one has the capacities to meet contingencies successfully.

Energy and commitment. Real leaders take seriously a fiduciary responsibility to the organization and don't perceive the job solely in personally exploitative terms.

Respect for achievement as distinct from status ascribed by birth. Contemporary managers understand that one earns deference by performance, not by class, race, family, or connections.

Concern with and responsiveness to time. Organizations are systems of human effort coordinated by time. Therefore responsiveness to time and its pressures must be of paramount concern.

---

[2] Obviously, selection for a given managerial position first of all requires matching the demands of that job with the capabilities of the individual. Here we are seeking to identify less specific personality characteristics. For a review of a pioneering, long-term study of the kinds of personal attributes that predict executive success based on AT&T's internal research, see Ann Howard, "Cool at the Top: Personality Characteristics of Successful Executives," which was presented at the American Psychological Association annual meeting, Toronto, 1984.

Flexibility and pragmatism. Management requires creativity, in contrast to presuming that immutable natural laws or company regulations should govern all decisions.

Our modern industrial world presupposes these attitudes, and presumably family, school, and society seek to imbue everyone with them. Insofar as that is true, they don't help us instinctively distinguish the effective from the ineffective manager, except to say that the former must be steeped in contemporary values in contrast to the values of more traditional societies. In the latter, for example, time is infinite, loyalties are primarily to family, status comes from birth, and there is a strong fatalistic belief that the individual can do little to shape the future.

Values aren't central to what most of us consider personality. On the other hand, personality, as measured by personality tests, does not seem to relate to executive effectiveness.[3] Many tests, of course, rely heavily on self-assessment and are based on questions that have helped distinguish the mentally ill from the "normal."

What aspects of personality, then, are likely to bear on job success in the kind of organizational environment that has been described? Given what has been said about the pressures, and frustrations, and action patterns required, it would seem that these approaches to personality might be fruitful in predicting who will be successful:

Level of cognitive development
Orientation toward time
Interactional capabilities
Problem-solving abilities

We shall explore these four, quite different approaches.

LEVELS OF COGNITIVE DEVELOPMENT

As we have described the manager's job, it is obvious that there will be countless frustrating incidents involving the need or desire to do something blocked by a rule, a stabilization require-

---

[3] A comprehensive monograph that seeks to summarize efforts to correlate personality tests with managerial effectiveness concludes that the record is poor, as have many reviews by leading psychologists. J. Campbell, M. Dunnette, E. Lawler, and K. Weick, *Managerial Behavior, Performance and Effectiveness*, McGraw-Hill, New York, 1960, p. 133.

ment, or the opposition of another group with differing objectives. Managers will be asked or motivated to go in one direction but find that organizational forces are constraining. Similarly, as we've seen, the modern organization requires actions but often doesn't provide direct control or even access to the necessary resources; one is responsible but lacks the authority. There are so many laterally imposed requirements from diverse staff and other managers that it is inevitable that there will be contradictions among these. The fabled "Catch-22" becomes more the rule than the exception.

How do managers cope with contradictions and inconsistencies? Watching the very profound differences in reactions suggests differences in cognitive style. This corresponds to more systematic studies of how adults cope with ambiguity and contradiction.[4]

Rigid and Simplistic

Naive managers, without much ability to deal with complexity, are perplexed, if not angry, when they view an organization with inconsistencies, one which does not follow the precepts of the traditional model (authority matched to assigned responsibility). At the outset, such managers are likely to assume there is some mistake. Either top management is shortsighted, an order has been misstated, or someone is "cheating":

> They couldn't expect me to complete this job without having ordered that other group to get me those files by Thursday. Either there has been a slipup or the accountants are pulling a fast one.

Many managers are, in a sense, frustrated engineers. For them management is simply the making of "correct," deductive decisions. The process is an obvious and logical one. When any problem occurs you first consider your goal, how the problem affects that, and what steps are necessary to go from the problem to a solution that will move you toward your goal.

To these managers everything is either "right" or "wrong," "true" or "false." They are puzzled, baffled, and distressed when problems turn out to have large areas of "gray." They keep

---

[4] See M. Rokeach, *The Open and Closed Mind*, Basic Books, New York, 1960; and J. B. Rotter, "Generalized Expectancies for Internal versus External Control of Reinforcement," *Psychological Monographs*, vol. 80, no. 609, 1966, pp. 1–28.

expecting the organization to go back to the good old days when everything was clear-cut: "You knew exactly what you were supposed to do and were given the wherewithal to do it."[5]

Aside from believing there must be some mistake and longing for their lost black/white world, these managers are likely to be obstructionistic:

> A subordinate requests that a project running out of space temporarily use an adjacent room. There is a policy that all space assignments are made at the time of project inception. The boss turns down the request flatly, citing the rule. In an almost parallel case, another R&D manager goes to the space committee and argues that a project running out of space because of additional top management–imposed requirements has become the equivalent of two projects. She justifies the need for additional space by exhibiting photos and diagrams of how conscientiously and completely existing space had been utilized to capacity.[6]

The modern organization with its plethora of stabilization and audit groups, each with distinct and sometimes conflicting criteria and with the need to shift and modify objectives in the light of changing demands, appears to these managers as a topsy-turvy world. When another group makes a demand that is inconsistent with its needs, it will be accused of disloyalty, of failing to understand the organizations's real needs or objectives: "Management ought to be homogeneous; there is a rational answer to this problem with which every sensible person will concur."

The typical reaction of these rigid, simplistic managers is to be angry—at the organization and at their "opposition"—or to

[5] Fred Goldner studied a large sample of managers in a major corporation. He was able to show over an extended period of time that those managers who viewed their world simplistically (one boss, authority equal to responsibility, staff with no power, one clear-cut goal, and the like) were less likely to promote as compared with those who saw the inherent complexity and contradiction in the modern corporation with its overlapping and often conflicting groups, requirements, and instructions. See Fred Goldner, "Success versus Failure: Prior Management Perspectives," *Industrial Relations*, vol. 9, no. 4, October 1970, pp. 453–474.

[6] In philosophic terms, these simplistic managers are adopting an Aristotelian, in contrast to Galilean, view of the world. Ideas, requests, and orders are either right or wrong, desirable or undesirable; new management techniques are simply superimposed on existing approaches.

give up: "How can I do it without the authority?" or "The rules forbid it; my hands are tied."

Adversarial

With almost the same preconceptions, there are those managers who become cynics. They see themselves in a dishonest or, at the least, untrustworthy world in which the one chance for survival is getting their enemies before their enemies get them.

These Machiavellian managers emphasize threats and power plays and see themselves as the equivalent of jungle fighters: "You're either for me or against me."[7]

Their day-to-day life consists of building alliances and proving their power. Decisions are made almost solely on the basis of the eventual impact on their personal power and their unit's visibility and influence:[8]

"I know when to find or even create a tough problem that is going to threaten our schedule or performance and then miraculously find the solution."

"Top management pays a lot of attention to those kinds of troubles and you are a hero when you can put the show back on the road. I purposely encouraged that standards group to try to stop us on the grounds we were deficient."

"I knew that there were enough powerful people who would side with us on that issue that they would be beaten. In the future they won't try any more of that nit-picking with me."

"We often end up with many hours of maintenance time that are difficult to allocate, so we just tack them on to the charges of those departments that act unfriendly."[9]

---

[7] Michael Maccoby, in his book *The Gamesman* (Simon and Schuster, New York, 1977) states that these managers were often successful in earlier, more traditional organizations where pure power, as distinct from sophisticated understanding of the "system" and how to work its interfaces, made the difference.

[8] Seeing some of these managers in action, a few observers of modern organizations have overgeneralized and assumed that management and politics are almost synonymous.

[9] Melville Dalton observed similar shenanigans in his classic study, *Men Who Manage* (Wiley, New York, 1958). A good study of managerial politics is R. Ritti and G. Funkhouser, *The Ropes to Skip and the Ropes to Know*, Grid, Columbus, Ohio, 1977. An extensive case study is found in Andrew Pettigrew, *The Politics of Organizational Decision Making*, Tavistock, London, 1973.

One expects to find managers like this in a highly politicized environment—say, in Washington—where status, respect, and clout are all-important.

Super-sales-oriented

Very similar in assumptions about the need for besting the other guy are those managers who seek to win with super sales techniques. Usually highly articulate and dominant inter-actionally, they learn that shrewd and pressuring tactics will gain them enough concessions to get their job done. These forceful talkers often overwhelm their more reticent colleagues, but over time this builds resentment and a backlash. Neverthe-less, for short periods these verbal persuaders can be highly successful—as long as the situation doesn't become too com-plex and catch up with them.

> Henry T. had been a highly successful sales manager in the en-cyclopedia business, and when his company was absorbed by a larger corporation, his reputation for being an energetic and per-suasive "doer" got him the job of divisional vice president. As the larger company began incurring economic problems, as more internal controls and audit and stabilization groups were added, his super-salesmanship was less successful. He never did grasp the new management system and was eventually de-moted.

These are the same managers who are always jumping on the bandwagon of some new management technique, be it MBO, job enrichment, or participative management. Rather than seeing these as elements of a larger pattern of managerial action, with the need to integrate them into a total management process, they han-dle them as isolated, mechanical procedures. They perceive the new forms as magical "gimmicks" which will transform indiffer-ent subordinates into highly motivated workers. They are at-tracted to those courses and executive programs which present these as superselling techniques, only it is the selling of loyalty and productivity, not products. Needless to say, because they are simply superimposed on an existing organizational process, not really understood, and often perceived as insincere by subordinates, they usually are not very effective after the "Hawthorne Effect" wears off.[10]

Compromising

The first three levels of cognitive development described above are characteristic of those who see the organizational world simplistically in black and white terms. A higher level is seen when managers can conceive that most problems don't have a right or an egocentric answer. Most decisions will have both favorable *and* unfavorable effects, no matter how carefully conceived. There is no perfect truth, only partial answers. While, for example, getting permission to utilize overtime will mean that the schedule will be maintained, many employees will grow accustomed to the extra earnings and even believe that working more slowly produces more lucrative overtime pay.

So these managers believe in compromise—that is, giving a little to get a little, splitting many disputes down the middle: "The other people probably have legitimate reasons for wanting it their way; if they get half a loaf, then I'll get the go-ahead."

Creatively Integrative

As Mary Parker Follett sensed in the 1920s, highly effective managers can solve apparently insoluble contradictions by creative syntheses, a higher level of cognitive development. A case from *Fortune* illustrates her type of managerial problem-solving skill.

> An RCA product manager with a failing product was caught in a squeeze between corporate cost-cutting requirements and the need to improve the competitive position of the product. He

[10] The "Hawthorne Effect," conceived in the now-famous Western Electric studies, is the short-lived responsiveness of subordinates to the appearance of management concern and interest in their lives and welfare. For a more complete analysis of the tendency for managers to look for gimmicks in solving leadership problems, see Leonard Sayles, "Whatever Happened to Management: Or Why the Dull Stepchild," *Business Horizons*, vol. 13, no. 2, April 1970, pp. 25–34.

sought to lower costs by getting vendors to cut the price of some key components, but company policies forbidding inventory accumulations constrained his ability to gain price concessions for volume purchases.

His solution was to show other managers that this particular component could replace the higher-cost elements they were using, thus increasing the volume he could offer vendors. He also surmounted the inventory constraint by signing a contract for a large quantity to be delivered sequentially over several years, thus limiting the total held in stock.[11]

Creative managers, using motivational patterns like those discussed in Chapter 4, find methods for reaching their goals that enable others—upon whom they depend or who control needed resources or authorizations—to attain theirs as well. They understand the larger system and the need to work organizational interfaces—perseverance, ingenuity, iteration, quick responsiveness. The interests of many groups have to be integrated.

> There are perhaps a dozen other managers who must concur with any change in plans I propose. Each one of these, in turn, probably has several or more different departments to whom they are beholden. So after I line up A, B, C, D, for example, I'll discover that E can't agree to that new program so I have to go back to A, B, C, and D with a a new proposal. Often after you do get your ducks all in a line, F or G comes along because of some demand made on them and wants some modification in the new plan. Well that's how you keep going 'round the circle—remodifying and renegotiating. There are just too many interests and interdependencies to do it all at once. The new managers find this extended sequence and the iteration drives them bananas, but that's what you've got to do to keep any complex effort alive and healthy.

Of course, managers with this sophisticated view of reality don't simply respond to pressures; they seek to change what

---

[11] Adapted from a *Fortune* article (February 1977, p. 129) that described RCA's efforts to be more competitive in portable "telephone" radios for trucks. One of the earliest and most lucid statements on the importance of "situational" leadership was that of Mary Parker Follett. See Henry Metcalf and L. Urwick (eds.), *Dynamic Administration: The Collected Papers of Mary Parker Follett*, Harper, New York, 1940. The current proponents of "contingency" theories of management rarely cite the seminal work of Follett, published nearly fifty years ago.

pressures there will be in the system, so they're not repeatedly coping with the same problems. (See Chapter 8.)

In Perspective: Professional versus Managerial Ability

An older study of bank officers helped show the contrast between the ability to cope with ambiguity and complexity and a "principles" approach to problems. The bank in question sought to develop more customer orientation among loan officers in order to improve the bank's reputation and business.[12] The loan officers with a professional orientation could only see their job as one of applying the bank's standards and criteria to the customer's financial position and then deciding whether or not to grant the loan request. Other loan officers saw their jobs as involving extended give-and-take with customers, developing their interest in the bank, and applying criteria flexibly. The managers in the first group saw their jobs as "professionals":

> [The officers are typically] aloof, suspicious . . . [and] the customer is appropriately seen as "figures," not as a person. "[C]lients will cheat you if you accept them on any basis other than a rigid test of their financial strength." . . . They tended to describe themselves as one or another kind of "professional."[13]

These rigid, technically oriented managers could not conceive of asking another manager or their boss to modify a rule or standard in order to try out an appealing innovation. They had an "impersonal, technical, arithmetic view."[14]

In contrast, the successful managers were the other type, the ones who saw the need to evolve a unique solution to each customer challenge, and this meant that they had to engage in extended give-and-take with the customer. In the interaction, new possibilities and new problems would emerge requiring new accommodations. Unlike the distant, reserved, and autonomous "professionals," these managers utilized interpersonal skills to develop each situation's distinctive possibilities. Here is how one of them described his job "strategy":

[12] David Moment and Dalmar Fisher, *Autonomy in Organizational Life,* Schenkman, Cambridge, Mass., 1975.
[13] Ibid., p. 24.
[14] Ibid., p. 47.

If I do a good job for [my customers] they spread the word around [the community] that I am a good loan officer. . . . I am cultivating the friendship of several young lawyers . . . [who] are in on big financial transactions . . . [and] of new accountants. [I]n the future these people will grow, and . . . there will be a lot of reciprocal sharing [of business]. . . . [15]

These managers were not afraid of confrontations, even arguments with potential customers, and they sought challenges that might give them a chance to prove what services and advantages their bank might provide.

They are much more likely to understand the value of what we call middle-level controls—monitoring the organizational system—and the need for continually introducing organizational change by utilizing leadership skills.

The table below summarizes these different levels of managerial cognitive development:

Type	Conception of organizational world	Managerial style
1. Rigid, simplistic	Everything right or wrong; one best way; pure rationalism	Getting their own way or paralysis
2. Adversarial	Win/lose: "me against them"; cynical	"Jungle warfare"; beating the other person
3. Super-sales-oriented	Win/lose: "me against them"; optimistic	High pressure; dominance; manipulation
4. Compromising	Everything a partial truth; trade-offs needed for survival	Negotiation; split down the middle
5. Creatively integrative	A complex system of dynamic and changing tension; an open system	Changing parameters of the problem; working interfaces to modify organizational pressures; problems seen as opportunities

Thus type 1 is the most rigid and the most likely to be hung up and unable to move. Types 2, 3, and 4 recognize the need to make a commitment in a world where there is no absolute truth

[15] Ibid., pp. 36–37.

or right or wrong. Type 5 represents the highest level of cognitive development, being able to conceive of new syntheses which creatively change the parameters of a problem.

PAST, PRESENT, OR FUTURE ORIENTATION?

Another way of looking at how personality shapes managerial behavior is to consider how the individual copes with past, present, and future states. The four categories we shall describe are familiar to anyone who has observed managers in action. Unlike the levels of cognitive development where there is a scale extending from less to more desirable, the modern organization seems to require a mix of time-oriented "types." In fact, it is not unusual to see three or even all four types composing a top management team, with each supplementing the distinctive skills of the other. All four may be necessary for the most successful management process.[16]

Thinking Types

These are the managers who appear quite frequently at top management levels—when they have been successful. Such executives often are former lawyers or technical people who are known as tough, unemotional, even ruthless. They get promoted to root out sources of inefficiency and to apply rational procedures to correct traditional and habitual practices.

Their strength comes from two sources. They are incredibly logical and consistent. They are never, or almost never, shaken from this consistency and the ability to think sequentially. In other words, they can recall, order, and assess the implications and consequences of past actions (e.g., a policy that was instituted—why, when, and with what implications) for today's problems and the likely future consequences and events. They are always extending this time line into antecedent conditions and future implications, assuming logical, sequential progres-

---

[16] Our analysis is substantially based on the reinterpretation of Carl Jung's work by Dr. Humphrey Osmond and John Osmundsen in *Understanding Understanding*, Harper & Row, New York, 1976. For excerpts from the original essays, see Joseph Campbell (ed.), *The Portable Jung*, Viking, New York, 1971, pp. 178–272. The widely used Myers-Briggs has the same heritage.

sions. At times this arithmetic orderliness and rationality can lead to overscrupulousness: insistence on absolute conformity.

At top management levels, their flair for planning, for formal analysis, and rational problem solving and unemotionality makes them appear the ideal executive. This ability for cool calculation, however, is not complemented by any ability to cope with the human needs and foibles of their associates and subordinates. Few subordinates will sense any understanding, rapport, or support emanating from these detached figures.

> Mr. N. was considered the most powerful of the top executives because of his ability to influence and control colleagues and subordinates. Whenever there was a dispute or confrontation, he not only remained cool and detached but was able with great articulation and patience to explain the origins in past actions, commitments (and mistakes), and the exact consequences that would likely follow each and every one of the proposed and opposed points of view. His mastery of the logic of the situation and his ability to place every fact and opinion in this matrix of history, technical interrelation, and indisputable implication made him a feared and respected opponent. While his reasoning powers attracted many of the younger people in the organization—as did his abilities to design sensible, logically complete and well-thought-through plans—he never developed any commitment to them except for being correct and rational.

As long as they can simply give uncontested orders or expert advice, be decision makers, with no need to build a consensus, they do well. But where feelings and interpersonal relationships are important, as they are at most middle levels of the organization and even, at times, within top management, these executives will need complementing.

Feeling Types

These managers tend to look backward: to values, traditions, commitments, and critical experiences and incidents. They relish reminiscing about both the good old days and the bad, and they thus embody the norms and values of most members of an organization. They are usually perceived as kindly, thoughtful, and "warm." While sometimes inarticulate, they make up for this in their absolute respect for previous agreements and un-spoken understandings. They are often the behind-the-scenes fixers and negotiators who help develop a consensus in troubled times—the liaison, advisory, and responsive managers, widely liked although often not very powerful.

> Joe Kelly was the most successful labor negotiator any of us had ever seen. While always in trouble with his boss for not being able to write reports and certainly incapable of giving a formal presentation that would appear well prepared and powerfully persuasive, he was unbeatable in one-to-one persuasions.
>
> While his major responsibilities involved developing close and good relationships with key union officials who otherwise distrusted and even despised the company, he was also used to help resolve difficult intramanagement disputes. He knew everybody in the industry, the union movement, and the corporation and treasured old acquaintances. He never forgot a favor or a friend or a secretary's birthday. He was constantly telling long, wonderful stories about the company's history and key men who had built or had helped shape the organization. He loved long lunches and never seemed to be in a hurry, particularly if it meant time for an old friend. He was absolutely trustworthy with a confidence or an assignment.

Rather obviously, "thinking" and "feeling" types represent almost perfect opposites. But there are two other opposites as well, with very different time perspectives. Remember, the "thinking" type tied past, present, and future together. The "feeling" type looked backward in solving today's problems. The "intuitive" type, whom we discuss next, looks almost entirely forward, and the "sensation" type deals just with the immediate present.

Intuitive Types

True "intuitives," as we use the term, are rather rare. They too often appear in top management as the source of brilliant new strategies that are not simply a slight modification or extension of what has been done before. They are great synthesizers—taking a large quantity of current information about tastes, trends, and demographics and sensing what the real implications will be that others can't see because they're too close to the present. Sometimes their breakthroughs fail miserably because they ignored the need for some foundation in the present (in terms of competency and resources), but it's likely that every truly new product and program—the Land (Polaroid) camera, the supermarket—was conceived by intuitives who could leap ahead of their contemporaries.

Obviously such people often become the successful entrepreneurs, although they may live unhappy lives when they are too much ahead of their time or don't have an implementer to put their ideas to work.

Intuitive managers can have communications problems too. Unless they are careful and have high interactional energy levels, they often will not be understood. They may fail to explain systematically and logically how one idea follows another, and the potential supporter is often mystified as to what is expected or why something is so important. Their conclusions appear arbitrary and capricious, unlike those of the "thinking types," who carefully and meticulously explain in easy-to-understand, 1-2-3 fashion the whys, hows, and whens of any issue. Thus intuitive managers may need help in making formal presentations and in dealing with associates on day-to-day problems.

Sensation Types

Here is the epitome of the here-and-now person. Some sensation types almost throb with intensity, responding to every nuance of the moment. Quick to sense any and all cues, quick to act and often (but not always) engaging—even entertaining—they often make superb negotiators and deal makers. Given their abilities to concentrate completely on the present, they can "wheel and deal." Many are superb at fund raising, at charming—as well as persuading—outsiders that the cause is needy or profitable.

There may be too much love of action and influence—even of power—to where crises are created in order to be solved and others sense that they are being manipulated for the personal gain of the sensation-type leader.

Some project managers and many entrepreneurs seem to fit this type. They are extraordinary at getting support from other line groups and top management and funding sources. They relish launching a new product or business. Any resource they need, they can beg, borrow, or steal; and as long as they don't become too manipulative and incur the distrust of their colleagues, they will gain the reputation of being fine fire fighters and resource getters. Work is a game in which each day brings a new set of challenges which will be dealt with in an opportunistic fashion, as though there were no memory of past problems or commitments or future worries.

Depending on one's own personality, it is easy to have favorites among these Jungian types. But organizations appear to be able to use all four and, in fact, need all four. Obviously many people do not fit easily into one or another category: they are mixtures. But these "ideal types" help us to identify critical differences.

Top Management Teams

Occasionally one observes top management teams which seem to work in great harmony because they are the perfect admixture of these types. There is no need to find the all-perfect leader. Each executive fills a needed role and complements the other, and each has a crucial role to play.

Most often this involves combining on one team:

1 An intuitive type to be the organization's genius. The genius may be in the scientific or engineering or even entrepreneurial world. This type is extraordinarily prescient in identifying ideas and trends, a capability that enables the organization to best its competition.

2 A thinking type to design and oversee the administrative procedures. This executive assures that solid rational approaches are utilized to plan, budget, and control the intuitive's great ideas. This type gets things done.

3 A feeling type to provide the responsiveness that motivates and reassures staff and aides. This type provides the sounding board, lightning rod, wailing wall, and "human touch" essential to build a human organization. This type also provides early warnings of pending organizational disasters.

Together the team covers all the important bases, and the whole is much greater than its parts.

INTERACTIONAL DIFFERENCES AMONG MANAGERS

Another way of looking at personality differences among leaders concentrates attention solely on the manner in which managers interact, that is, handle their conversations with other managers and subordinates. Research suggests that almost every managerial job requires great quantities of interactional energy, the ability to talk with large numbers of people every day—all of whom may be quite different in how they want to be handled and may, in their own way, be provoking and frustrating. There is no question that most successful leaders have extraordinary interactional energy, the ability to keep acting long after more average individuals grow tired of talking, arguing, and cajoling.[17] A few top executives can endure by being laconic, reclusive, and difficult to interact with, but they are not fulfilling the demanding leadership role described in Chapter 1.

Contrasts in Interactional Energy

Here are two vignettes drawn from our own research files which illustrate rather typical extremes: a high-energy, filled-with-initiative woman and a very-low-energy male. Both were hardworking, bright, and certainly conscientious. Their differences in interaction patterns caused them to shrink and stretch their respective jobs to fit their different personalities. (Of course, the absence of good middle-level controls for these jobs permits this type of job manipulation. See Chapter 8.)

Jane Fitzgerald was hired to handle the X Company's printing, to collect and transmit the printing requirements of various department heads to outside print shops—a semiclerical task. In a matter of months she had reorganized the whole operation. Noting that different departmental schedules and lackadaisical planning reduced the volume of any one order, she got permission to set

---

[17] See Eliot Chapple and Leonard Sayles, *The Measure of Management*, Macmillan, New York, 1969.

quarterly deadlines for all departments. Instead of using the usual outside source, she put the work up for bid. She discovered that printing costs could be further reduced by modifying and standardizing many of the forms and announcements the various departments demanded. Within a year company printing costs had been cut in half and deliveries expedited. (Jane was later promoted to manager of administrative services.)

Phil Foster was a well-trained engineer who, as manager of standards, had to approve all engineering drawings before they were sent to the field. His office received dozens of drawings each day, and when he found a mistake he circled it and sent it back to the drafter with a mimeo note, "REDO." The result was that the Y Company had almost double the number of drafters that their competitors had—and didn't know why. Foster had no initiative and found it difficult to telephone or discuss mistakes: he couldn't help train the drafters or show them what he wanted or why they had been wrong.

Specific Interactional Skills

Aside from raw energy, successful executives need differentiated interactional skills with which to fill the leadership roles we have described. These qualities include:

1 Initiative—the ability to originate contacts. When problems emerge, information must be transmitted, cooperation secured, and feedback provided. The leader must have the ability to respond to environmental cues with interpersonal action.

2 Quickness—the ability to initiate contacts, often in large numbers in a short period of time. This is of special importance to managers occupying crossroads, or "switching point," positions where rapid dissemination of information and instruction is needed when breaks in routine occur.

3 Perseverance—the ability to keep going back to the same people and raising the same issues when a worthwhile project is involved. Managers must maintain their own enthusiasm in order to persuade, negotiate compromises, and propose new possibilities.

4 Flexibility—the ability to adjust one's pattern of give-and-

take to the pattern of others. Managers must talk freely and then listen. And encourage others to do the same.

5 Dominance—the ability to keep talking, although others seek to interrupt and take over. This is essential if one is to present ideas and viewpoints and obtain an adequate hearing.

6 Listening—the ability to remain silent over reasonably long periods. The good manager listens so that others can present a complex or highly emotional view and address delicate or embarrassing issues.

7 Equanimity—the ability to maintain one's interactional capabilities even when others are unresponsive to orders or ideas or seek to pressure or dominate. Managers cannot overreact in stressful situations.

Handling Stress One of the most disabling personality traits in a manager is vulnerability to stress. As we have described, the typical managerial day provides numerous incidents that will be stressful for the susceptible manager; such experiences can put managers "out of action," that is, impede their natural way of talking and listening for some period of time. Others in contact with them will find the experience unpleasant or even intolerable. Stress usually shows itself by increased reticence, or just the opposite—great volubility. Either state is upsetting to other people and thus the stress spreads like a contagion through the organization. Here is a typical example.

> Ella is stressed by nonresponse. She believes in everything that's said about the value of delegation. She gives broad, meaningful assignments. However, lacking interactional energy, she often does not explain fully what is expected of subordinates and what they need to know. As soon as the subordinate appears to be faltering, making a mistake, Ella senses nonreponse and moves in to take over. Being under stress now, she is unable to explain at all what went wrong, what she wants, or what the hapless subordinate should do. The latter, detecting the stress as hostility, will be loath in the future to accept very much responsibility. In turn, this will confirm to Ella that while delegation is good in theory, it doesn't work in practice, given her inept subordinates. To complete the cycle, Ella, delegating less and doing more herself, has even less time to train, counsel, and provide

feedback to others, which means they will appear increasingly more inept. Now under almost constant stress, Ella will run faster and faster and accomplish less and less. Her stress reactions will further injure her relationships with other managers and throw more work on her own shoulders.

This type of vicious circle is repeated over and over by managers with no sensitivity to the importance of interaction.

Stress is easy to observe in yourself and others, and it is highly destructive of the complex web of coordination that keeps managerial work flows intact. Successful managers are those who have a great deal of "elasticity," that is, they can be pulled and pushed out of their desired interaction patterns without detectable changes occurring in how they handle their other relationships. Since the manager's job is primarily relationships, the ability to withstand buffeting by difficult, stubborn, domineering, and incommunicative people is absolutely critical to success.

Job-Specific Skills   Obviously there are differences in the interactional requirements of jobs: some are fast-paced (like a project manager's job, where dozens of interfaces may need reworking each day and there are few, if any, routines); others are much slower because of built-in regularities. Some require great initiative; others are largely positions where the executive is responding to the initiatives of others. The great value of the middle-level controls (discussed in Chapter 8) is that the manager can see what patterns of interrelationship are required, and there can be some matching of personality and job since both can be described in precisely the same behavioral terms.

PROBLEM-SOLVING ABILITIES

Managers are doers and decision makers; they make things happen, which means they solve problems. What personality characteristics contribute to this basic skill? First we need to define problem solving and decision making.

The myth that decision making is the act of a thoughtful, isolated manager who meticulously weighs the alternatives and works through cost/benefit trade-offs dies hard. As many studies have shown, a decision is the end result of a lengthy organizational process, rather than something that occurs at one point in time as the product of an omniscient executive.[18]

Also, as we have noted, problem solving can easily be confused with analysis, that is, with rigid, disciplined logical thinking. The rationalist model is well developed in managerial training, of course, but problem solving in organizations (as distinct from the classroom) involves more than analysis. There are at least three steps: (1) problem (or opportunity) identification; (2) analysis, including data collection; and (3) decision making and implementation.

Problem (or Opportunity) Identification

In our earlier discussion of controls, we sought to develop a systematic procedure for identification of managerial problems where intervention was necessary. More profound managerial issues may be identified by less systematic procedures. Truly basic questions concerning the type of product or service rendered or methods of distribution and advertising are often raised by "intuitive" managers who are sensitive to vast quantities of both qualitative and quantitative information. They can process this in ways no computer can emulate and often thereby identify otherwise hidden trends, opportunities, and contradictions. Their brilliant and incisive abilities provide "leaps" forward that cannot be compared to the rationalists' step-by-step manner of thinking.[19]

Gaining Information

Most executives find that direct personal contact provides critical supplementary information to any formal reporting system. The information is more timely, less likely to be manipulated to improve the appearance of the formal control reports, and thus more candid. Getting people to talk openly and at some reasonable length requires:

---

[18] See Graham Allison, *Essence of Decision*, Little, Brown, Boston, 1971; and Leonard Sayles, *Managerial Behavior*, McGraw-Hill, New York, 1964.

[19] Within the university this is especially noticeable when a student or faculty member must select a problem to study. The more pedestrian projects seek to carry a line of work one step further; the more brilliant find strategic problems that open up whole new areas.

1 The ability to listen, to be silent for long enough periods to draw out the other person.

2 The ability to synchronize one's own speech pattern to the pattern of others. This flexibility of interaction, in which the interviewer speaks only after the respondent has finished expressing an idea or series of ideas but then speaks long enough to give the respondent a chance to regain the ability to speak, is critical to eliciting reliable feedback. It means avoiding overlaps, any "talking down" to the other person, and stressful gaps of silence. When properly synchronized, most individuals will speak extensively and openly with ease and comfort.[20]

Gaining information also requires the interactional energy to meet with a wide variety and large number of people to accumulate ideas, data, and insights. In the modern organization there will be widely dispersed experts with technical information, other managers who have seen part of the problem and have ideas, and, of course, subordinates who are often closest to the problem.

Analysis

Some period of time is also necessary to digest, work through, and analyze the resulting data and opinion. Managers who are too peripatetic, too anxious to always be "on the go" and on the firing line, often can't sit still long enough to think and assess.

> Even here there are multiple styles. The systematic problem solvers: " . . . size up the situation, decide what the main problem is, organize a method of solution, and devise step-by-step procedures to carry it out. . . . [They] begin with a system or concept of how to arrange and weigh information, as if they had a mental picture at the outset of the kinds of information that are important. . . ."[21]

---

[20] Of course, this is the major strength of what has been called "nondirective" interviewing, listening with "the third ear."

[21] David Ewing, "Discovering Your Problem Solving Styles," *Psychology Today*, December 1977, pp. 60–70. Ewing, in part, is citing the work of James McKenney and Peter Keen, "How Managers' Minds Work," *Harvard Business Review*, vol. 52, no. 3, May–June 1974, pp. 70–90. See also Daniel Isenberg, "How Senior Managers Think," *Harvard Business Review*, vol. 62, no. 6, November–December, 1984, pp. 81–90. The author finds that successful senior executives often combine intuition with analysis and accomplishing some of their analysis while they're actually working through the solution.

In contrast, there is another group of people who carry out successful analysis in more unsystematic, less rigorous but often more creative, ways:

> [They work by] . . . trying out one idea after another in a process of free association . . . often quick and brilliant on some occasions, indecisive and disorganized on others. . . . [They] focus more on details, digest and ponder individual facts and clues, without trying to fit them into some conceptual scheme . . . [and] they suspend judgment and avoid preconceptions.[22]

In fact, many people have sought to develop methods for developing these unsystematic problem-solving skills for problems which resist "logical" solution.[23] Presumably some would argue that such skills are partially a product of the right hemisphere of the brain.

Unfortunately, some organizations are not particularly tolerant of this less orthodox style of thinking and tend to favor the clear-headed systematic analysis which can be articulated in an appealing and logical fashion. They allow analytic-minded managers to reject ideas for which there is no quantitative data, model, or equation. Yet, at least in the public arena, the ability of such managers to cope with the complex and ambiguous problems of the modern world can be questioned.[24]

Many executives who can "feel" the situation and "sense" the answer through unsystematic mental techniques may come up with better answers.[25] (But as important as "the" answer, of course, is the ability to implement it.)

Decision Making and Implementation

As we saw in Chapter 9, few decisions that involve change are welcomed, at least by all who will be impacted. Many consulting firms have earned their high fees simply by interviewing

---

[22] Ewing, loc. cit.

[23] See Edward De Bono, *Lateral Thinking,* Harper & Row, New York, 1972.

[24] See David Halberstam, *The Best and the Brightest,* Random House, New York, 1969.

[25] This line of reasoning is well expressed in two articles by Harold Leavitt, who questions the overemphasis on quantitative techniques in MBA education: "Beyond the Analytic Manager" (Parts I and II), *California Management Review,* vol. 17, nos. 3 and 4, Spring and Summer 1975. My Columbia colleague James Kuhn is now studying these creative "artistic" decision-making capabilities.

everyone in an organization who may have some knowledge of a problem, then sifting and weighing the combination of fact and opinion they have obtained and writing it up in a systematic report. Effective leaders can do the same—if they have this ability to draw people out, to listen, and to keep initiating contacts.

"Selling" a Course of Action A major shift in interaction pattern is required to move from ideas, alternatives, to acceptance of a solution. The modern organization produces diverse interests and, thus, viewpoints. While some decisions can be made unilaterally, many must be "sold" to those who must implement them. This doesn't mean that everyone shares in the decision process, or votes, but only that conviction and acceptance are necessary for reasonably enthusiastic implementation by those in critical positions.

So at this point the decision maker shifts to persuading and exciting people who are able to moderate among opposing factors (as "feeling" and "sensation" types can do) and serving as a catalyst to generate agreement. The successful managers we have observed could "sell" new programs by communicating their excitement, their conviction about eventual enormous success and generous rewards for all. There was usually contagious enthusiasm when they eloquently and extensively described the merits of the decision. Having many of the skills of Jung's "sensation" type, they were quick to sense reservations and doubts and would vigorously explain, justify, and reassure the other person and move among divergent interests to pull them together.

Again, they had high interactional energy, perseverance, and enough dominance to keep circulating, talking, and "selling."

Implementation As we have seen in Chapter 9 any important change decision will require modification and a good deal of support because the initial plan is always faulty, has omissions, and requires modification. Again, interactionally this means applying initiative and perseverance in the face of a stream of frustrating problems. Many weaken when so many things go wrong, so many people fail to follow through as expected, so many unanticipated crises occur. It is the manager with enormous quantities of interactional energy, who keeps repersuading, reassessing, and explaining new orders, who is likely to be successful in implementation.

The process is done piecemeal; it involves improvisations and getting "one's ducks in line." Here is a description of an executive who handles this process with distinction:

> Whenever an important decision comes up, Phil spends a great deal of time sounding out his managers. When it looks as though a choice is close, he sees everyone who is likely to be affected and lobbys like hell. He doesn't want any surprises if there is going to be a meeting. By doing his homework, convincing them one by one, before there is any formal decision, he avoids being ganged up on and usually then it's smooth sailing.
>
> Now once in a while he can't pull it off. One of the old guard with a big following who is used to having his own way just won't go along. Then it's beautiful to watch Phil's finesse. He takes the fellow into his office, lets him explode about this "crazy new move," and then takes over the conversation. By this time, having had his say, the fellow is usually ready to cool down. Gradually Phil shifts the discussion around to some unsolved problem this fellow is coping with, something he still needs to do and is vulnerable on. Before you know it, the guy is explaining why his problem is taking so long and the other matter is passed over.
>
> Phil just knows these decision take weeks to work through, not a quick hour or two.

Problem Solving and Neuroses

As we have described the personality requirements of problem solving, it is obvious that there are substantial stresses on managers who would exercise real leadership. Our themes here re-echo materials presented earlier. Managers are "contingency factors," having to cope with unanticipated and unanticipatable problems. As we saw in our discussion of both controls and lateral relations, there is no such thing as doing everything right. Decisions inevitably reflect trade-offs, willingness to sacrifice something to gain more of something else. Managers are thus always vulnerable, both to internal guilt and external criticism. Further, managers can always be highly critical of others, peers as well as subordinates, who have to make trade-offs too. Each is doing this from a distinctive vantage point and with goals and values slightly different—in some cases very different—from the objectives and values of any particular manager.

It becomes important to know how managers adapt to this world of imperfection, of more to do than there is time to do, of more requirements than can be met. Those who will never be leaders suffer from one or another neurotic trait that distorts the problem-solving process.

Obsessive-Compulsives One of the paradoxes in the identification of managerial potential is that personality traits that appear to be the most promising may also be disabling. Those selecting future executives for new positions or promotion typically favor the brightest: high grades, finely researched and reasoned reports, projects handled to perfection. Often those who are most successful in this type of achievement are obsessive-compulsive when it comes to implementing a decision. They are driven to accomplishment and achievement. They are the ideal professional: always setting higher standards for themselves, hardworking, grade-conscious, and perfection-minded. While they are suited for a professional career, their strengths may interfere with managerial performance.[26]

Managers, as we have seen, must be satisfied with imperfection, with incrementalism—half a loaf today and the rest tomorrow or next month. Those with a strong need for completion may be frustrated when it comes to major organizational changes. Introducing change requires patient persuasion, tolerance for delay and for divergent views and fragmented efforts.

Starting the day with a fixed program and schedule, resenting any deviation from what has been planned, and finding intolerable any failure to attain the day's planned accomplishments is a sure way to obtain ulcers. Such rigidity is also responsible for lashing out at subordinates and colleagues who appear to have blocked these accomplishments. To be sure, sensible managers respect and conform to time requirements, but they also know that, realistically, contingencies will occur, the unexpected is likely, and that a manager's job is to cope with that.

[26] See Waino Suojanen and Donald Hudson, "Coping with Stress and Addictive Work Behavior," *Atlanta Economic Review*, March/April 1977, pp. 4–9.

Reasonable decisiveness and an action orientation are necessary. Successful managers are not those who get hung up on too finely balanced alternatives and timidly avoid risk-laden choices. As we saw with our project managers, there is a time to cut debate, to force choices, and to maintain the momentum of the work flow. But there is a distinction between a neurotic compulsion to finish every task that one first planned for the day—regardless of the new problems and obstacles that appear that must *be worked through other people*—and a recognition that time is important and choices have to be made. The typical manager's day cannot be planned like the professional's—so many experiments completed, so much data collected and analyzed. But the tempo of a work process can be maintained through monitoring and intervention; this, however, requires a great deal of human interaction.

"Driven" managers will lack patience and not be able to work through the numerous organizational interfaces. Impatient, they will neglect informing some key person, be unwilling to cajole and persuade, and find delegation difficult when it means careful explaining, training, and coaching. They will end up with narrow spans of control and create unnecessary levels and checks and balances because of their impatience and drive. In the short run, they will appear to accomplish things because of their tough insistence on immediate performance, but there will be no organization to support their single-minded ambition.

Power versus Approval   At the same time, managers cannot expect to be loved. There will be the need to discipline, to refuse requests, and to place constraints on people. Managers too eager to be accepted by subordinates, too fearful of hostility, cannot be effective in an organizational world filled with contradictory and conflicting goals and interests. Earlier studies of entrepreneurs suggest that leaders have to be willing to "leave home." Managers too dependent on fixed and supportive social relationships—not simply parental but also collegial—will be less willing to promote, to be mobile, and to risk animosity by having to make unpopular choices.[27]

---

[27] The importance of need for approval has been most carefully explored by Karen Horney in *The Neurotic Personality of Our Time*, Norton, New York, 1937.

As David McClelland suggests, successful managers do want power; they recognize the need for power to accomplish their organizational goals.[28] They recognize the need for this to manipulate the diffuse, contradictory, and often unwieldy organization. But this is not power in the sense of personal aggrandizement. Subordinates, as we have noted, are quick to sense and resent leaders who seek and utilize power for personal gain, who are self-important, unapproachable, and "on the make."

The reader will quickly recognize exceptions to what we have been saying: ruthless, self-important leaders who have grasped for and won power, introduced imperialistic trappings of office, terrorized subordinates into abject deference, and even accomplished great things. There are many such leaders in history with a limitless drive for personal ascendancy. Such strategies can be successful, but they are less likely to work in modern diffuse organizations with their entrenched professionals, their need for a great deal of technical expertise and fine-tuned coordination. Such leaders are most frequently seen in the political arena and in organizations which have become desperate because of past failures. Of course, timidity in commitment (decisiveness) can be fatal in most organizations. Subordinates and colleagues are quick to sense those who "waffle" for fear of antagonizing some group or making a costly mistake that can be attributed to them when the results are in. But implementation also involves overcoming explicit objections on the part of those who say they "can't until next month."

Assertiveness versus Aggressiveness Female managers are often exposed to assertiveness training to build confidence in their ability to hold their own in relationships with other people. Unfortunately, there is often a tendency to confuse assertiveness with aggressiveness, particularly in managerial situations. Aggressive managers cope with the frustration of other persons' uncooperativeness by "blowing their stack," showing hostility and emphasizing that the others are being unfair, disloyal, lazy, or in some way inadequate. The emphasis is

[28] David C. McClelland, "The Two Faces of Power," *Journal of International Affairs*, vol. 24, no. 1, 1970, pp. 31–36.

on the other persons' selfish motives and what they *should* do if they are to be decent, loyal people.

Thus when the others fail to cooperate in the implementation of a new program, they are told something like:

"If you really wanted this job or believed in what we are doing, you wouldn't be so reluctant."

"After all I've done for you, you're willing to let me down when I need that so desperately?"

In sharp contrast, assertiveness is impersonal, neither castigating nor demeaning of motives, but explicitly insistent. Remember the example of the programming manager who wanted to transfer into marketing and was at first refused? (See Chapter 7.) She sought to get the job by firmly presenting the specific means by which the other person could help her reach her objective and the mutual benefits involved:

You will have to pay my salary, but I'll try to arrange it so that I continue to be listed on programming's budgeted personnel count. Make it a temporary appointment and we can see how it is working out after six months.

I can act as a liaison between marketing and programming which should improve the quality of service you get from them.

In other words, rather than arguing that not getting the transfer would be "discrimination," "unfair," or somehow show that the marketing manager had poor motives or other inadequacies, the programmer showed how the job transfer could be effectuated with a minimum of fuss and cost, laying out the steps for the other person to take and citing specific advantages.

"Tough Guy" Managers Many floundering organizations mistake the aggressive for the assertive, and there the price in inadequate leadership can be very high.

Tough-guy managers are often brought in to turn around sick companies. Sometimes bringing a strong personality to make the hard decisions and perform the difficult surgery of getting rid of deadwood, high costs, and lethargy does indeed work where management has been indecisive in the past. But many organizations hire a tough-*talking*, instead of a tough-

minded, manager. The result can be a disaster. The tough talkers usually have destructive characteristics that are very obvious.

1 They like to use tough language (often shocking obscenities), but the toughness is often turned to outside, irrelevant targets—how corrupt the unions are, the younger generation's sloth, and government inefficiency. The tough-talkers like the sound of their own voices. They've gotten ahead, in part, by making persuasive speeches on what's wrong with everybody else.

2 They usually surround themselves with sycophants. They fear strong people being too close and very much play favorites.

3 Most destructively, they like confrontation and "shoot-outs" for the thrill of the risk and the feeling of power they provide. For them, most of the world is the "enemy" that must be vanquished.

These tendencies put their organizations into constant turmoil. Small issues get blown up into major confrontations because they see compromise and negotiation as weakness. With little tolerance for constructive give-and-take, they create an air of anger and distrust that destroys confidence in them and in the organization.

In extreme cases, the confrontations they create inhibit amicable settlements. Many are sadists, personally insecure and unhappy. They get their satisfactions from humiliating and putting down everyone who seems weaker.

In sharp contrast is the strong-willed, self-confident executive willing and able to take on challenging situations in which some people inevitably are losers. But these managers like to solve problems, develop a smoothly functioning organization, and usually communicate a sense of trust to most of their colleagues. They use conflict and confrontation as a last resort, not as a preferred method.[29]

Management indeed needs executives who are willing to risk being unloved, who can choose unpleasant alternatives, and who "bite the bullet." Too many executives put social accep-

---

[29] See "The Toughest Bosses in America," *Fortune,* August 6, 1984, pp. 18–23, for vignettes of some tough-talking and tough-minded corporate CEOs. The descriptions are powerful. Also see David McClelland and D. H. Burnham, "Good Guys Make Bum Bosses," *Psychology Today,* December 1980, pp. 169–170.

tance and risk avoidance ahead of organizational welfare and misunderstand power. In seeking a decisive, tough-minded leader, organizations risk being taken in by the pathologically hostile. These people may look good and sound wonderful; they're great at manipulating superiors (including boards of directors who see them as saviors). But they can destroy the very business they claim to be saving.

Horney's Classifications

Many years ago a distinguished psychiatrist summarized what we have been saying in a far more cogent scheme.[30] Karen Horney noted that some people tend to deal with all of their relationships in a rigid fashion, while somewhat healthier people are able to balance their approach to the requirements of the situation. She described three types that view their world very differently.

Moving against. Like the "tough guys" and some of the more power-hungry managers described above, those "afflicted" with this syndrome see the world as composed of enemies who must be vanquished before they themselves are forced to succumb. For them, the best defense is a constant offense, perpetual battling, and criticism. This can intensify when the other person makes concessions or endeavors to mollify them and seek their approval. To them, such a response simply shows weakness.

Moving toward. These individuals seek approval; good and accommodating relationships are their constant goal. They want to please and be appreciated, and they believe that others will like them.

Moving away. Such managers seek to minimize their entanglements by avoiding both combative and supportive relationships. They usually have some sense of superiority. Even so, they fear both domination and affection; their ideal is detachment.

Because of its ambiguity and contradictions, the managerial world allows all three to find easy expression for their needs.

[30] See Karen Horney, *Our Inner Conflicts: A Constructive Theory of Neurosis,* Norton, New York, 1945. Horney's work anticipated many of the findings David McClelland would develop twenty-five years later when he talked about need for power, approval, and achievement.

The other person can always be seen as either wrong, unappreciative, or in need of "wooing." But, unfortunately, such exclusive views guarantee failure.

THE ISSUE OF AGE

Many managements debate the relationship of an executive's age to performance. At one time the balance appeared to be shifting toward young executives. Freshly minted MBAs were promoted quickly up the line and companies experimented with forced or voluntary early retirement. Then a *New York Times* story suggested a contrary trend: a growing preference for older, more mature, seasoned, and experienced executives who would bring better judgment to bear on the increasingly difficult and erratic business environment. The implication was that more youthful managers did best in a simpler economic world of easy and regular expansion.[31]

Which is right? Psychologists have long noted the obvious differences between the more ebullient, energetic, even dogged young executive and the more thoughtful, cautious senior. But more insight stems from recent work on what is called "adult development" (in contrast to child development) and specifically on the so-called midlife crisis.

While this is still somewhat controversial, many social scientists believe that men in their late thirties and early forties go through some kind of "crisis," or, better, a period of personal reassessment. Until then they have been driven by goals and aspirations often set in their teens. When they discover that life is more complex than expected, that their careers and incomes have not brought them untarnished happiness and infinite power and that life is finite, they feel the need to rethink their goals and life styles.[32]

For a few, the results can be traumatic, even shocking. Some drop out; change jobs and/or wives; seek a simpler, childlike world; or go on one last big fling. For most, however, there is a constructive resolution of these tensions. And this is where the benefit to management may be seen.

At this stage many executives become less driven, less ego-

[31] *New York Times*, May 25, 1977, p. 44.
[32] Daniel Levinson, *The Seasons of a Man's Life*, Knopf, New York, 1978.

centric and eager for personal aggrandizement. More at peace with themselves, more realistic about the world and its satisfactions, they can afford to be more broadly thoughtful about the needs of others, both institutions, and colleagues. It would appear likely that upper management particularly benefits from having managers who not only have perspective, based on extensive experience and intellectual maturity, but who are freed from the need to score big personal gains and climb above or over everyone around them. Such seasoned managers can fulfill the top management function of facilitating the development of others as well as the development of the organization. They are more likely to be perceived as true leaders and mentors, unselfish when it comes to choosing between personal gain and company progress.

One study of successful women executives suggests that, like their male counterparts, they feel freer at midlife to transcend narrow stereotypes of maleness and femaleness. Many had felt pressured to conform to a male environment; now they can adopt more supportive, less competitive, and even more feminine roles. They begin to delegate more effectively and facilitate the development of their subordinates.[33]

Where the organization requires hard-driving, constantly alert executives who can handle scores of tough negotiations and exchanges each day, who never tire of persuasion and exhortation and working through complex problems involving dozens of participants, it is more likely that relative youth will be important. Thus Texas Instruments, with its fast-changing technology, required its executive vice presidents to retire at 55, though the chief executive officer and members of the board of directors could stay on beyond that age.

CONCLUSIONS

Most human behavior experts have become wary of trying to correlate personality traits with executive performance, and for good reason. The typical personality test used as a selection device was never very good, and it was often prejudicial and misleading.

[33] Margaret Hennig and Anne Jardim, *The Managerial Woman*, Doubleday, Garden City, N.Y., 1977.

But this doesn't mean that we must reject all considerations of personality differences as predictors of managerial success. That would be absurd. Obviously, personality plays a critical role in determining how a manager's job will be handled, since so much of the job involves discretionary dealings with people. The job is not tightly constrained by a machine, a schedule, or a work method; in fact, what the job becomes is often a reflection of the personality of the manager holding that specific job. The job description is largely secondary. Assertive, skillful managers add functions and power; passive managers allow their positions to atrophy.

Historically, the trouble has been that most assessments of personality have concentrated on internal motives, mental health, and self-appraisal. In this chapter we have sought to get away from highly subjective motives and questions of mental health. Our several approaches to assessing personality and problem-solving capabilities have dealt with reasonably objective and, we hope, observable on-the-job behavior. We have presented categories that managers can use themselves in evaluating the promotional potential of their subordinates—can even use for self-evaluation. One doesn't need to call in a psychiatrist or psychologist to see the very obvious differences in how people handle their jobs and their human relationships. They are usually very obvious, very predictable, and recurring. On-the-job observation supplants the clinician's diagnosis.

CHAPTER 12

THE POINT-COUNTERPOINT OF MANAGERIAL STYLE

Can managers be taught an effective leadership style? And is there one style "for all seasons"? How much is effective leadership simply an unpredictable combination of a unique personality operating in a unique situation? How much is good leadership simply a matter of having some important strengths (i.e., skills) that more than compensate for any personality deficiency? Even if one can define good leadership, can it be taught and can it be learned?

One of the ironies of the study of management is the growing discrepancy between our field-research-based knowledge and our prescriptions for leadership success. The behavior described in earlier chapters suggests a wide range of subtle, finely tuned skills that must be situationally honed. Yet many popular prescriptions stress simplistic, one-dimensional cure-alls such as give rapid one-minute feedback.[1] Or managers are exhorted to adopt a "Y" or "Z" style of leadership.

---

[1] Kenneth Blanchard and Spencer Johnson, *The One-Minute Manager*, Morrow, New York, 1982.

A UNIQUE PROFESSION

The managerial job has a tempo unlike that of any other high-status professional position. Managers have the sense of living in a chaotic, hectic world, one often in turmoil and one in which the more placid powers of rational decision making can rarely be employed. There is little time to be reflective; instead there is a substantial need to keep on top of problems that threaten to explode at any moment into major catastrophes. And "keeping on top of" means continuous rethinking and re-adjusting.

In most professions one does different things at different times and what one does is relatively unambiguous. The belief that this was the case in management led early on to many fruitless efforts to determine the proper emphasis on "doing planning," "doing organizing," "doing controlling." But the business of management defied that kind of analysis. The basic managerial functions—like providing structure, getting and giving feedback, handling long-run planning—are too easily blurred because of the time pressures and operational contingencies that are "givens" in the manager's world. The successful manager soon learns to improvise, to do any number of things almost simultaneously, and to read multiple layers of meaning in any one interaction:

> As Jane's manager, Kira is anxious to build a sense of supportiveness into her relationship with her new employee. She sets up a "chance" meeting, and as she speaks to Jane she seeks to ascertain—through nonverbal cues as well as through the tone of the conversation—whether Jane has problems, whether she is comfortable with the work, whether she feels she is making progress. In addition, Kira uses this informal meeting to emphasize a critical element of Jane's job—developing outside contacts—something Jane may be neglecting in the pressure of day-to-day events. Then before she moves on, Kira reassures Jane that the reorganization being considered in the department will not affect her status at all.

Managers not only have to learn to make their contacts, meetings, and interchanges do double and triple duty but also how to "turn on a dime" as a conversation shifts from a technical to an organizational to a personality issue. Verbal interchanges, whether between superior and subordinate or between peer groups, can at one and the same time deal with:

1 Efforts to solve an immediate issue confronting them
2 Efforts to improve relative positions (i.e., power) in the organization's "pecking order" (see Chapter 6)
3 Efforts to resolve personality conflicts

LIVING WITH INCONSISTENCY AND CONTRADICTION

We have obviously come a long way in understanding leadership. However, as managers have come to see leadership in behavioral terms, it has been tempting to look for the "one best way." Even recognizing that an R&D setting may require a different style of leadership than a machine shop, managers would like to think there is a neat consistency for a given situation. But while there may be some similarities in the overall style of manager A and manager B, the core of managerial work appears to be based in inconsistency and contradiction. The manager's workday involves a wide variety of tasks, many of which are seemingly at odds, and good management often requires acting in inconsistent fashions.[2]

This is not to say that leaders should dissemble, push for one goal or value today and reject it tomorrow, take a clear position on a tough issue and retreat when it becomes too uncomfortable. No, by inconsistency we mean the ability to shift behavior from one leadership style to a style that may appear to be very different. The key question for the manager is *not* what style is superior but rather when to adopt what style.

The essence, then, of successful leadership is to have a broad repertoire of skills that enable one to do things which, to the outsider at least, will appear inconsistent if not contradictory. For example:

1 Managers should delegate. But it is widely recognized that there will be many times when the good manager will

---

[2] One of the first and most cogent sources of data on these contradictions can be found in Morgan McCall and Michael Lombardo, *Off the Track: Why and How Successful Executives Get Derailed*, Center for Creative Leadership, Greensboro, N.C., 1986. Also see Tom Peters and Robert Waterman, *In Search of Excellence*, Harper & Row, New York, 1982. This widely read study of America's most well-managed companies shows that their executives engage in nonlinear, nonsequential behavior.

"look over the shoulder" of a subordinate and will get involved—long before results are in—if catastrophe looms.

2 Managers should use the chain of command. But there will be times when good managers bypass the chain and contact a subordinate's subordinate or a superior's superior directly. Doing it too often can be disastrous, but never doing it can be just as destructive.

3 Managers are told repeatedly, "See the big picture; don't get enmeshed in details." But there are times when they must get deeply involved in the details of operations and technology and become "hands-on" managers—whether or not they've had direct work experience.

4 Managers must exude confident optimism that the current course is the right one. But at times caution, doubt, accepting the possibility of a hidden flaw are the order of the day.

5 Managers must take tough stands, be the curmudgeon, appear impervious to the human cost. But the effective manager is also able to show warmth and understanding and a concern for human values. And a manager can be fun-loving too.[3]

6 Managers must persevere, "tough it out," though there be problems and discouragements galore. But the manager must also have a sense for the situation that requires flexibility, "backing off," perhaps an admission of a mistake in judgment.

7 Managers must live up to the organization's rules and regulations. However, good managers know where—and when—rules can be bent.

8 Managers must alternate between high-risk and low-risk strategies.

9 Managers must be decisive, not waffle, not suffer "paralysis by analysis." But good managers let some problems sit, work them through cautiously, wait for additional data or resolution by others.

10 Managers must make solitary, unilateral decisions on some issues. On others it will be critical to involve all the parties, move by increment, seek consensus.

---

[3] For an important statement on the contradictions between exercising strong personal leadership and a more accommodative, tentative, "incrementalist" style, see Joseph Badaracco, Jr., and Richard Ellsworth, *Integrity and Leadership*, Harvard Business School Press, Boston, 1988.

11 Managers must devote an inordinate amount of time to getting immersed in an immediate problem. But at times, this kind of involvement must be shunned in favor of staying at arm's length and studying the big picture. Otherwise, pressing, short-run crises will dominate the longer-run strategic issues.

12 Managers must, almost at one and the same time, push the boss's agenda on subordinates while fighting for subordinate needs that challenge the boss's priorities.

13 Managers must share information, keep everyone informed, and demonstrate candor. But casual remarks can be misinterpreted and amplified and become threatening rumors. And there are issues on which the executive must keep his or her own counsel and *not* share vital information.

14 Managers have to know when to confront and when to compromise.

15 Managers must use specialists and value their expertise. But they cannot ignore the limitations of the experts, their biases and narrow points of view.

16 Managers must be action-oriented, time-driven, and communicate a sense of urgency. But there are times when the pace must be slowed, a reflective mood introduced, panic dissipated by thoughtful, careful, slow, even plodding steps.

17 Managers must forge a unified group whose members will stimulate one another to extraordinary performance to achieve a common goal. But at times they have to counter the narrow parochialism of the group and its resistance to outside ideas; they have to develop loyalties to the larger organization.

18 Managers must give subordinates autonomy and control in order to foster the sense of responsibility. But there will be times when critical functions (because of economies of scale or blurred boundaries) must be centralized—even within a decentralized organization.

19 Managers must use numerical targets to motivate high performance. But because such targets also mislead, encourage fudging and parochial, short-run activities, managers must appraise and give feedback in qualitative terms, some of which will denigrate the motivationally powerful "targets."

The list could be extended, but perhaps the point is made: no single set of principles or techniques will suffice for the successful manager. Most of what will be useful at any one time will have its counterpart, a sort of antimatter, that will be equally useful and relevant for other occasions. Note that this isn't because, as some critics would say, management is a field built largely on folklore. No, it's simply because the managerial world is too complicated for formulas.

MANAGING WITH FINESSE

In addition to having the behavioral skills and the organizational sophistication to alternate between what at the simplest level appear to be opposing means and methods, managers need finesse in carrying out their work. They must base their actions on something like the classical Greek "golden mean"— that is, they must always seek to avoid the extremes. Too much decisiveness becomes impetuosity; excessive confidence is perceived (often correctly) as arrogance. Moving too far in the direction of perseverance suggests rigidity; extreme optimism connotes lack of a sense of realism; too much doubt suggests lack of self-confidence. Managers who exude compassion and warmth, while well liked, perhaps lack the toughness necessary to operate in the "real world."

Finesse is the skillful movement back and forth between these opposing behavior patterns, a subtle orchestrating of mood, moment, and method. Finesse also involves the skillful use of participative management. This style of management cannot be measured simply by the number of decisions made jointly by subordinates and superiors. In reality, the "participative" manager is not necessarily the one who allows the most decisions to be made by subordinates. Nor are participative managers consistently participative. At any one time the manager may make some decisions unilaterally—i.e., without subordinate participation—and may even reject an employee's advice when it has been solicited. (Of course, when doing that the effective manager will give a full explanation for his or her decision.)

The sense of involvement and power sharing that is the mark of the participative style grows out of a number of managerial behavioral patterns:

1 In conversations with subordinates, how much time does the manager spend listening—in contrast to speaking?

2 How responsive is the manager to issues raised by subordinates—in contrast to issues on the manager's own agenda?

3 How frequently does the manager give subordinates visibility in meetings with outsiders (higher levels of management and staff groups)?

4 How much effort does the manager devote to resolving with upper management the issues raised by subordinates?

THE WORLD OUTSIDE COMPUTERS ISN'T BINARY

Of course, many executives find it difficult to accept a style of executive action and decision making that stresses inconsistency in finding "solutions" to vexing human and institutional problems. Managerial work is stressful enough without constantly having to make choices between leadership styles, and life in the executive suite would be so much more bearable with a simple (albeit less useful) catechism of do's and don'ts. This Newtonian view of management is, ironically, both the most popular and the least realistic. It supposes that managers do one thing at a time and that they are advocates of either one leadership style or another. This traditional view of leadership ignores the process by which leaders actually lead, which is a much more complex process of establishing and maintaining interactive relationships. It is much easier to assume the world is binary—either/or, you are or you aren't.

Managers have their own reasons for oversimplifying and relying upon a limited number of comfortable, set patterns. Most management positions lack many of the "creature comforts" of the typical high-status job. They offer instead the "hot seat," a position that requires gaining the cooperation of many reticent, recalcitrant subordinates (some of whom, called "professionals," are especially niggardly in giving deference). Getting things done through complex organizations and past Byzantinelike fiefdoms is frustrating, requiring much more than the patience of Job. It is easy for even the best-intentioned executive to become cynical about the predominance of politics and the evils of human nature, at least as they show themselves on the job. While most high-status professionals assume they can use the organization and expect autonomy and deference, the executive is locked into a web of interdependencies where even slight improvements can require extraordinary skill and stamina. Under such circumstances, combined with the pressures of competition, it is easy to empathize with the desire to simplify leadership to a few "tried-and-true" principles.

In a complex, even contradictory, organizational world, managers will have to forgo the luxury of having a few simple principles to cope with the frustrations of human behavior. They will have to accept the fact that it is the knowing *when* and *how* and *what* to do that is at the very heart of effective leadership. No formulas, no neat, pat answers or well-honed techniques will suffice. As in economics, "It all depends" are the watchwords.

INDEX